Dublin's Working Prams

Susan Weir

Published by Susan Weir 2012

ISBN 978-0-9574924

Printed by Naas Printing.

Author

Susan Weir was born and reared in Dublin. She is a graduate of Trinity College Dublin. For the last fifteen years, she has worked at the Educational Research Centre in Drumcondra in Dublin where she carries out research in the area of educational disadvantage. She is a keen photographer and painter. Since childhood, she has been captivated by the pram traders of her native city. Her book is intended to record and celebrate the unique contribution of these women to Dublin life. Susan lives on the north side of the city with her husband, daughter, and three cats.

Dedication

This book is dedicated to all of the street traders that feature in its pages.

CONTENTS

ACKNOWLEDGEMENTS

This book would not have been possible without the street traders. In particular thanks are due to Rita, Betty, Alice, Hannah, Kathleen, Teresa, Rose, Vivienne, and Hannah. Sadly, Rita did not live long enough to see the book published. While Hannah did not want to be photographed for the book, she was particularly helpful to me, even abandoning her pram one day to go home and get me a copy of the *Bananas on Breadboards* DVD about street traders! Thanks are particularly due to Ellen Preston, Lily Kearns, Vera Shortall, Carole Foley, Mary Holmes, and Marion White who gave generously of their time and memories. Thanks to Mary Maher of the Dublin Adult Learning Centre for her enthusiasm for the project and who hosted an exhibition of the photographs, and to Maureen O'Sullivan TD who invited me to exhibit the photographs in the Pillar Room at the Rotunda for the 30th anniversary celebrations of the 'Gregory Deal'. Thanks also to Fr Tom O'Keeffe of Cabinteely Parish for his recollections of Lena and her pram. Thanks are also due to Irene Stevenson of the Irish Times, to Michael Hinch of the Irish Independent, and Martin Walshe of John Hinde Ltd for assistance with images. Thanks also to Frank Fahy for his editorial comments and enthusiasm for the book. I am indebted to my mother for carrying out a couple of pieces of important detective work on my behalf, and to my husband Howard and daughter Daisy for allowing me space to work on the book in what is an already very busy life. Finally, I owe a huge debt of thanks to Hilary Walshe, not just for her expertise in formatting the book, but for her belief in the project from the very beginning.

Preface

Ever since I was a little girl growing up in Dublin, I have been fascinated by the old prams used by the street traders (the 'dealers' as we used to call them) to transport and display their goods. For as long as I can remember, I could never pass a dealer's pram without slowing down to admire it.

Some of the attraction, I'm certain, is born of nostalgia. In the early 1970s I was a young child growing up in Dublin. In those days it was common for quite young children to mind the babies of local families. I often knocked on neighbours' doors and asked if I could take the baby of the house for a walk in his or her pram. This was invariably greeted with delight by the mothers, who were grateful for a break.

To tell the truth, pushing the big bouncy pram down the street was at least as, if not more, appealing than taking care of the infant. On trips to town as a child, my friend and I would head for the basement in Roche's Stores on Henry Street. This was a veritable *Mecca* for pram lovers, stocking all the major names, including Silver Cross, Pedigree, Swallow, Marmet, Swan, and Restmor. We would spend hours agonising about the pram we would choose if we were mothers, and good suspension was one of the main considerations.

The growth in the popularity of the car as the preferred mode of transport, and the requirement for modern prams and buggies to be accommodated in cars, has led to the demise of the traditional pram. In fact, their use by the Dublin street traders provides just about the only opportunity to see these prams nowadays. The traders' prams range in age from the 1940s (the Walker pram on page 43) to the 1980s. While some have buckled wheels and the odd dent, they have, as I hope the photographs show, survived in remarkable condition.

As is the case with vintage cars, part of their appeal is a curiosity about their past. For example, where are the babies that once occupied the prams? It is very likely that they are now grown up with children and even grandchildren of their own. One of the traders I spoke to in Meath Street told me that she raised ten children in her pram, and that she paid for the pram at a rate of £1 per week when she was expecting her first child.

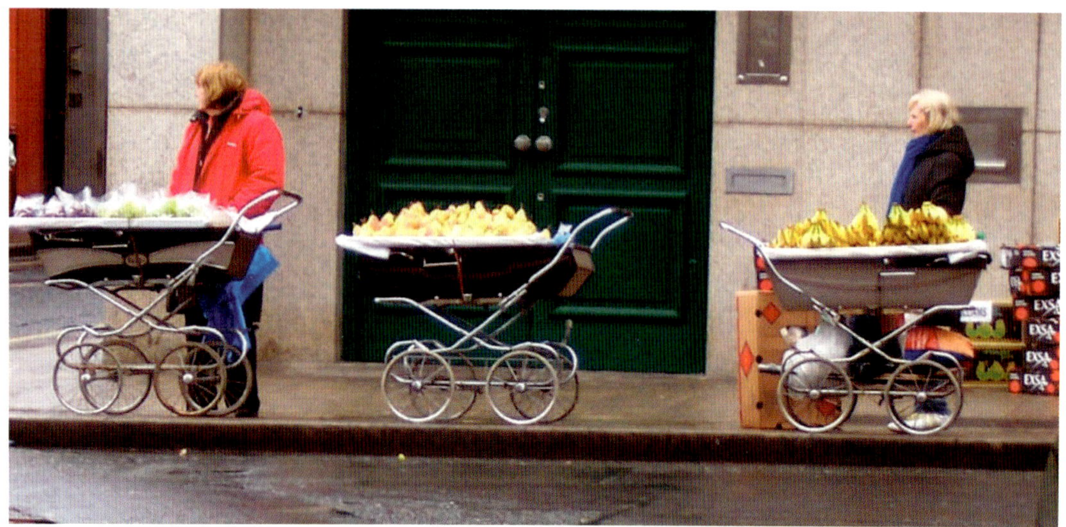

As far as I am aware, Dublin is unique in the prominent use of prams by traders to sell goods. I have often witnessed the bemusement of tourists at the sight of people buying fruit from old baby carriages. One tourist commented: 'When I first saw the gangs of women pushing these prams through the north side of Dublin, I thought it was some kind of protest. But no, it was just an ingenious way of moving and selling fruit'.

One day when I wandered down to Capel Street to have a look at the traders, I overheard some women tourists exclaiming with delight: 'Oh, my goodness – look at all the Silver Cross prams full of fruit!' Shortly afterwards, I decided that I would begin to take some photographs of the traders for posterity. Over the following few years, I rarely visited the city centre without my camera. This book is a vehicle for showing some of the resulting images.

Trading goods from prams has, of course, a long tradition in Dublin. The unofficial Dublin anthem 'Molly Malone' is a musical tribute to a street trader. As was the case with the heroine of the song, many of the street traders featured here continue the tradition of street trading from prams begun by their mothers and grandmothers.

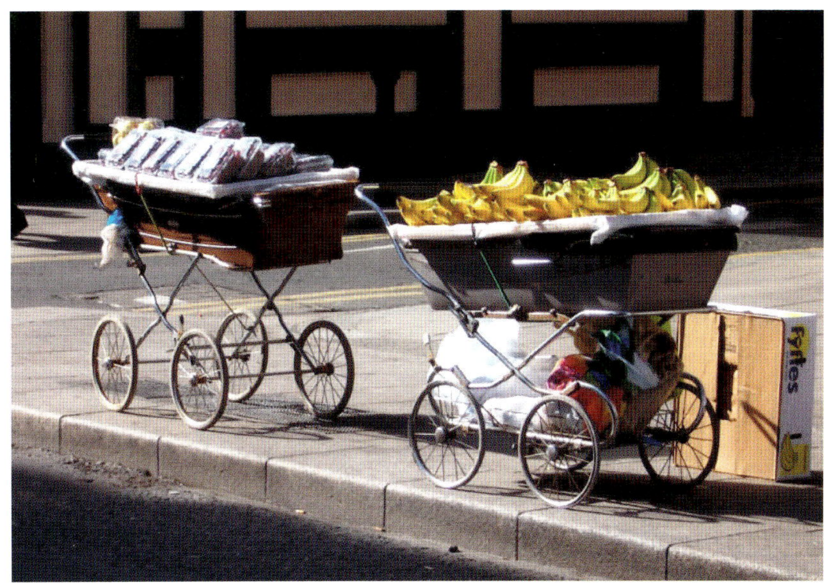

The photographs in the book were taken between 2008 and 2012 in various locations around Dublin, including Capel Street, Mary Street, and Henry Street, where the traders and their prams may be found most days. There are some photos of traders' prams in Moore Street and O'Connell Street, and in Meath Street in Dublin's Liberties, an area in which street trading has a strong tradition, and which was the homeplace of Molly Malone. A wide variety of goods feature atop the prams, from fruit and flowers to Easter eggs, Mothers' Day cards and mistletoe at Christmas time. The photographs are interspersed with interviews with traders in which they recall their lives trading on the streets of Dublin.

The collection of material for this book was prompted by a fear that, with progress, the traders and their prams will disappear. The following pages represent a modest attempt to provide some kind of record of them at the beginning of the 21st century.

Susan Weir, November 2012

The Pram

The pram holds a special place in the hearts of many Dubliners. Most people born in the 1970s (and certainly before that) remember the old-fashioned prams of the day with great affection. In those days, every family with young children had a pram.

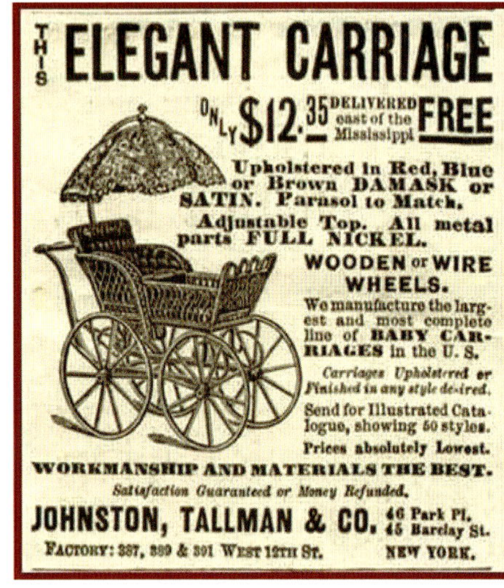

An example of an early baby carriage from 1891.

The word pram – a contraction of the longer *perambulator* – is a formal reference for an old-fashioned baby carriage. The shorter term came into common speech in late Victorian times, and now refers to any kind of wheeled vehicle used to transport infants. The first carriages for children were constructed in the mid-19th century, and had three wheels with a built-in wicker chair in which children capable of sitting upright were placed. At that time, carriages for babies did not exist, as medical opinion advised against exposing infants to an excess of fresh air! When Queen Victoria bought three of these 'child carriers' for her own children, she created the 'must have' accessory for wealthy parents of the day. By the late 1870s, the medical community had changed its collective mind and begun to advocate the benefits of fresh air for babies. This led to a demand for prams in which babies could lie flat. However, because these prams lacked features such as rubber tyres and a sprung chassis that were typical of prams made a century later, they were almost certainly uncomfortable to travel in, not to mention difficult to push.

The addition of rubber tyres and springs meant that the later baby carriages were much more comfortable vehicles. The prams of the 1950s and onwards were masterpieces of engineering. Their bodies were metal, usually steel, and they sat on springs or straps above their gleaming chrome chassis. In motion, they appeared to roll along effortlessly despite their weight, while the spokes on their great wheels glinted in the sunshine. Unlike the mass-produced prams and buggies of today, each pram was made by a team of craftspeople involving, among others, wheelwrights, coachbuilders, springsmiths, iron founders, upholsterers, and finishers. The finisher's job was to paint the stripes or coachlines onto the finished pram body.

One of the main manufacturers, Silver Cross, traded on its association with royalty, and several royal babies were transported in prams made by the company. Also, conscious of its reputation for exclusivity and status as the market leader, Silver Cross named various pram models after cars made by Rolls Royce, such as the *Silver Shadow*, *Parkward* and *Mulliner*. The advertisement on page 7 for the *Silverdawne* model in 1955 even features a Rolls Royce in the background. Silver Cross prams were as strong as they were glamorous. On one occasion, a pram which had been in a collision with a car was returned to the Silver Cross factory. The pram had absorbed the impact of the collision and the infant inside was unharmed. The factory replaced the chassis, resprayed the pram body, and returned the pram to the owner 'as new'. Prams from the main makers such as Silver Cross and Pedigree could also be customised, enabling clients to choose the colours of the pram bodies, as well as the type and colour of apron and hood fabric.

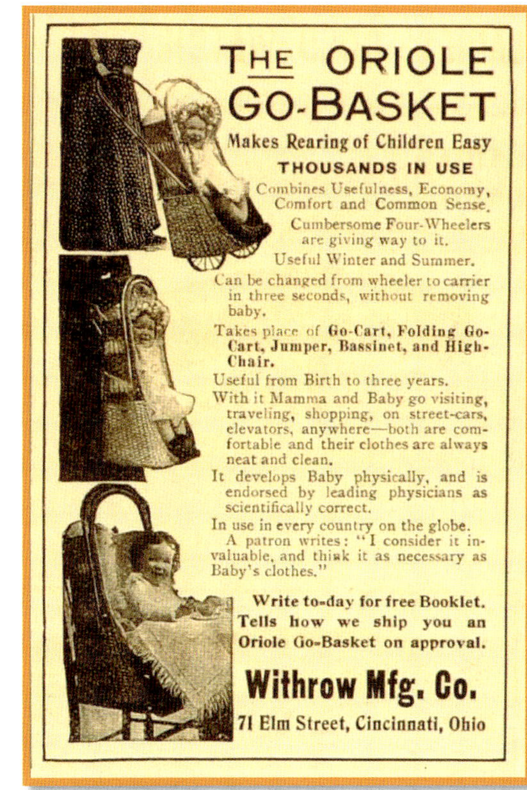

A different design of baby carriage from 1906.

All of this craftsmanship came at a price. For new parents, the investment was so significant that many people could not afford to buy their pram outright, instead opting to pay for it on the 'never never' (payment in instalments). The Silver Cross model on page 7 would set a purchaser back £29 in 1955, a very large sum at the time. Pedigree prams were also hugely popular in Ireland, and in 1964 the *Vantage* model shown on page 90 retailed at 17 pounds, 10 shillings, and sixpence. Both Silver Cross and Pedigree also produced dolls' prams (Pedigree owned the Triang toy factory), which were miniature versions of the larger prams and were highly sought after as children's toys. Indeed, the Silver Cross factory still produces coachbuilt dolls' prams as luxury items with each pram costing in the region of €500. Ireland also had its own pram manufacturer called Walker Industries. One of the oldest prams currently in use by a street trader in Dublin is a Walker pram manufactured in Dublin around 1940 (see page 43).

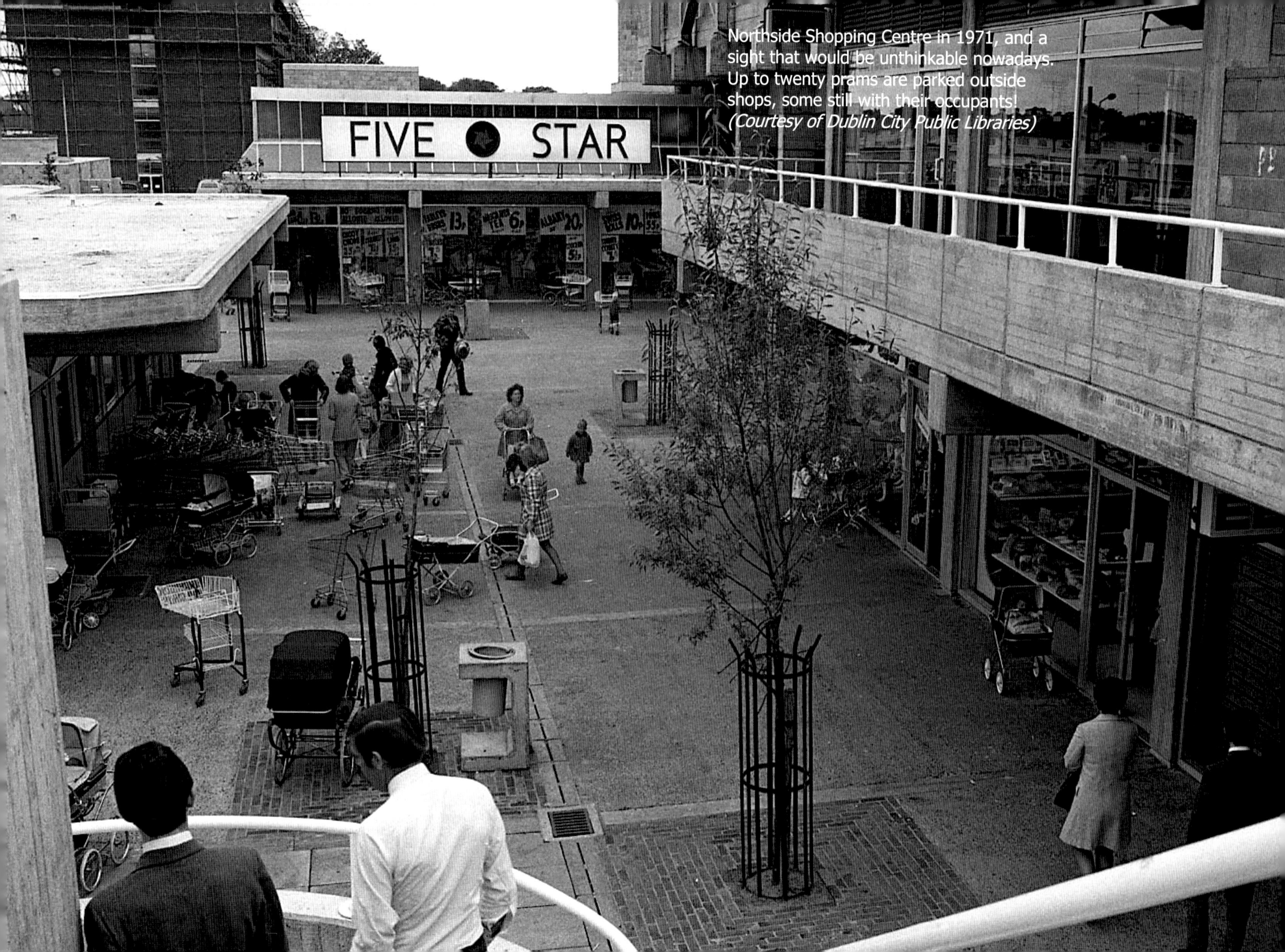

Northside Shopping Centre in 1971, and a sight that would be unthinkable nowadays. Up to twenty prams are parked outside shops, some still with their occupants! *(Courtesy of Dublin City Public Libraries)*

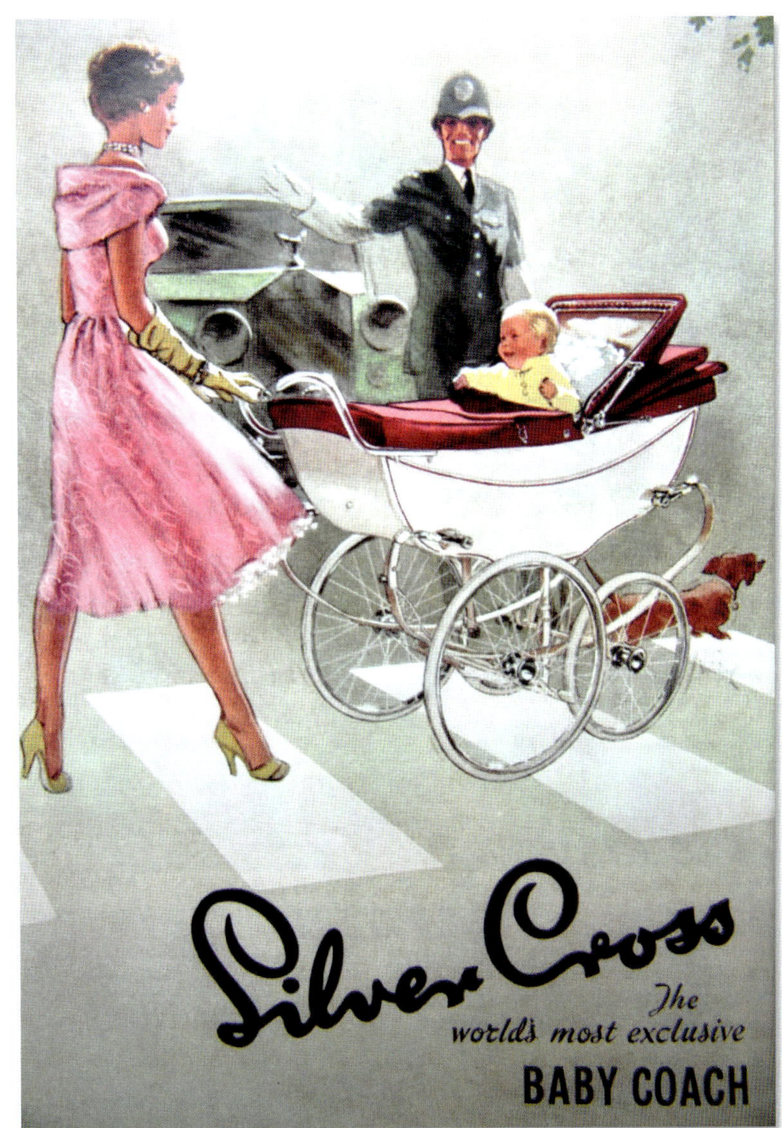

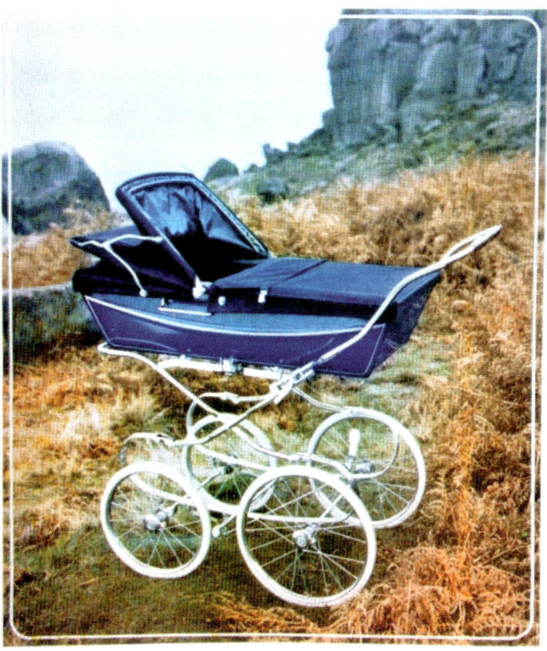

Left: An advertisement for a Silver Cross *Silverdawne* pram from 1955 showing a Rolls Royce in the background. This model cost £29.

Above: The *Grosvenor* pram in the Silver Cross catalogue from 1977. Several of these prams are still in use by the street traders. See two examples of this model on page 63.

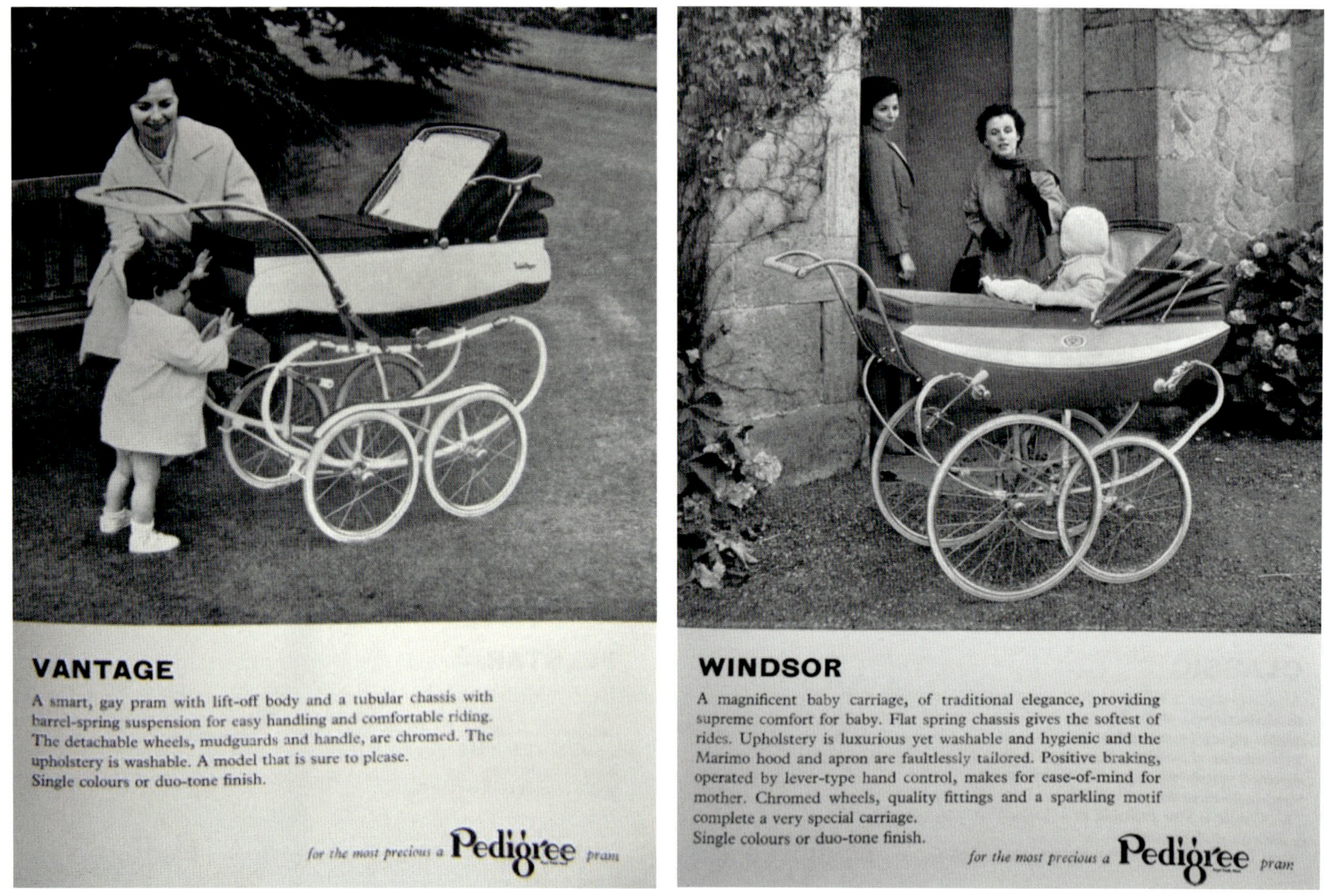

Above: Two excerpts from a Pedigree pram catalogue in 1964, which featured fifteen different pram models. The prams ranged in price from 15 pounds, 19 shillings, and sixpence for the modest Vantage model on the left, to 27 pounds, seven shillings, and sixpence for the most elaborate model, the Windsor, on the right. A Pedigree Vantage pram may be still seen in action on Dublin's Mary Street on page 90.

The pram was a highly versatile vehicle. In addition to its use as a baby carriage, the spaciousness of the pram and its metal basket underneath meant that it lent itself to all sorts of uses, from transporting turf from the local depot to taking the family dog to the vet. While many families did not have a car, almost all families with children had a pram, despite the cost. The same pram tended to be used for all the children in the family in succession, and when the newest arrival took up residence inside the pram, the next oldest sat on a specially designed seat above the apron, while another ran alongside holding the handle. When the prams' days as carriers of children were well and truly finished, their wheels were sometimes removed and used by children to construct wooden 'go-cars' – makeshift vehicles steered with rope. More importantly from the point of view of this book, some prams took on a new lease of life as perfect mobile stalls for the street traders of Dublin.

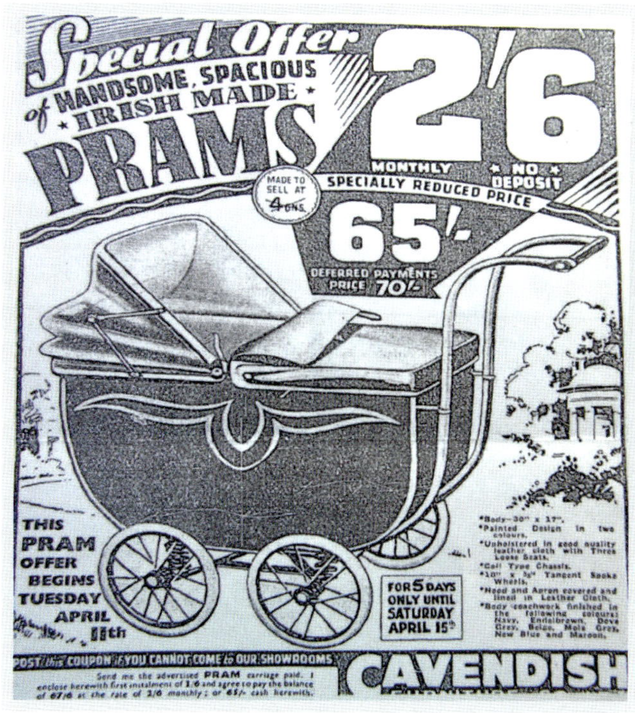

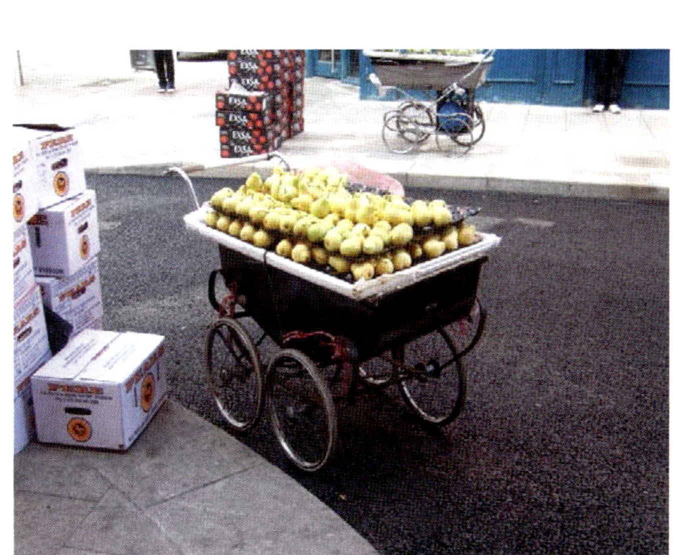

Above: A newspaper advertisement for Irish-made Walker prams from April 1939.

Left: A Walker pram dating from the middle of the last century in action as a mobile fruit stall in Mary Street.

Molly Malone: Dublin's most famous street trader

In Dublin's fair city,
Where the girls are so pretty,
I first set my eyes on sweet Molly Malone,
As she wheeled her wheel-barrow,
Through streets broad and narrow,
Crying, 'Cockles and mussels, alive, alive, oh!'
'Alive, alive, oh, Alive, alive, oh',
Crying 'Cockles and mussels, alive, alive, oh'.

The character of Molly Malone, celebrated in the song, is synonymous with Dublin city. The song tells the tale of a beautiful fishmonger who traded on the streets of Dublin. She is typically represented as a street trader by day and a woman of dubious virtue by night. Another view is that she was one of the few chaste female street traders of her day. According to the legend, Molly Malone lived in the 17th century and died of a fever in 1699. However, there is no evidence that Molly Malone ever existed. Despite this, in 1988, as part of the celebrations of Dublin's Millennium, a statue by Jeanne Rynhart was erected in her honour at the bottom of Grafton Street.

The statue's merits have been the subject of much debate among Dubliners, who, renowned for applying irreverent nicknames to some of the city's best known features, refer to it variously as 'The Tart with the Cart', 'The Trollop with the Scallops', and 'The Flirt in the Skirt'. The statue, nonetheless, draws enormous numbers of tourists, many of whom pose to have their photographs taken with it. Ironically, the tourists that flock to the statue do not realise that if they took a ten-minute walk across O'Connell Bridge to the north side of the city, they could witness the modern equivalent! Arguably, it might have been much more appropriate to site the statue near Moore Street or in the Liberties, places where street trading still exists.

Opposite: The statue of Molly Malone at the bottom of Grafton Street, Dublin.

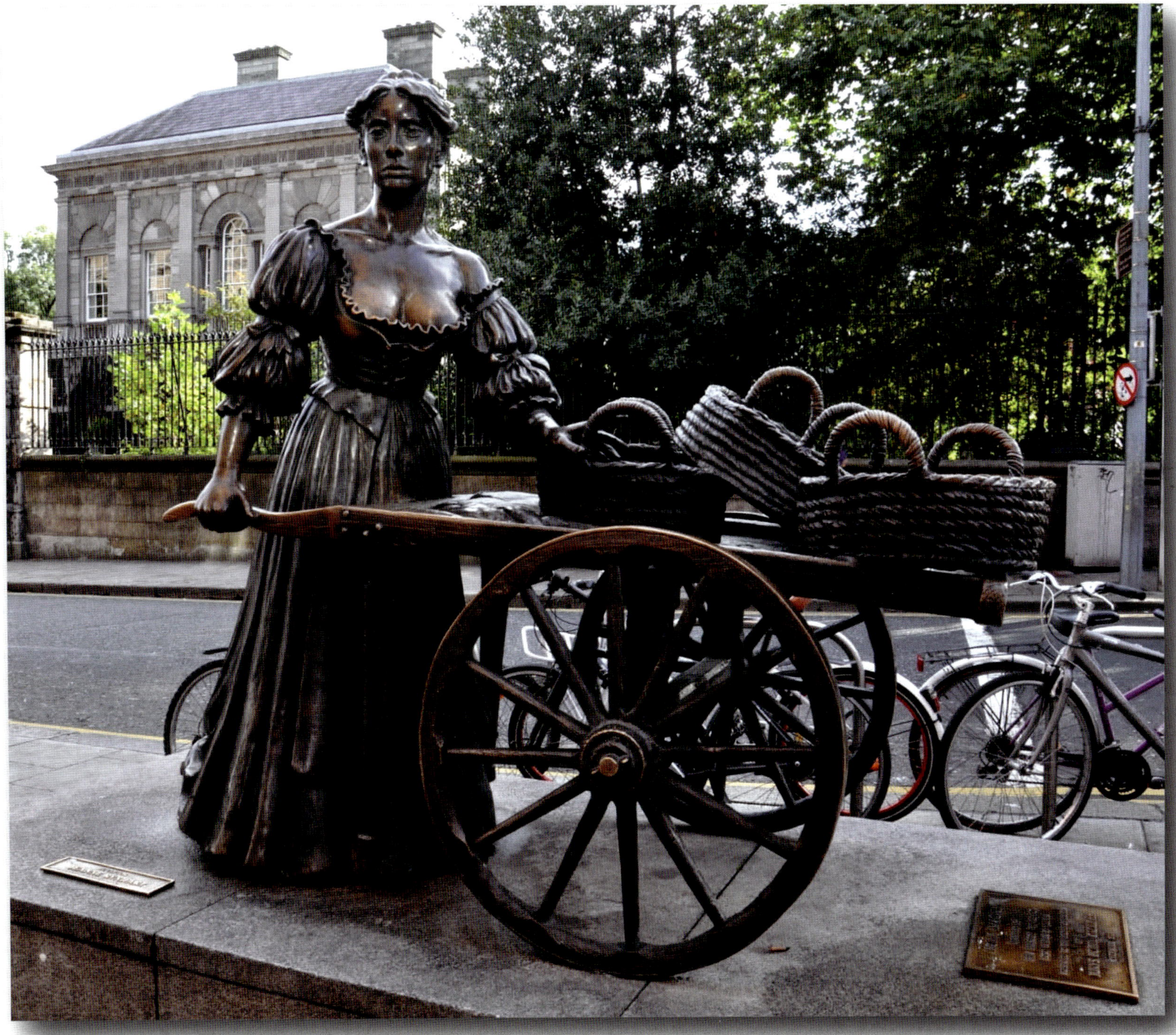

Dublin's Working Prams: Early- to mid-20th century

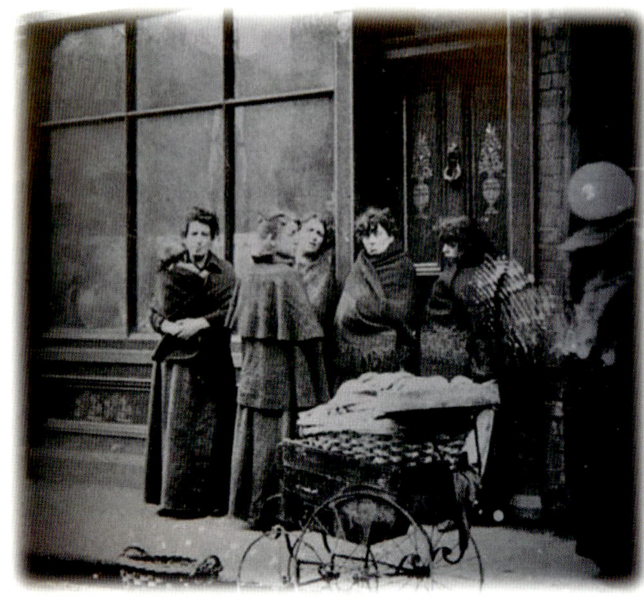

In the mid-20th century, the streets around Moore Street and Henry Street were thronged with shoppers. While Moore Street was the main shopping street for fresh produce, other surrounding streets such as Parnell Street were also populated by an array of butchers' and grocers' shops. A multitude of little interconnecting streets and narrow lanes were home to individual stallholders as well as markets of varying quality and size. Cole's Lane, which ran parallel to Moore Street and linked Henry Street with Parnell Street, was one of the most popular locations for street traders. Although Cole's Lane still exists, and even retains a few trading stalls, it was truncated when the Ilac shopping centre was built, and it is now used mainly by people as a secondary entrance to the centre.

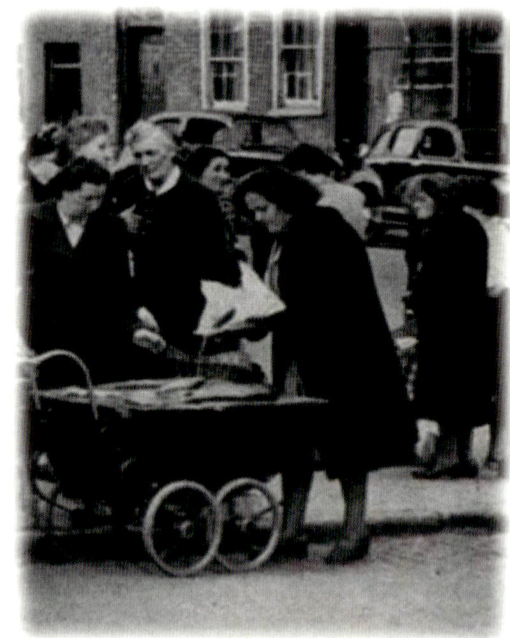

Above left: Selling fish from a pram outside a pawn shop in Dublin, circa 1900.

Above right: Fish seller in Dublin in the 1940s. Such is the propensity for Dubliners to use babies' prams as fish stalls, it has led to the following saying in Dublin: 'Take the child out of the pram and let the woman see the fish!'

While street trading was a very common occupation (particularly among women) in the last century, it is beyond the scope of this book to describe more than a few examples. In that respect, it is difficult not to include a small section on what was to become one of the most high profile street trading families of all – that of one of Ireland's best known businessmen, Bill Cullen. In his autobiography, *It's a long way from penny apples,* he gave a wonderful and evocative insight into the living and working conditions experienced by some of Dublin's street traders in the middle of the last century. The book also describes post-war Dublin as a place in which few people had any money and where people worked very hard for what they had. However, despite these difficult conditions, the Irish retained their characteristic warmth and humour, and this was never more evident than at Christmas time. Christmas was a magical time in Dublin city, and a bit of a bonanza for street traders. It was then that Henry Street came into its own under the sparkling festive lights. The street would be abuzz with people and noise, all buying decorations, Christmas novelties, and 'fancy goods' from the prams of the street traders.

'The pram' is mentioned frequently in Cullen's book, underscoring its pivotal place in the lives of street traders. He described how his mother, Mary Darcy, acquired a trading pitch in Cole's Lane just opposite the main entrance to Arnott's department store. He told how the tailor Louis Copeland Senior would often buy bananas from the pram when he and his mother were passing Copeland's shop on Capel Street on their way from the market to their pitch in Cole's Lane. Louis would give Bill a shilling for the six bananas, and sometimes slip the youngster a penny for himself. Such was the warmth of the relationship between them that the famous tailor of bespoke suits to 'the gentry' quietly went about making Bill's First Communion suit in his workshop, later presenting it to Bill's mother at a bargain price that she could pay off in instalments. With regular alterations involving taking the suit up and in, and letting it down and out, that suit went on to serve her six sons for First Communion and Confirmation over the next fourteen years!

Bill's granny, Molly Darcy, herself a street trader, also had a pram. On Fridays, Bill would often accompany his grandmother as they pushed the pram in the darkness to Amiens Street station to get the 5.00am train to Howth where the trawlers landed their catch. They were often the first customers, and as a result, had their pick of the catch. The haul would be loaded onto two flat fish boxes on top of the pram and covered in ice powder. The pram would make its return journey to the city in the goods wagon of the train. Molly Darcy sold fish off her pram outside her home in Summerhill for thirty years.

In the course of gathering material for this book, I was contacted by Father Tom O'Keeffe from Cabinteely in Dublin who told a story of a street trader he knew. As a young priest, he had been Chaplain in Holles Street Maternity Hospital from 1971 until 1980. For a number of years before and during that period, practically every baby born in the hospital was brought to Westland Row church for Christening. In those days, it was unthinkable that a mother would bring her baby home and then arrange the ceremony in the local parish church, weeks or even months later as happens now. The reason for the haste was an irrational fear that if the baby died before it was baptised, he or she would not go to heaven, but end up in *Limbo*. The custom, therefore, was that the newborns had to be christened in Westland Row church shortly after birth, while the poor mother lay in her hospital bed totally uninvolved in the ceremony.

A local woman, Lena Redmond, grasped this as a business opportunity. She offered her services to transport the babies in an old pram that she used to sell fruit in Moore Street at weekends. It was a large framed pram with buckled wheels – probably not the most hygienic mode of transport! Lena could fit eight babies into her old pram at once, and the fare was modest enough at half a crown per baby. With a full capacity of eight passengers, the total payment for the round trip amounted to one old pound, nicely augmenting her income as a street trader. Father O'Keeffe recalled an elderly priest from Westland Row telling him that he had once baptised twenty-eight babies in one session – all transported from Holles Street hospital to the church in Lena's old pram.

Because I was born in Holles Street hospital in the 1960s myself, I asked my mother if she remembered the practice. Indeed, she did! In fact she clearly remembers Lena coming into the ward and leaving with four or five babies in her arms to take them to the church. (I was, however, just a little disappointed to be told that that I had not been one of those babies that travelled in Lena's pram). Many others remember Lena with fondness. Locals in that area of the city recall her as an amazing woman, who was hardworking and kind to everyone. Lena was also to be seen regularly with her pram piled high with clothes on her way to Tara Street wash-house where she would do laundry for neighbours.

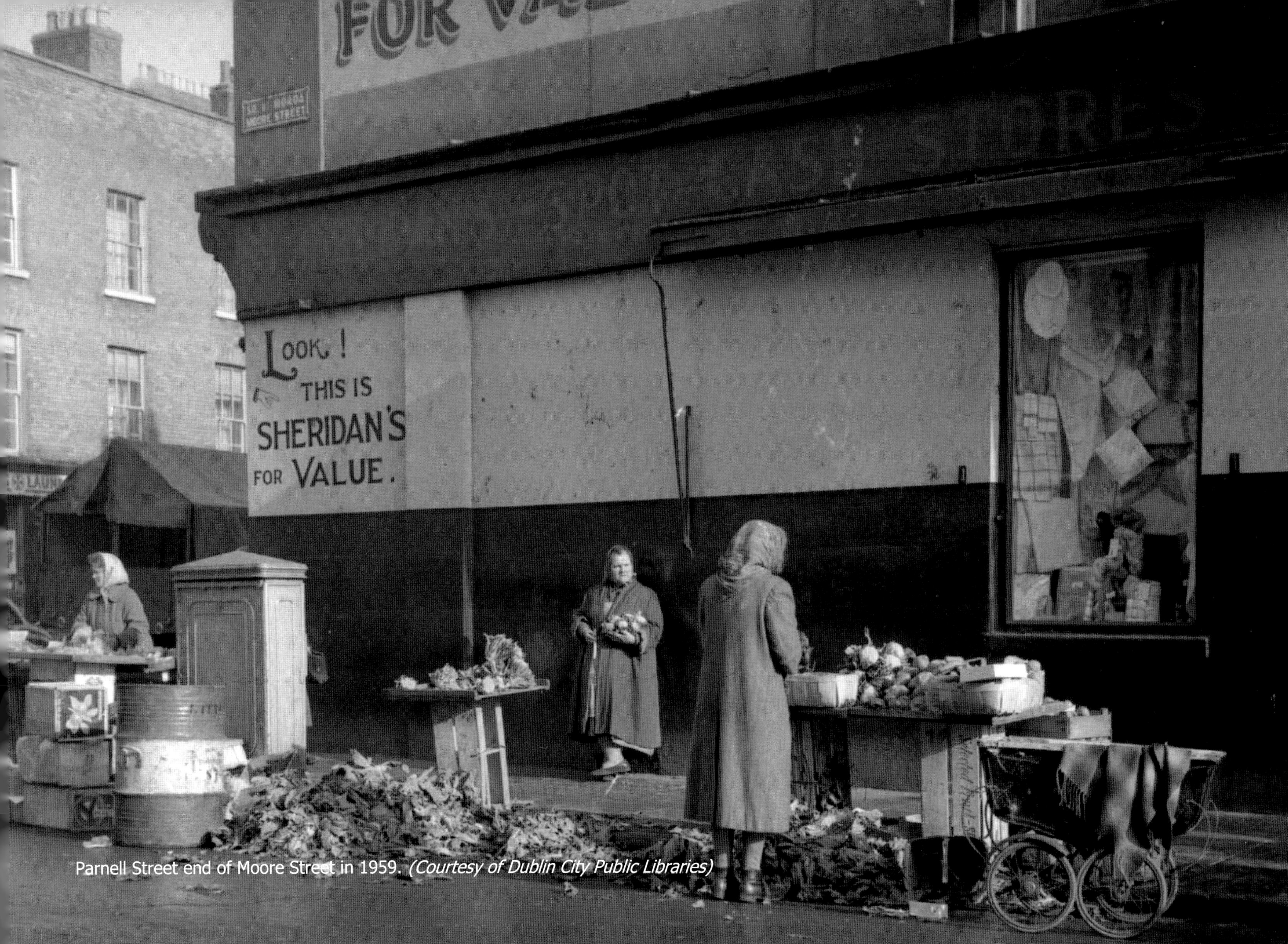

Parnell Street end of Moore Street in 1959. *(Courtesy of Dublin City Public Libraries)*

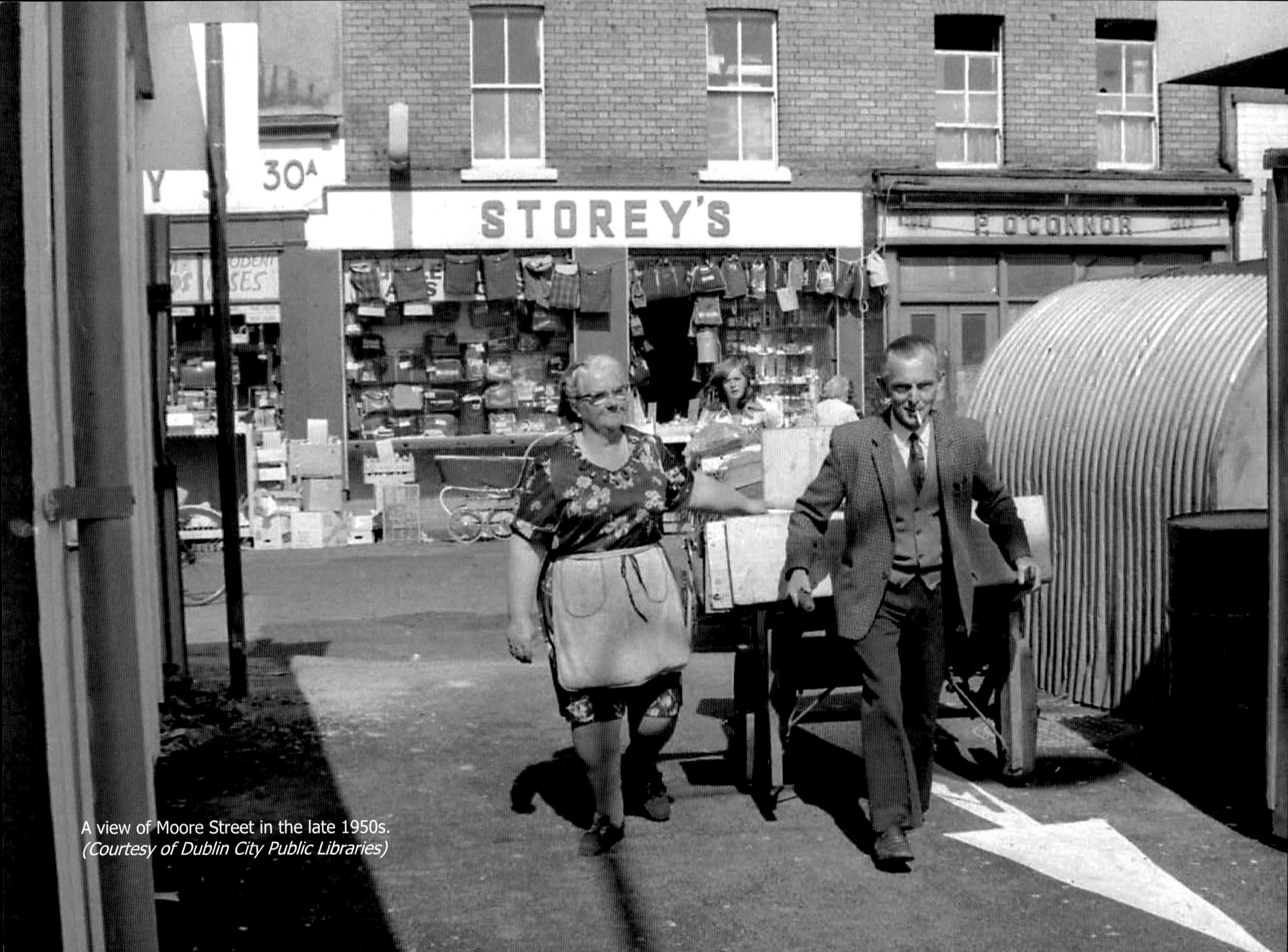

A view of Moore Street in the late 1950s.
(Courtesy of Dublin City Public Libraries)

People of an older generation might also remember a street trader called Hanna Moran, who sold fruit and confectionary from a pram outside Heuston train station between 1925 and 1993 – a period of almost 70 years. Her nickname 'Beauty' (which she carried into old age) had its origins in her striking good looks as a young woman. Over the course of her life as a street trader, she saw out a total of eight station masters, and built up a huge circle of customers and friends, including many of the station staff. In 1993, at the age of 81, Hanna was finally forced to stop trading following a prolonged battle with the authorities. At the time, Hanna lived alone in a little flat off the quays (her husband had died and she had no children). Her old pram now stood at the end of her bed for fear it might be stolen from the porch outside. In an interview with the *Irish Times* after she had been forced to stop trading, she asked: 'Why couldn't they have left me for the short time I had to go? If they saw the friends that I saw at that railway...I can't stick the loneliness now'.

By her own admission, she did not make much money ('...the price of a smoke, and if I fancied a little cake on the way home I could buy it'). What made Hanna Moran's life worthwhile was being able to chat to the passersby and tourists, sing a little song in her chair, and have a laugh with her customers. During the interview she revealed that since she stopped trading, she rarely left her flat and was barely surviving on her small state pension. Out of that, she paid £6 a week to an insurance company to ensure she had a decent burial when the time came. What is striking about Hanna's story is not her undeniable strength, but the coldness with which she appeared to have been treated by the authorities. It is particularly regrettable in cases like hers, where the individuals concerned knew no other way of life. They had begun street trading before the modern laws were made and before those who made them were even born.

The following pages show the pram in action in Dublin from the 1950s to the 1970s. Many of the photographs in this section show an inner city Dublin which is difficult to recognise today.

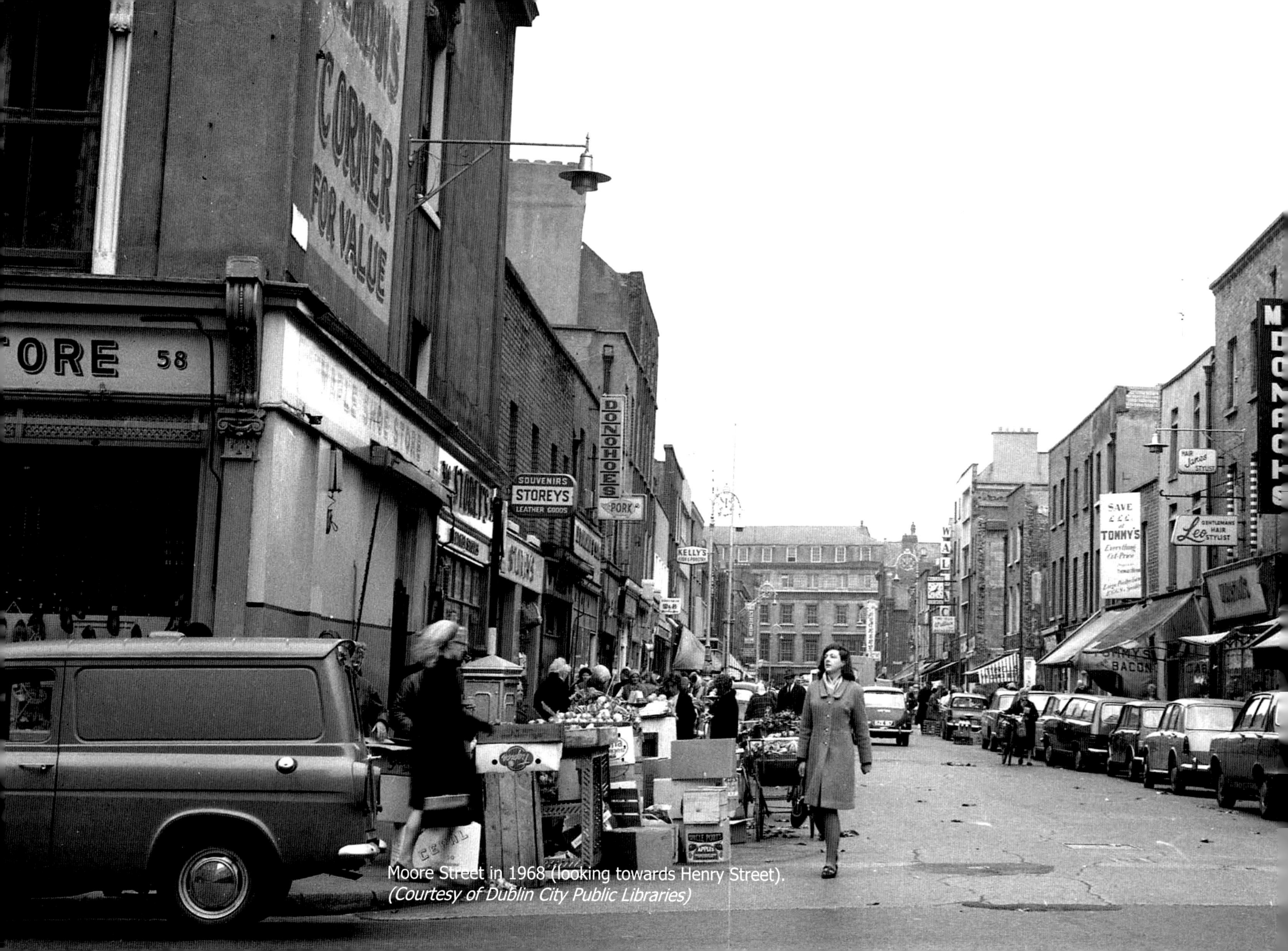

Moore Street in 1968 (looking towards Henry Street).
(Courtesy of Dublin City Public Libraries)

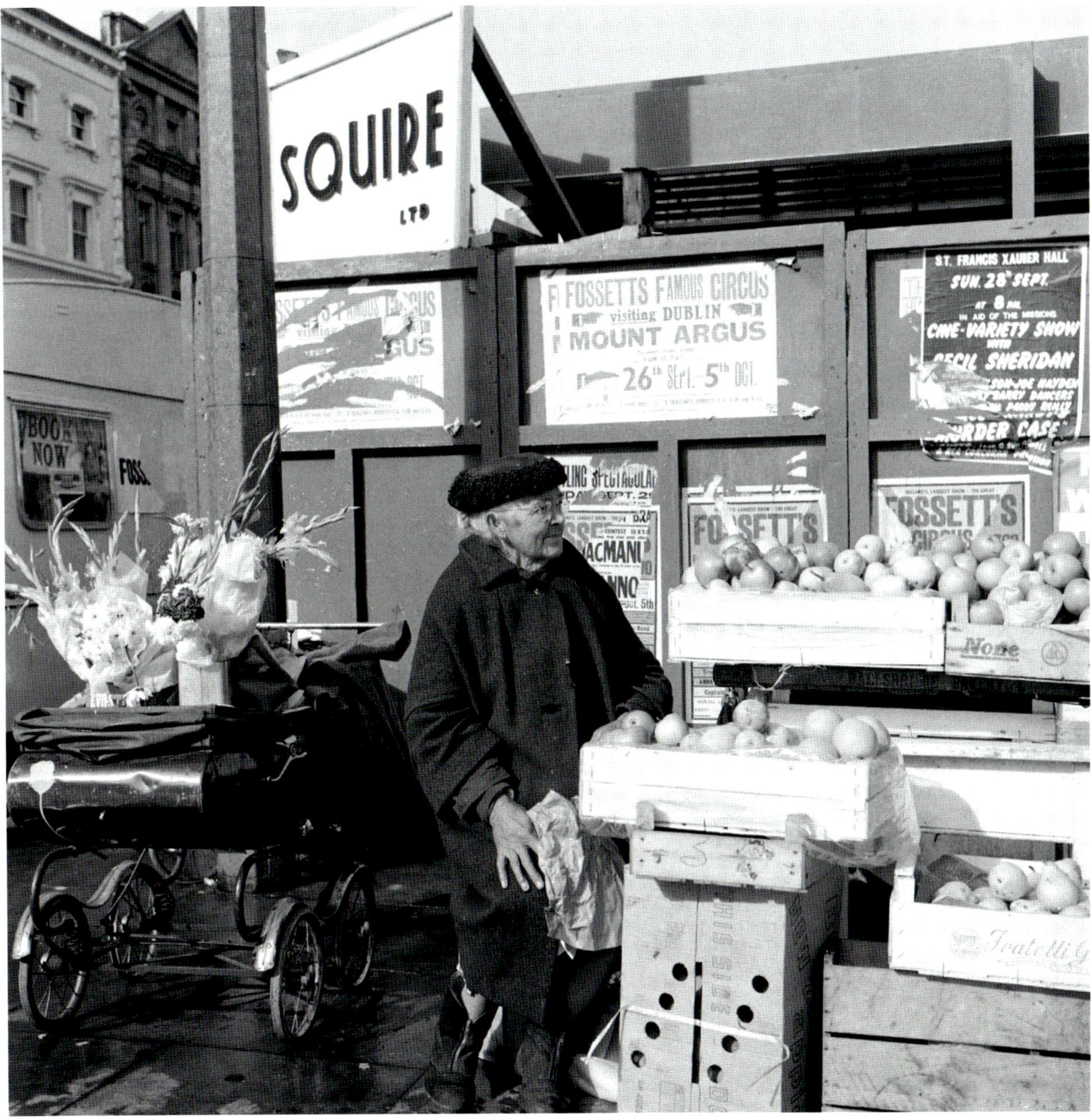

Fruit and flower seller in 1969 at the foot of what was Nelson's Pillar, in O'Connell Street, Dublin. The Pillar was blown up three years earlier in 1966. The 'Spire of light' now occupies the same spot. *(Courtesy of the National Library of Ireland)*

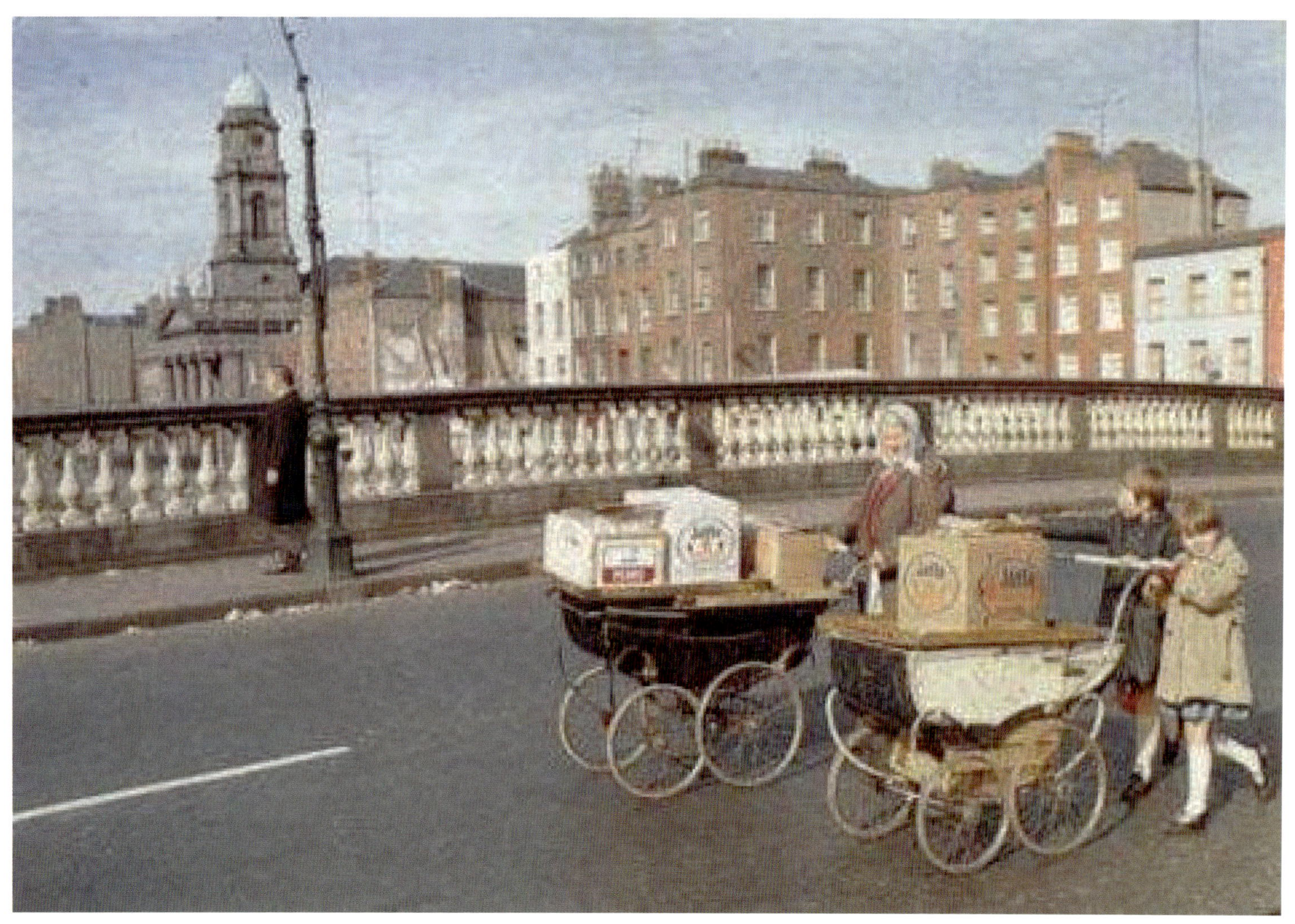

Above: Traders with their prams (probably coming from the fruit market) crossing Father Matthew Bridge over the Liffey in 1961. In those days it was common for children to begin street trading at a very young age. *(Courtesy of John Hinde Ltd)*

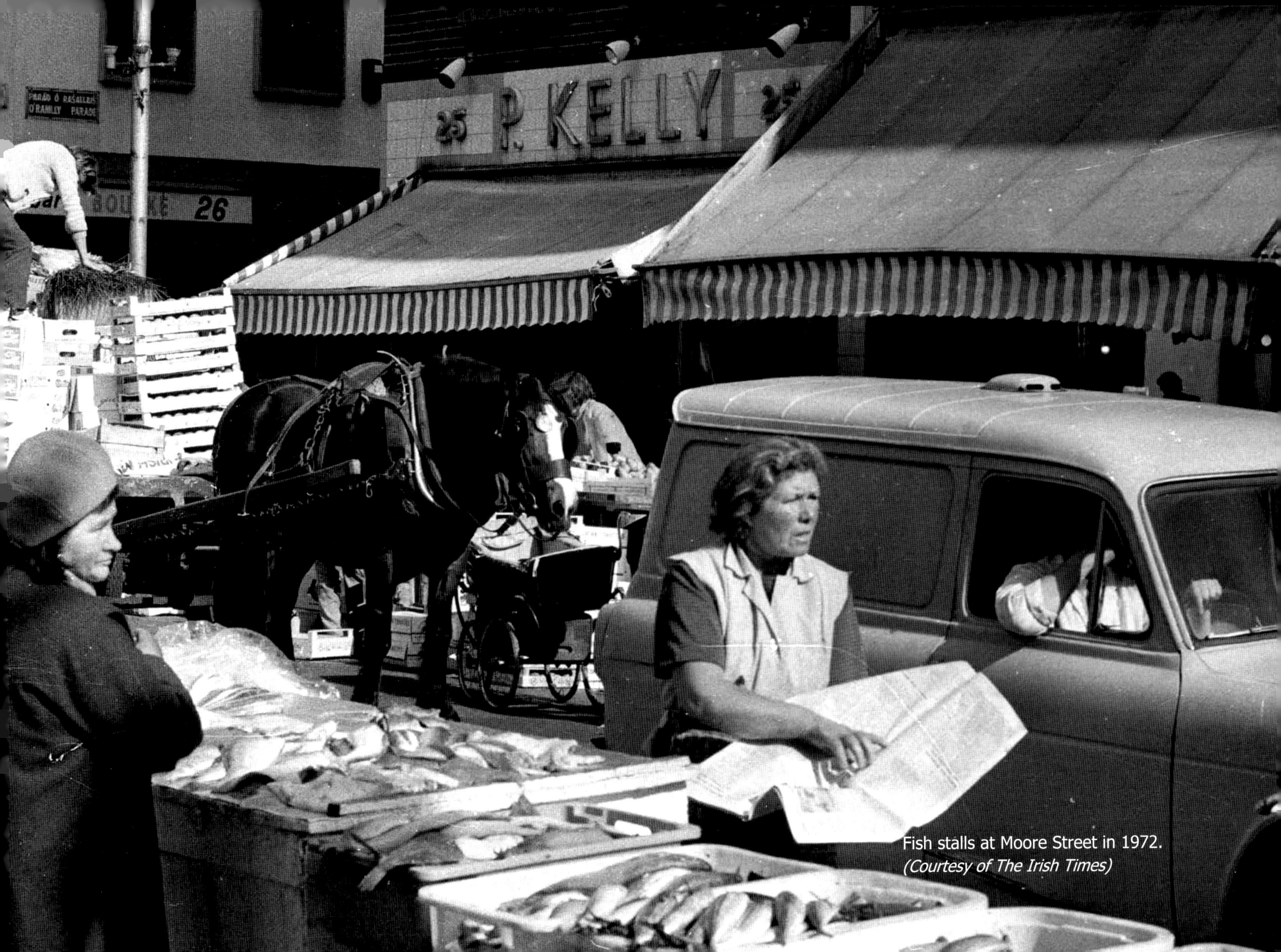

Fish stalls at Moore Street in 1972.
(Courtesy of The Irish Times)

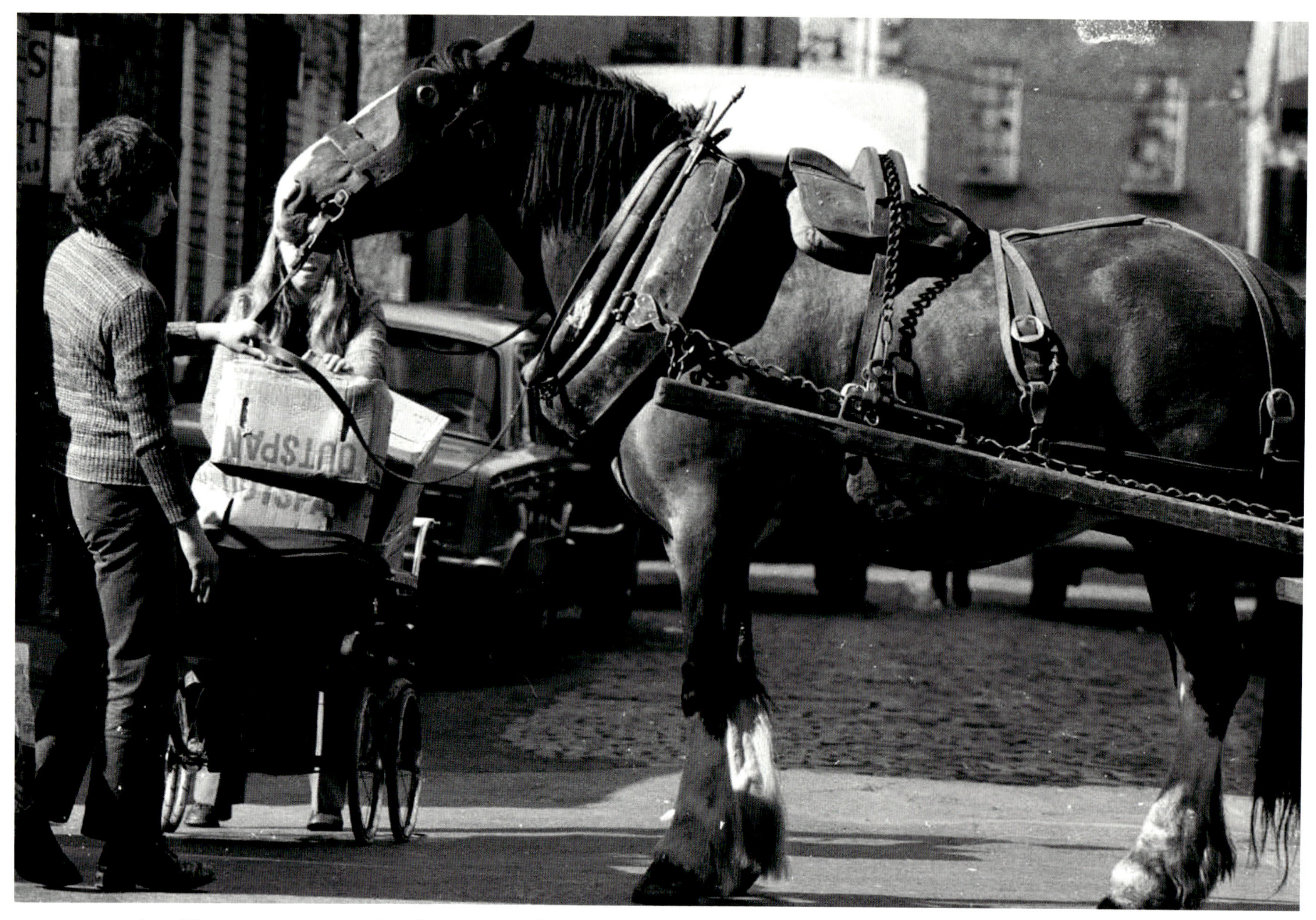

A sight no longer seen. Unloading oranges from a cart onto the pram at Moore Street in September 1972.
(Courtesy of the Irish Times)

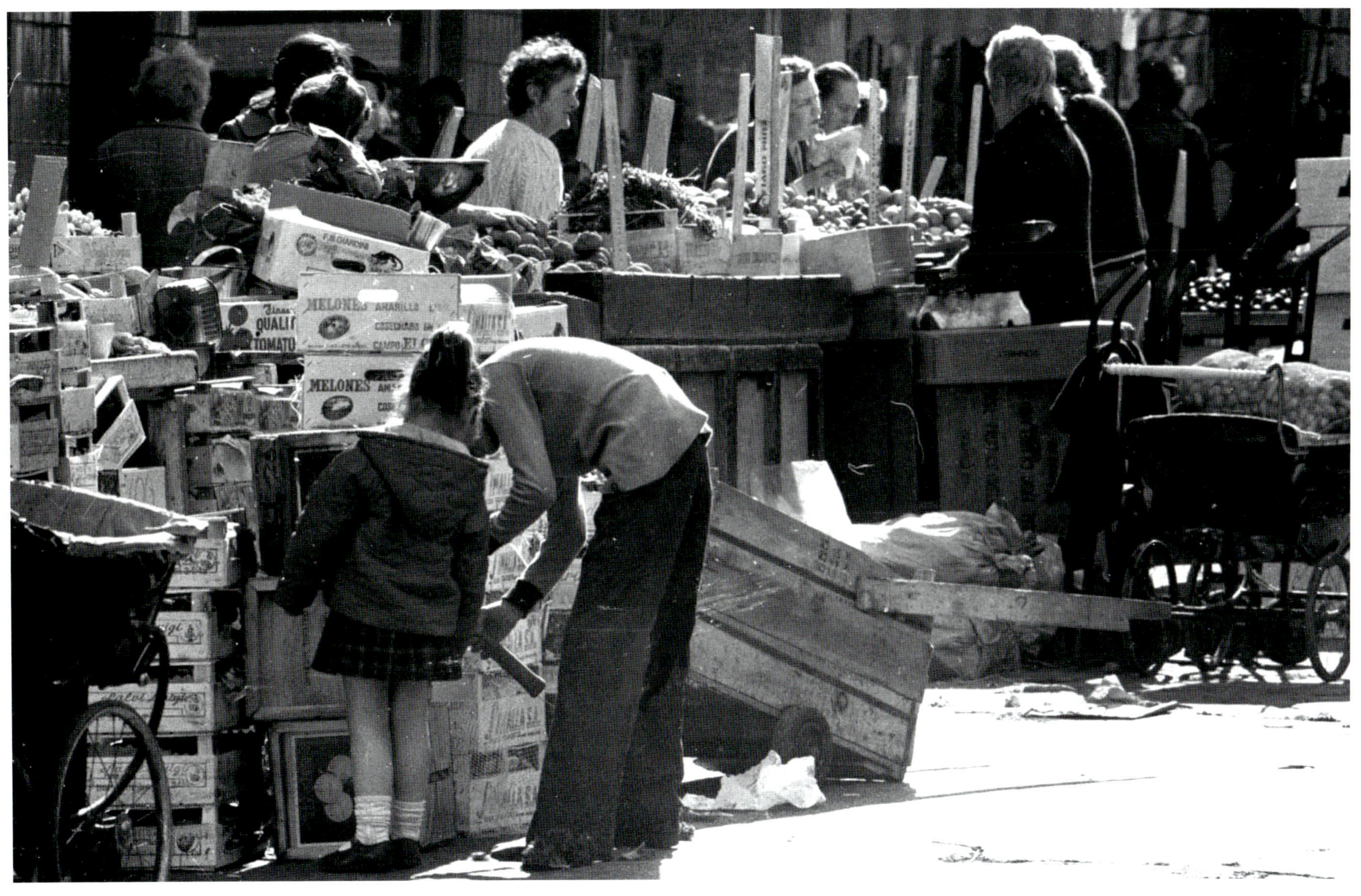

Early morning sunshine in Moore Street, September 1972. *(Courtesy of the Irish Times)*

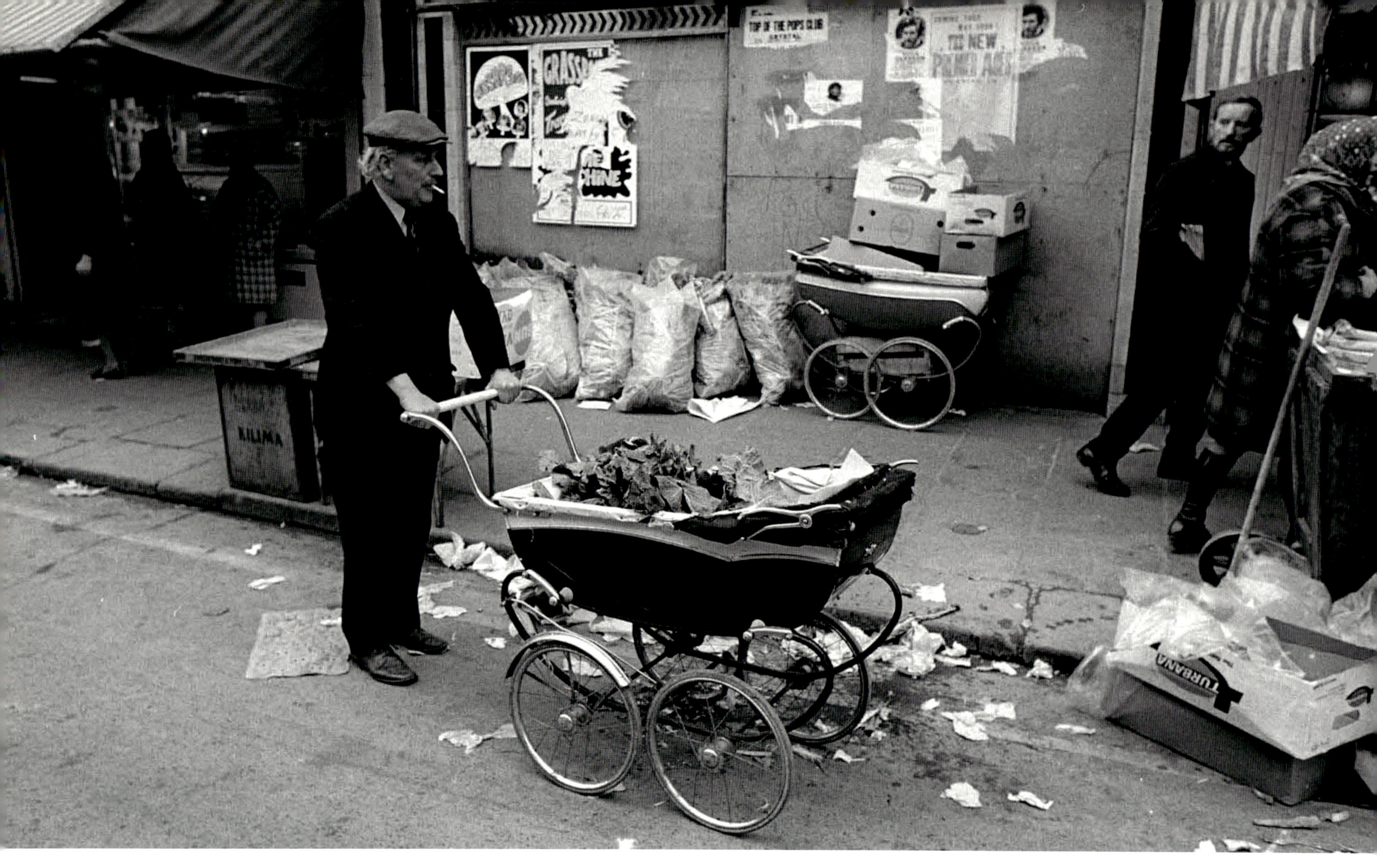

Cecil Sheridan, a well-known Irish comedian, takes a pram full of cabbages for a stroll in Moore Street in 1973 - much to the bemusement of passersby. *© RTÉ Stills library.*

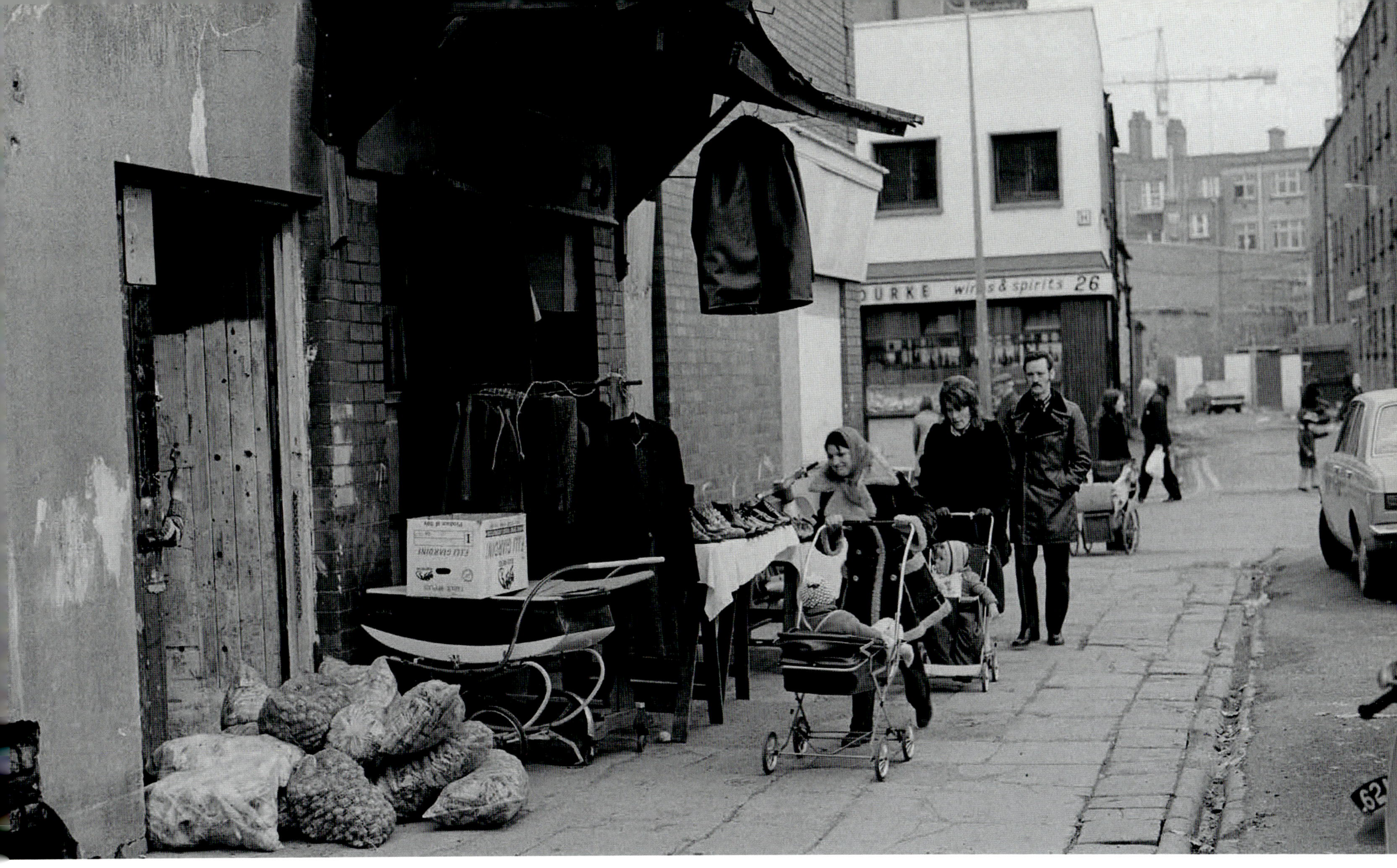

The Anglesea Market off Moore Street in 1974. *© RTÉ Stills library.*

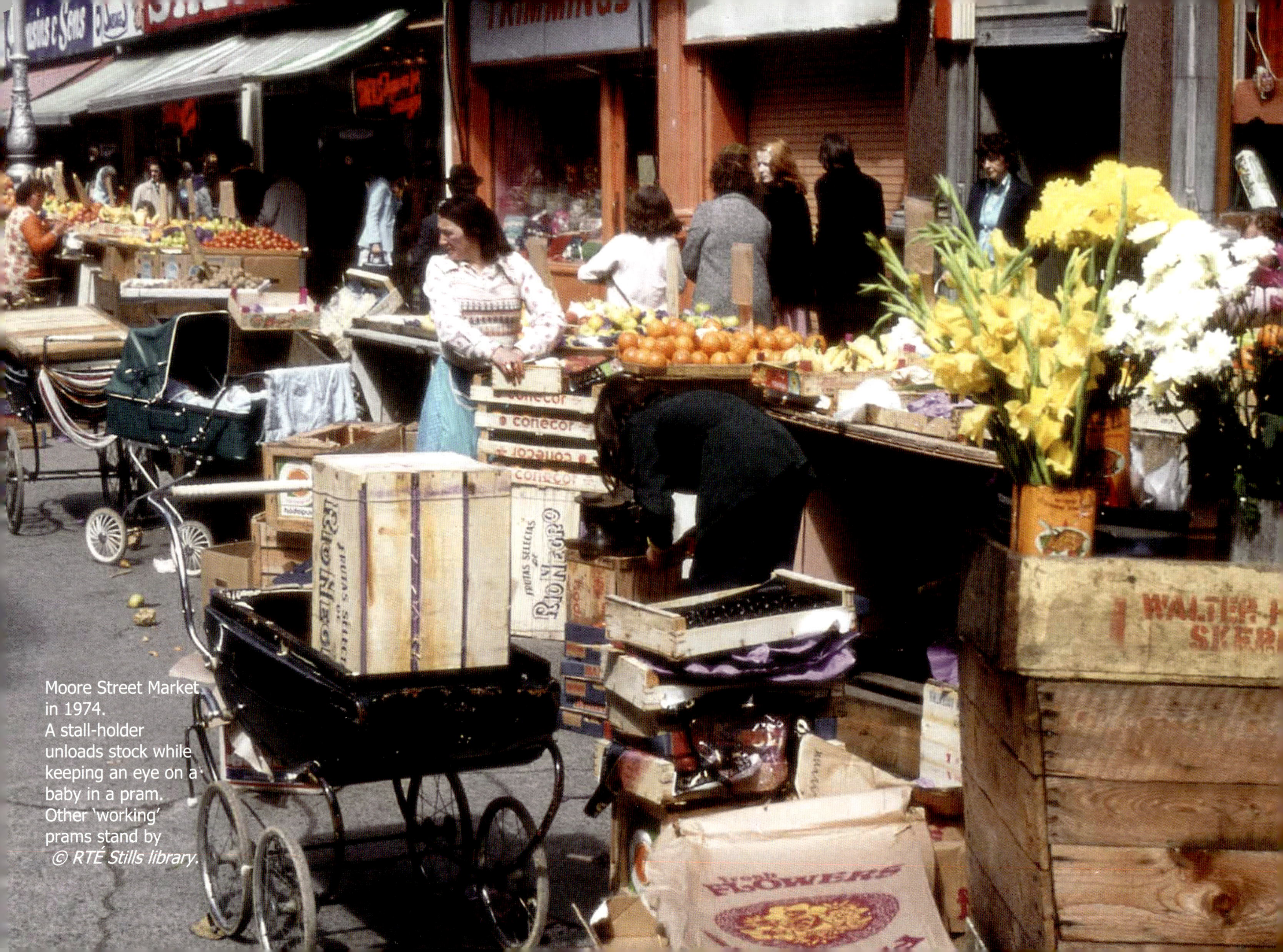

Moore Street Market in 1974.
A stall-holder unloads stock while keeping an eye on a baby in a pram.
Other 'working' prams stand by
© RTÉ Stills library.

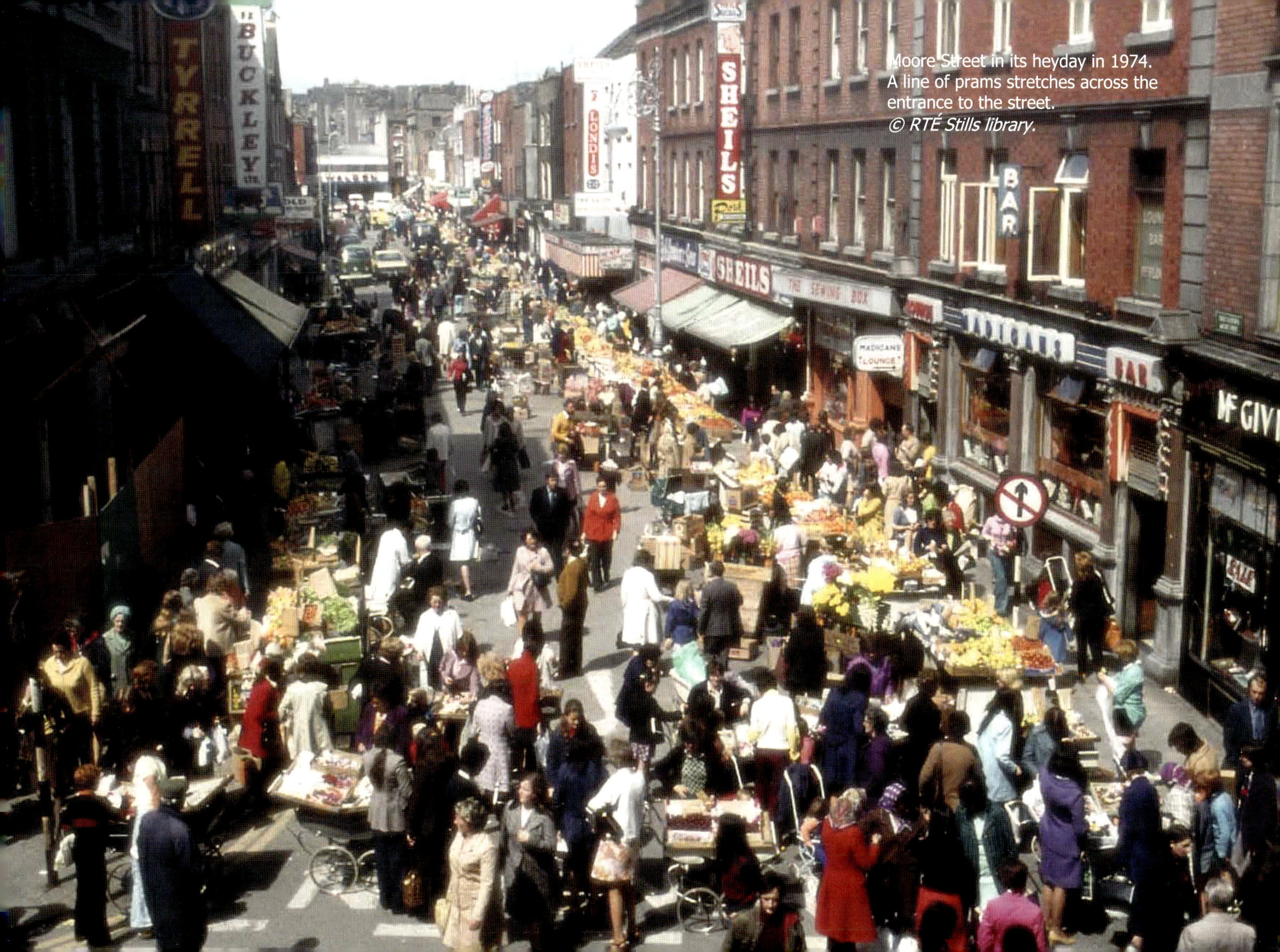

Moore Street in its heyday in 1974.
A line of prams stretches across the entrance to the street.
© RTÉ Stills library.

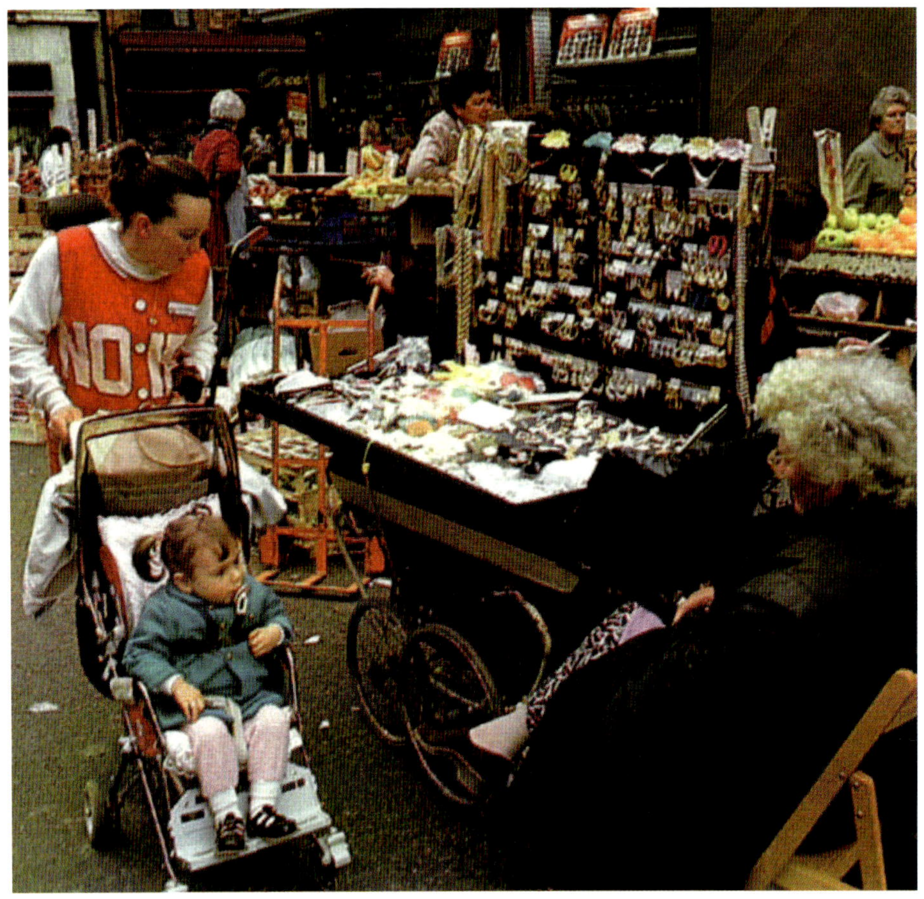

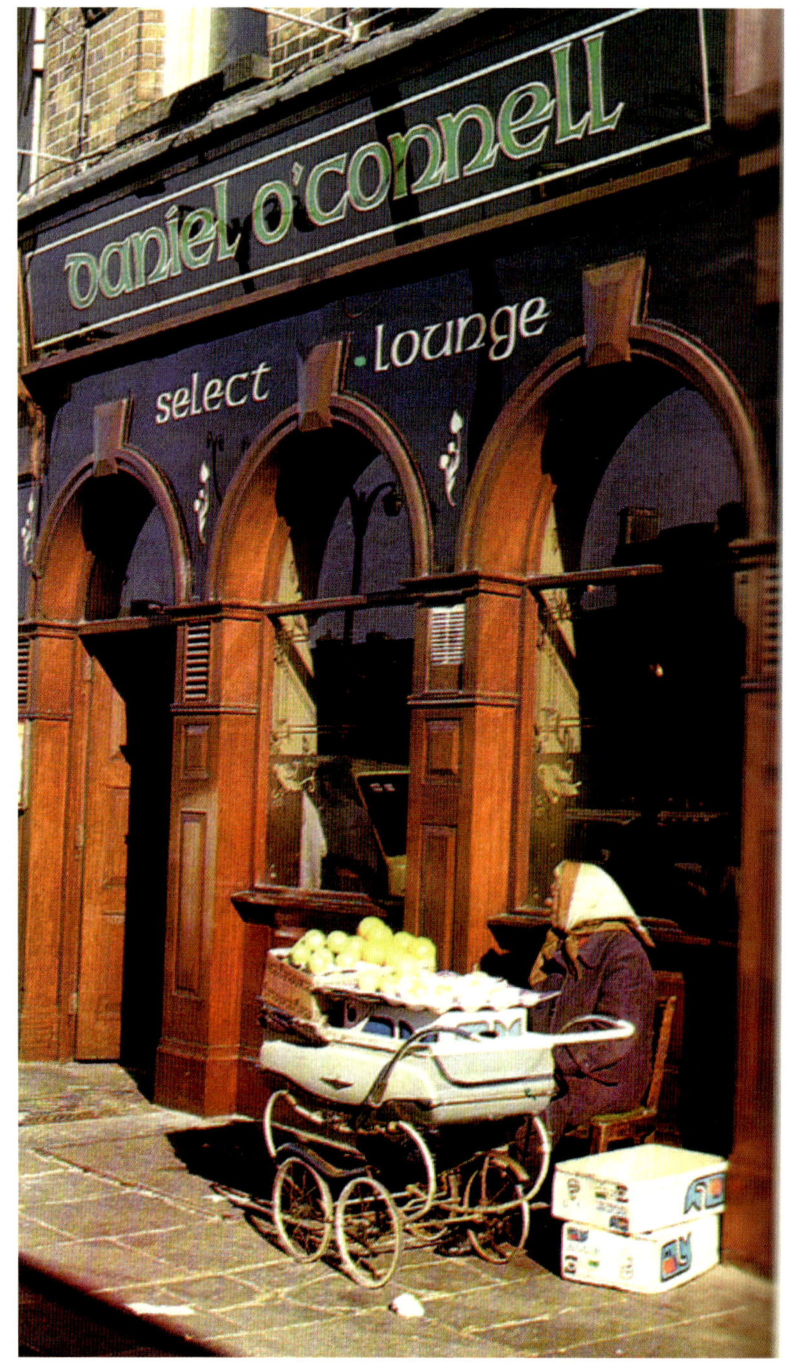

Above: A pram serves as a jewellery stall in Moore Street in 1988.

Right: A fruit seller on Aston Quay in 1988.
(Courtesy of Ireland of the Welcomes)

Dublin's Working Prams: The closing decades of the 20th century

While trading from prams has been a Dublin tradition for many years, a crisis arose in the mid-1980s which seriously threatened the future of street traders. At that time, powerful business interests considered street traders to be a threat to other businesses in the city centre, and pressure was put on the Gardaí to get the traders off the streets. A major problem for the traders was that they required a license to trade, and few of the traders possessed one. One of the reasons for this was that, if a person had committed more than two illegal trading offences, they were prohibited from getting a license in the future. The fines for an individual would sometimes accumulate to large amounts, and if the trader could not afford to pay the fine, she or he would be sent to Mountjoy prison for a couple of days.

I clearly recall seeing the somewhat ridiculous sight of women selling from prams being rounded up by the Gardaí and being marched to Store Street station with prams full of bananas or chocolate. Some Gardaí removed the wheels from the prams in order to immobilise them, while one Garda earned the nickname 'spokes' because he carried a pliers with which he cut the spokes on the pram wheels. Stock would be confiscated so that any money spent by the trader on the initial outlay for the goods was lost and not recoverable. Alternatively, stock was temporarily confiscated and returned after it had become valueless (fruit being an obvious example).

The greatest supporter of the street traders was undoubtedly the late Tony Gregory T.D., who fought a campaign to uphold the constitutional rights of street traders to earn a living and provide for their families. Tony Gregory considered the arrest of street traders to be an attack on inner city communities and an attempt to destroy traditional livelihoods. He was particularly aggrieved that the drugs trade was rampant in the inner city, and rather than arresting street traders, he felt that Garda effort should have been focused on catching those involved in the drugs trade. Street trading was an issue that Tony was involved in up to the end of his career, and one of his last political appearances was in *Bananas on Breadboards* – a film about street trading in the markets area of the city. When he died in 2009, Tony Gregory was mourned particularly by the street traders.

In early 1985, Tony and the local Garda Superintendent organised a mass meeting on the issue of street trading. At the meeting, it was agreed that a solution needed to be found to the problem of the numerous arrests that had occurred in 1984. However, despite the best intentions, Tony and fellow councillor Christy Burke continued to be called on to represent women who had been arrested for street trading. In July 1985, matters came to a head when a perceived increase in the harassment of street traders by the Gardaí led to a protest by street traders in Dublin city centre. Following the arrest of three women traders for the non-payment of fines imposed for trading illegally, several women blocked O'Connell Street with their prams. The Gardaí attempted unsuccessfully to move the prams, and then summoned reinforcements from Store Street Garda Station. Following the arrival of about 10 Garda vans and 50 Gardaí, one of the vans attempted to drive a wedge though the crowd of people who were sitting down in protest. At this point, violent scuffles broke out between those gathered and the Gardaí which resulted in several people, including some women street traders, being injured. As a result of the disturbances, at least seven people were arrested, including three with high public profiles: Tony Gregory, Christy Burke and Joe Costello.

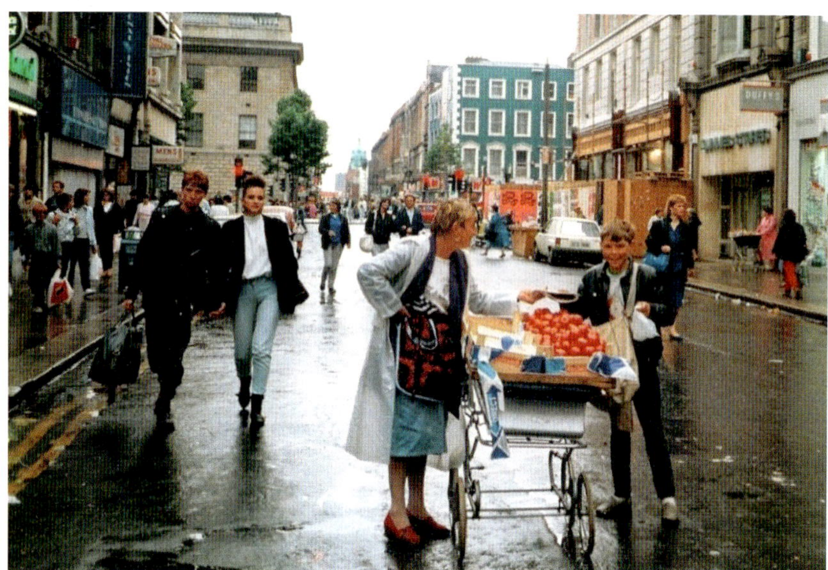

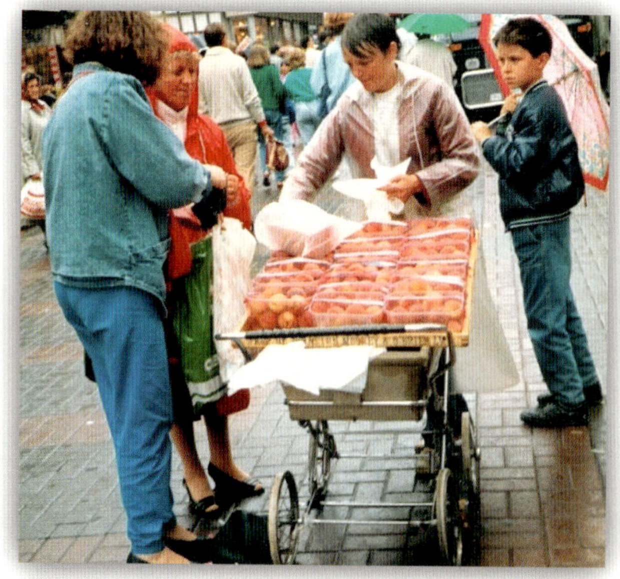

Street traders in 1988. **Above Left:** North Earl Street. **Above Right**: Henry Street.
(Courtesy of Lily Kearns)

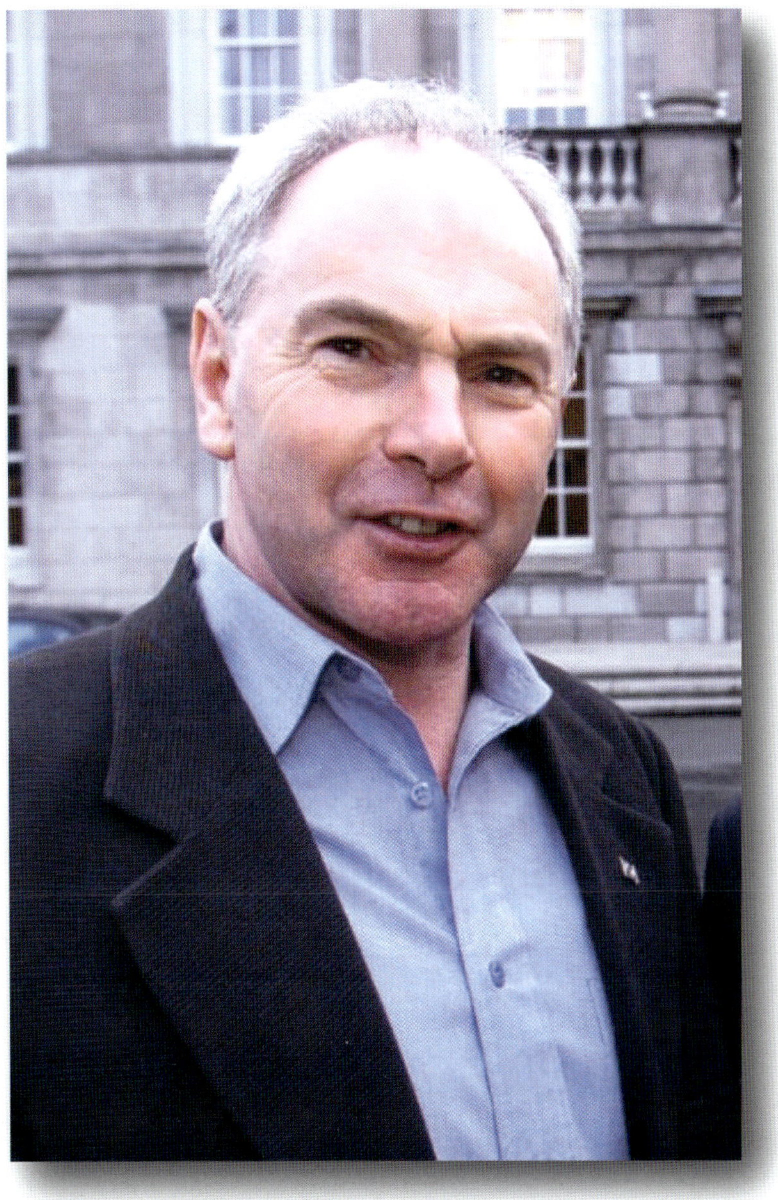

Tony Gregory was subsequently charged with causing a breach of the peace and obstructing traffic. When later convicted of both charges, he refused to sign a bond to keep the peace for six months, stating: 'I represent some of the poorest people in the country and I'm not going to give a guarantee that I will not involve myself with protests on their behalf'. His refusal to sign the bond, along with non-payment of the fines incurred, led to his imprisonment for 14 days in January 1986. Christy Burke joined Tony in Mountjoy prison for his involvement a few days later. While Gregory served his prison term, those whom he had supported at the protest the previous summer turned out in numbers outside Mountjoy prison every evening. They marched to Mountjoy with their prams at six o'clock every evening, singing 'Molly Malone' and a variant of the well-known Dolly Parton song 'Stand by your Pram'! A more formal concert was organised by the protesters on a bitterly cold afternoon at which the greatly appreciative audience was treated to music provided mainly by local inner city groups, with a guest appearance by Ronnie Drew of the Dubliners.

Left: The late Tony Gregory T.D., a great champion of street traders. *(Courtesy of Independent Newspapers)*

The protests were embarrassing for the government and served to greatly raise the profile of the street traders' situation. However, the whole episode did not lead to any great change in the approach of the authorities to the street trading issue. Over the next decade or so, Tony's commitment to the street traders never faltered. Then in 1993, in a gesture that was considered significant by all concerned, the Ilac Centre, Dunnes Stores and Roches Stores presented twelve new stalls in Cole's Lane to the street traders.

The street trading issue returned to prominence a couple of years later and became the subject of a heated debate in the Dáil in the summer of 1995. On this occasion, it was not the 'pram women' that appeared to be the target of the proposed legislation, but the more transient and unscrupulous casual traders that set up business one day and were gone the next. The reason that the debates are of interest here is that the Dáil transcripts seem to reveal a softening in attitudes towards traditional street traders of Dublin on the part of contributors. The contributions of several speakers were characterised by affection and respect for the traders.

The then Minister for State at the Department of Enterprise and Employment, Pat Rabbitte T.D., highlighted the important role that street traders had played in the life of the city. He noted that the Moore Street traders had 'made their contribution in a special way' and 'had been there as long as the shops against which they compete'. Support for the traders also came from Senator David Norris, who noted that 'these women have to pay to be arrested. Every time they and their goods are brought to the Garda station, they are charged for the dubious privilege. They then have to pay again to get their goods back – goods for which they have paid legally with their own hard-earned money'.

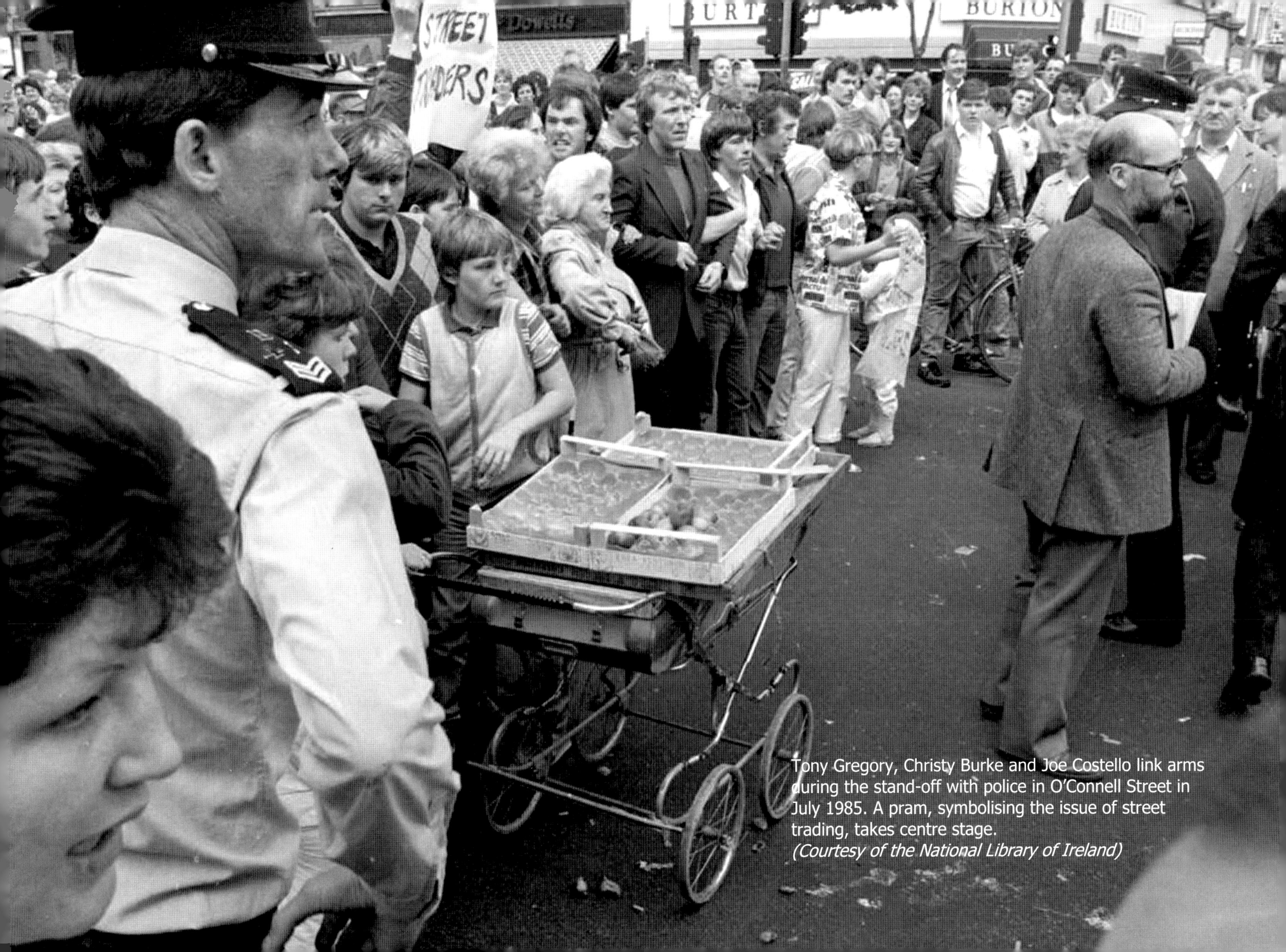

Tony Gregory, Christy Burke and Joe Costello link arms during the stand-off with police in O'Connell Street in July 1985. A pram, symbolising the issue of street trading, takes centre stage.
(Courtesy of the National Library of Ireland)

The contribution to the debate by Senator Joe O'Toole underscored further the extent of solidarity with the traders: 'Markets and street trading are an essential part of the atmosphere and colour of a city. People come to Dublin and they visit Moore Street because they have heard and read about it'. He went on to say: 'In the inner city, there is great support for the street traders as the Minister will be aware. They are considered a focal point of the city and are also considered to be honest and decent. These people are barely making a living or are not making a living. They are topping up their income. Many people in the city, including street traders, would say that it is better to see people employed – in the narrow sense of the word – in street trading than doing nothing or being involved in some socially unacceptable activity'. He went on to describe the traders as people 'who worked outside in all sorts of weather, day after day, year after year'. Furthermore, they 'have to pack their materials out of the way every night; they have to hustle for business; they have to stay out in all weathers; and they have to be on duty from the time they start in the morning until they finish in the evening. It is not a regular or ordinary situation'.

It seems, therefore, that while the efforts of those such as Tony Gregory did not result in huge improvements in the conditions in which traders operated, there certainly seemed to be something of a change in attitude towards them. To me, the pram traders might be regarded as authentic entrepreneurs, people who bring fresh fruit and other produce closer to the people of Dublin and in doing so make a small profit. They are part of what makes Dublin city what it is.

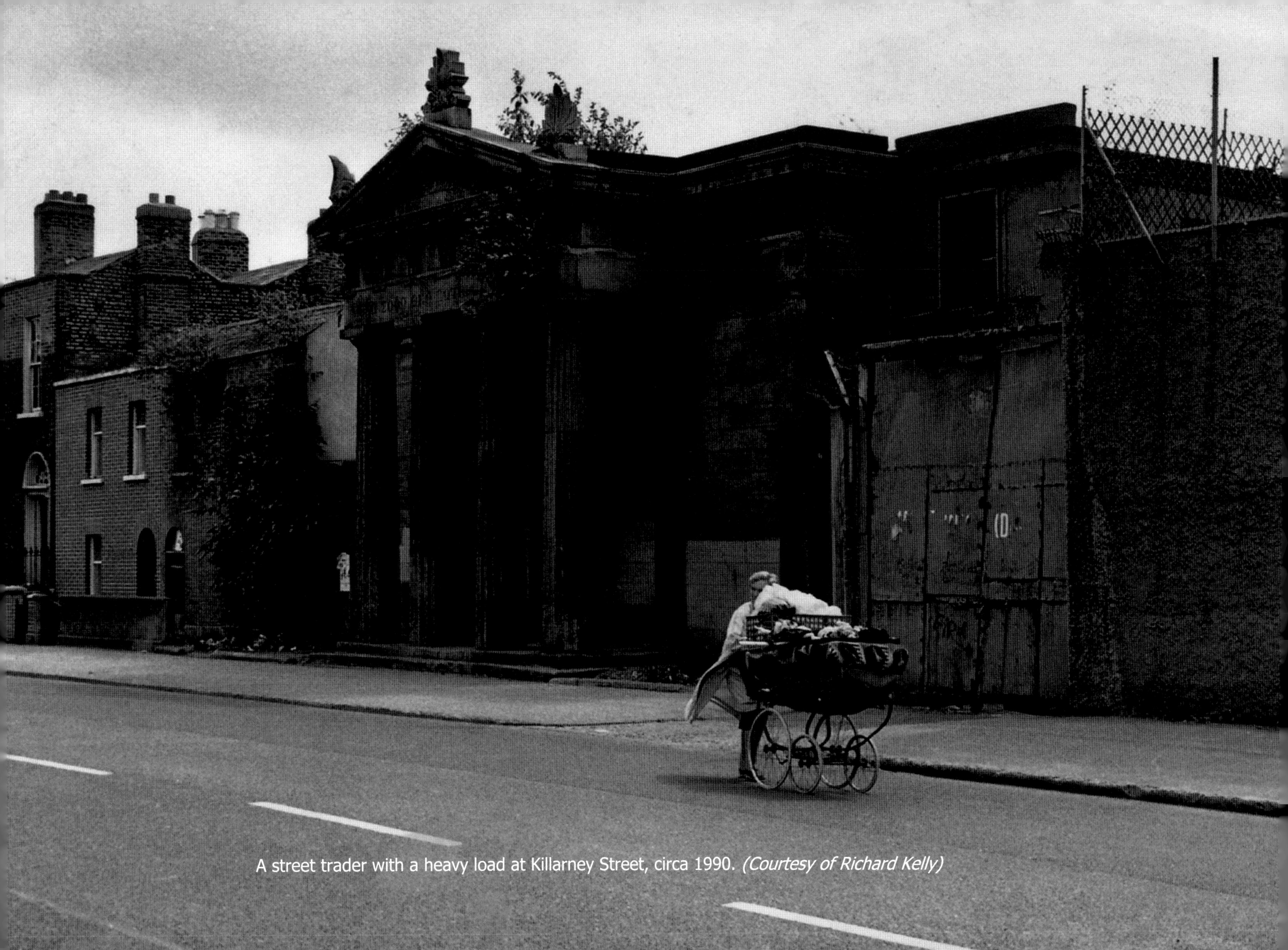

A street trader with a heavy load at Killarney Street, circa 1990. *(Courtesy of Richard Kelly)*

Dublin's Modern Street Traders and their Prams in Words and Pictures

Ellen's Story

Ellen Preston is a tiny woman with a huge spirit. Now aged 84, she has been married to her husband, Peter, for 64 years. They have twelve children (seven boys and five girls), 36 grandchildren and 32 great grandchildren. Over the course of an afternoon, sitting in her cosy kitchen, and accompanied by several pots of tea, she told me about her life as a street trader. One of the first things she told me is that she reared her twelve children by selling from her pram.

Ellen is the fourth generation of women in her family involved in street trading (indeed, her own daughter is the fifth). Her great grandmother lived on High Street in Dublin's Liberties, and had been a street trader on Meath Street, and her daughter (Ellen's grandmother) followed in her footsteps. The family eventually moved to the north side of the Liffey, and Ellen's mother got a stall outside Kearns' butcher shop in Parnell Street from which she sold fruit. However, she stopped trading altogether following the tragic death of her young son in an accident. Ellen's older sister took over her stall, and Ellen helped to run it. By the time Ellen was an adult, the fruit stall she and her sister ran together could no longer support the two of them. Ellen decided to get herself a pram.

In those days, prams were very easy to come by. They were to be found in attics or for sale in second hand markets, such as the one in Cumberland Street. Armed with her pram, Ellen made her way to the fruit market in Smithfield. There she bought a box of bananas, a box of oranges and a box of pears. She headed for the arcade near the General Post Office, a place that was to become her regular trading spot. She also pushed her pram up Grafton Street where she sold the best of strawberries to regular customers such as the comedienne Maureen Potter. For St Patrick's Day, she would spend hours picking shamrock in the fields in Artane and selling it later from her pram in town. At Easter, she bought lots of little chocolate eggs and dressed them up in little baskets to sell from her pram. The profits were small, but it was enough to buy dinner for the children and a loaf of bread and some butter.

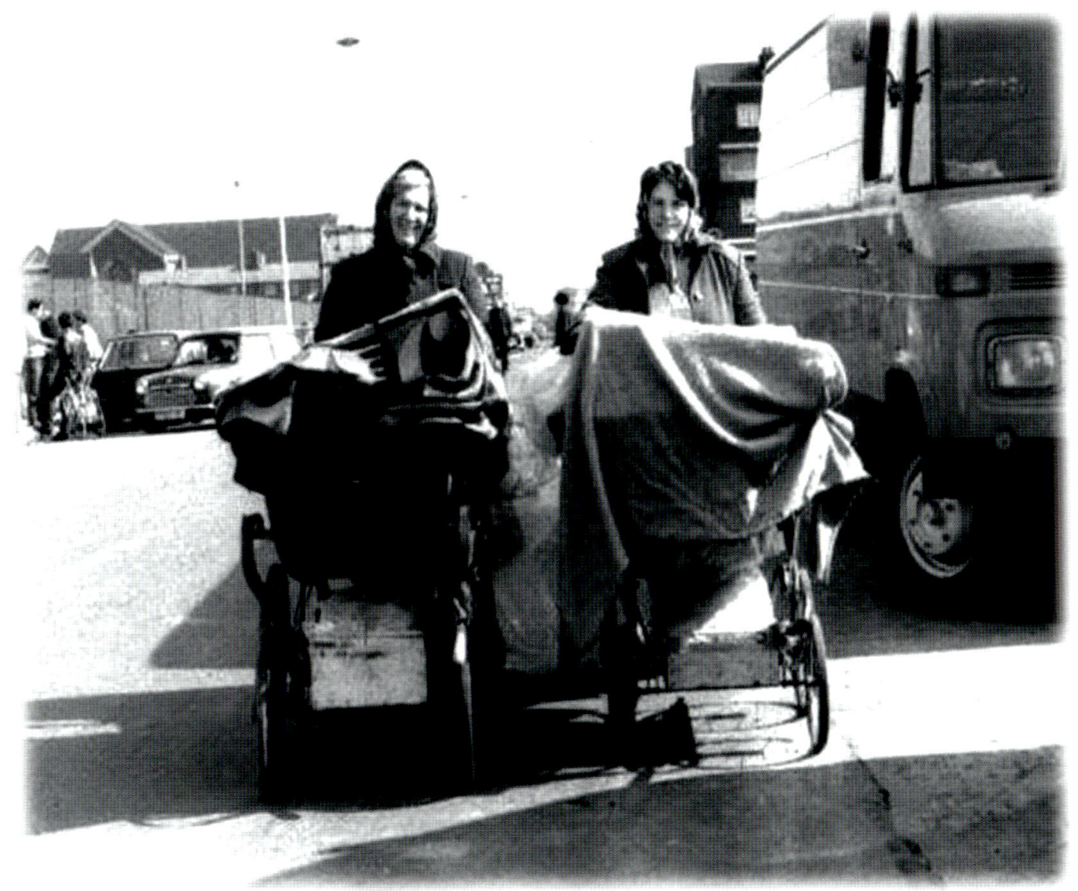

Ellen (right) and her friend Esther Mangan push their prams along Seán McDermott Street, Dublin, circa 1981. *(Courtesy of Pat Farrell)*

In those days, there was a great sense of friendship and unity among the traders. They would help each other out if anyone was in trouble, and it was not uncommon for the traders to lend each other the money to buy fruit and be repaid when the fruit was sold. Ellen particularly loved the Christmas trading season, when Henry Street was lit up and alive with carol singers and street traders. On one occasion she recalled how an entrepreneurial 'Santa Claus' who was charging a small sum for children to have their photographs taken with him was arrested in Henry Street and marched by the Gardaí down to Store Street Garda station. However, the children were so angry that Santa had been arrested that they followed him in *Pied Piper* fashion to the station. Eventually – and one would hope in the spirit of Christmas – the Gardaí were forced to release Santa without charge.

When Ben Dunne Senior opened his first big shop in Henry Street, the people of Dublin city came in their droves for the bargains. The pram traders spotted this as a sales opportunity and lined up with their prams each day outside the newly opened Dunne's Stores. Ben Dunne respected the traders, and considered them entrepreneurs like himself.

'How did you do today, girls?' he would ask as he left the shop in the evening, occasionally buying a bit of fruit from one of them.

'Grand, thanks Mr Dunne,' they would say.

'Fair play to you, girls,' he would add.

When the current flagship store opened on the same spot decades later, the traders feared that they might not be welcomed by the new management. However, the new CEO, Margaret Heffernan, welcomed them as her father had done before, telling them: 'My father loved every one of you, and you are welcome to stay and trade beside the shop'.

Life was very hard as a street trader. With a growing family to look after as well as her work as a street trader, Ellen often did not get to bed until two or three in the morning, not long before she had to get up again to get the children dressed, washed, and out to school. Due to her circumstances, the local priest wrote a letter to the children's school seeking a special dispensation for them to leave the school at lunchtime to go home for their dinner. Ellen would be there with dinner ready, having spent the morning selling from her pram. When the children returned to school in the afternoon, she took to the streets once again with her pram.

Ellen traded every day. One day, heavily pregnant with one of her children, she went out trading in the snow and brought her hospital 'parcel' containing personal items and things for the baby with her (just in case). Later that day she walked straight from work through the snow to the Rotunda hospital and had her baby. A week later, she was back on the street, earning a living. Although life was hard, Ellen loved her life as a street trader. Firm friendships that survive to this day were made with other traders.

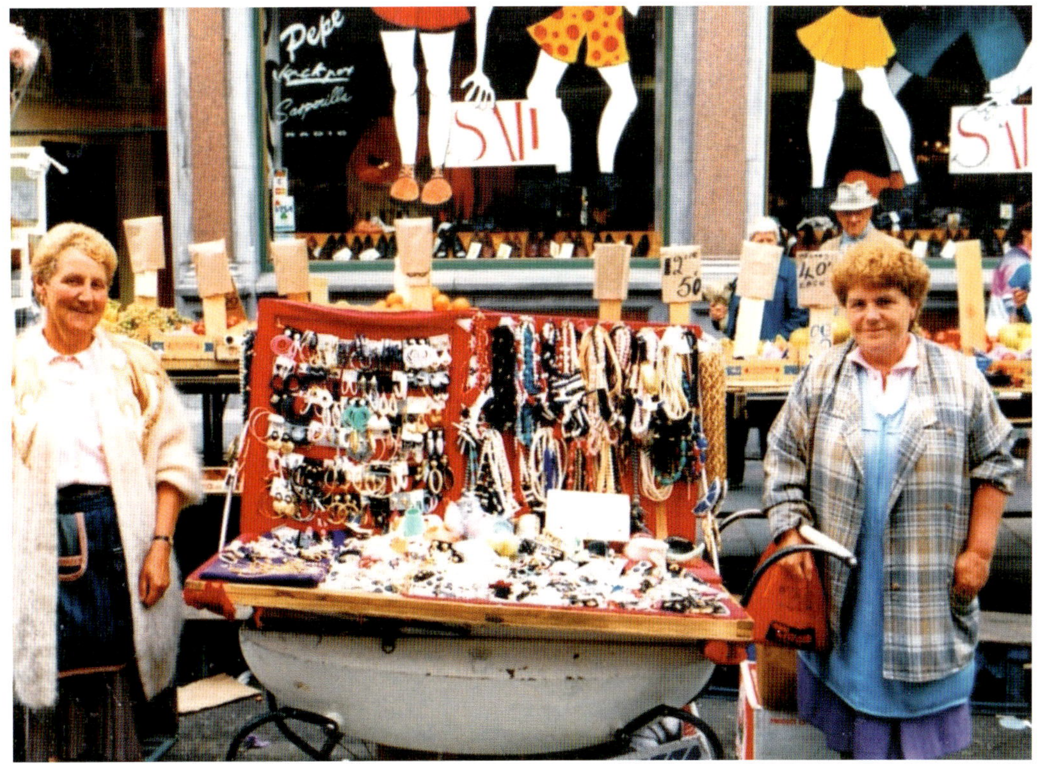

Ellen (right) and May Hutch with a pram full of jewellery at Moore Street in the 1980s. *(Courtesy of Ellen Preston)*

Court appearances were also a common occurrence. During one of Ellen's appearances, the judge inquired as to why the women were being brought in front of him. The attending Garda, pointing to one of the accused, replied 'This woman was found selling strawberries outside Clery's, your Honour'. The judge was outraged and dismissed the case, saying that they were only hard-working women trying to earn a living for their families. The street traders were often dealt with compassionately by the courts, and the judges' attitudes would usually soften when they heard about the women's circumstances. 'How many children have you got?' they would enquire of each of them. Ellen recalled how on one occasion Justice O'Grady fined each woman before him half a crown before instructing them: 'now go on about your business'.

When relations between the authorities and the street traders deteriorated to an all-time low in the summer of 1985, Ellen recalls the Gardaí being dispatched in riot gear to face the traders. When Garda Paddy Boylan asked Ellen and five other traders to move on from their spot in Moore Street, they refused to move. Instead, they engaged in a sit down protest, demanding stalls from the Corporation. In the melee that followed the clashes, Ellen and her friend May were mystified as to what had become of their prams which were nowhere to be found. After looking everywhere for them, the prams eventually were located in the morgue of the old Jervis Street Hospital!

There was a lot of fun to be had too, not to mention many escapades involving *cat and mouse* games with the Gardaí. Encounters with them were a regular occurrence for all street traders. Because many, including Ellen, did not hold permits to trade, they were regularly chased by Gardaí through the streets with their prams, arrested, and put into vans to be brought to Store Street station. Some of the Gardaí were particularly kind to the women they arrested, and when they arrived at Store Street station they would make them pots of tea, and even go to the local takeaway and buy chips for them!

In the 1960s, Ellen often sold fruit from her pram on O'Connell Bridge and sometimes caught the eye of the Garda directing traffic from a pointsman's box in the centre of the street. It was not unknown for him to abandon his station in pursuit of the traders and their prams. On one occasion, the Gardaí swooped on Ellen and several other traders when they found them trading in Henry Street. Ellen ran up Dominic Street and into the church where she hid in a confession box until the danger had passed. Others who took a detour into Dominic Street flats were not so lucky and were apprehended by the Gardaí. One particular Garda sergeant had the specific job of dealing with the street traders in the 1980s, and he knew the name and family circumstances of each of them. When he retired, the traders held a collection for him to show there were no hard feelings!

I spent the afternoon listening to Ellen tell stories about her life as a street trader. Before I left, she brought me out to the yard to show me her pram. It is a beautiful *racing green* Silver Cross pram with white coach lines, and of course, it has a breadboard on top. Then, she brought me into her sitting room and showed me a table covered in framed photographs of her children, grandchildren, and great grandchildren. As I looked at all the faces, I could not help wondering how different it all might have been had it not been for Ellen and her pram.

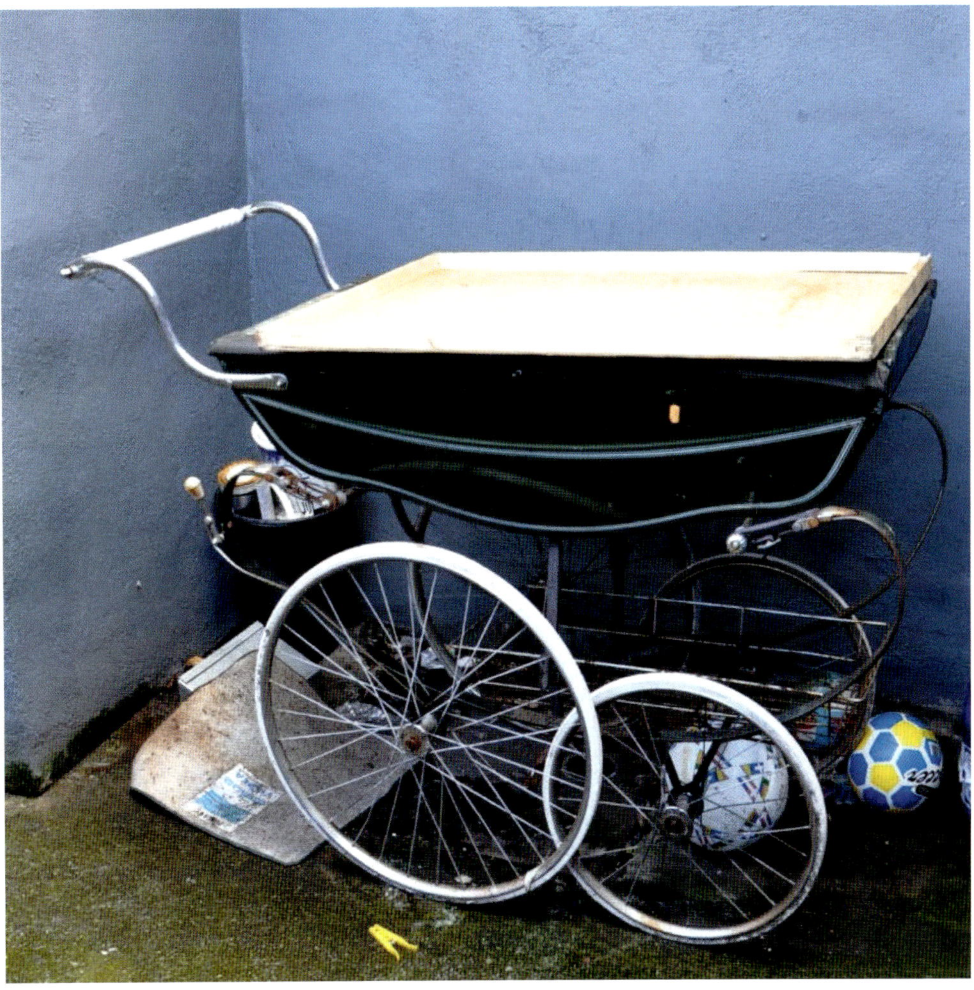

Left: Ellen's pram that she keeps in her yard.

PHOTO GALLERY 1: DUBLIN'S WORKING PRAMS IN THE 21ST CENTURY

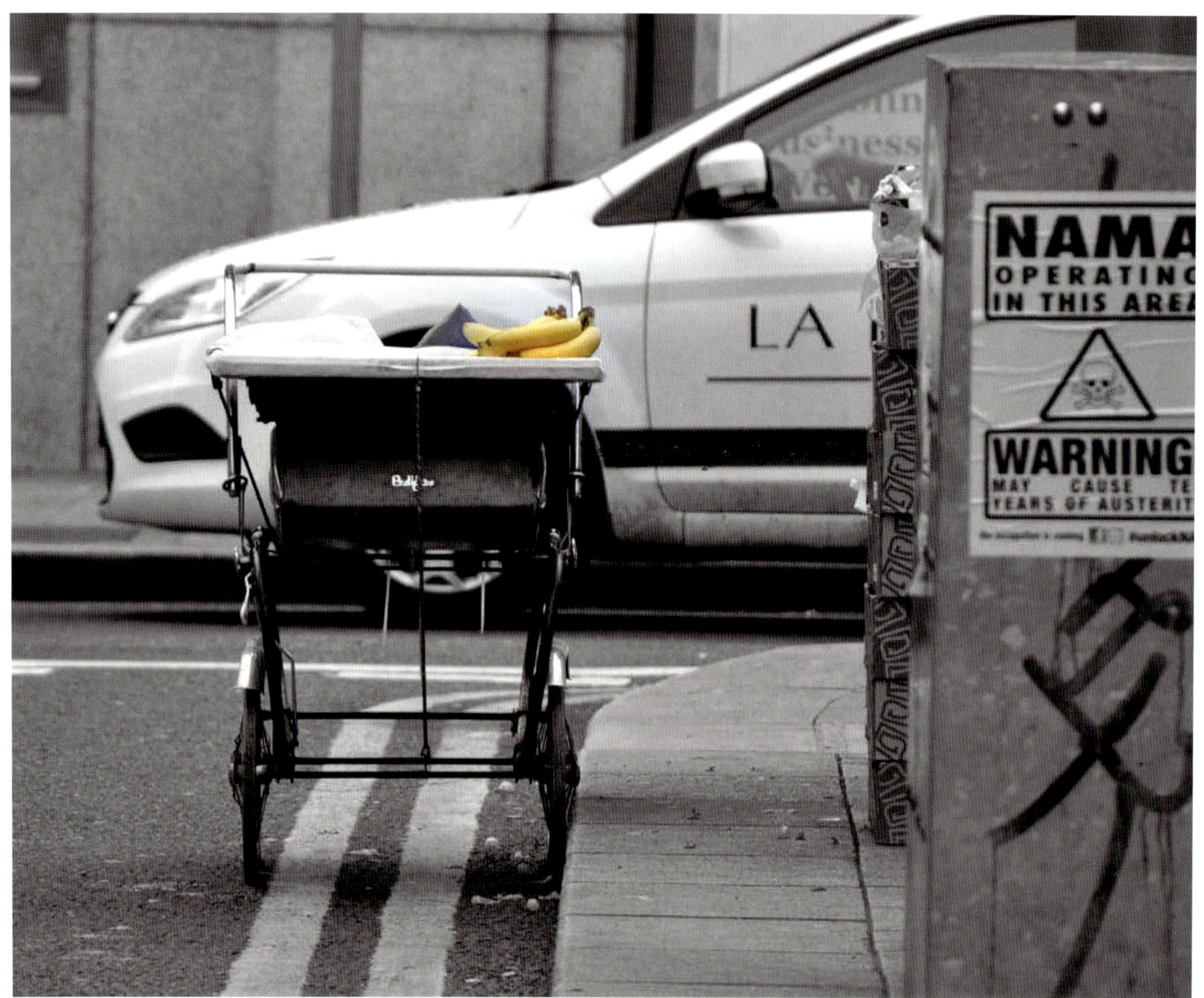

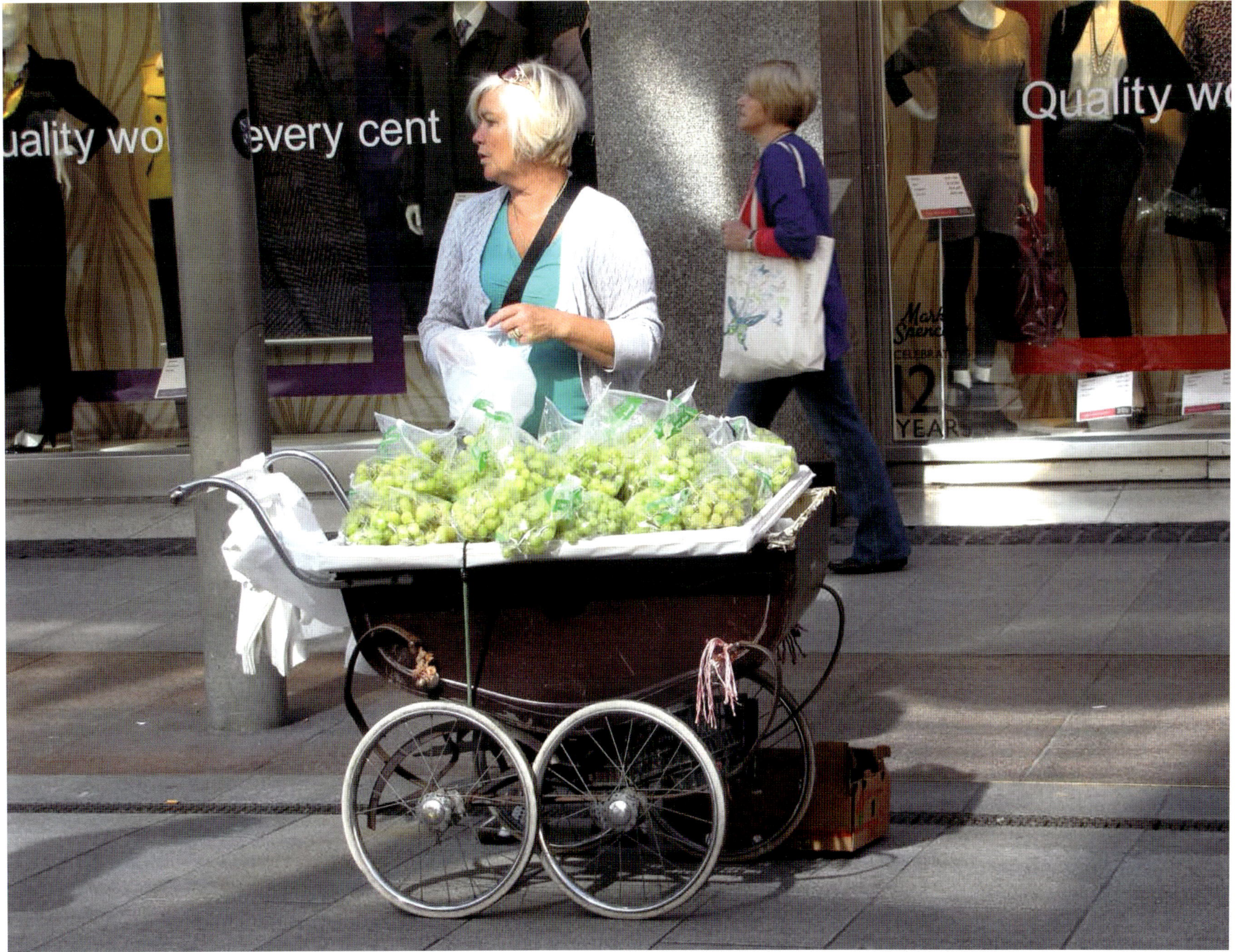
uality wo
every cent
Quality wo
12
YEAR

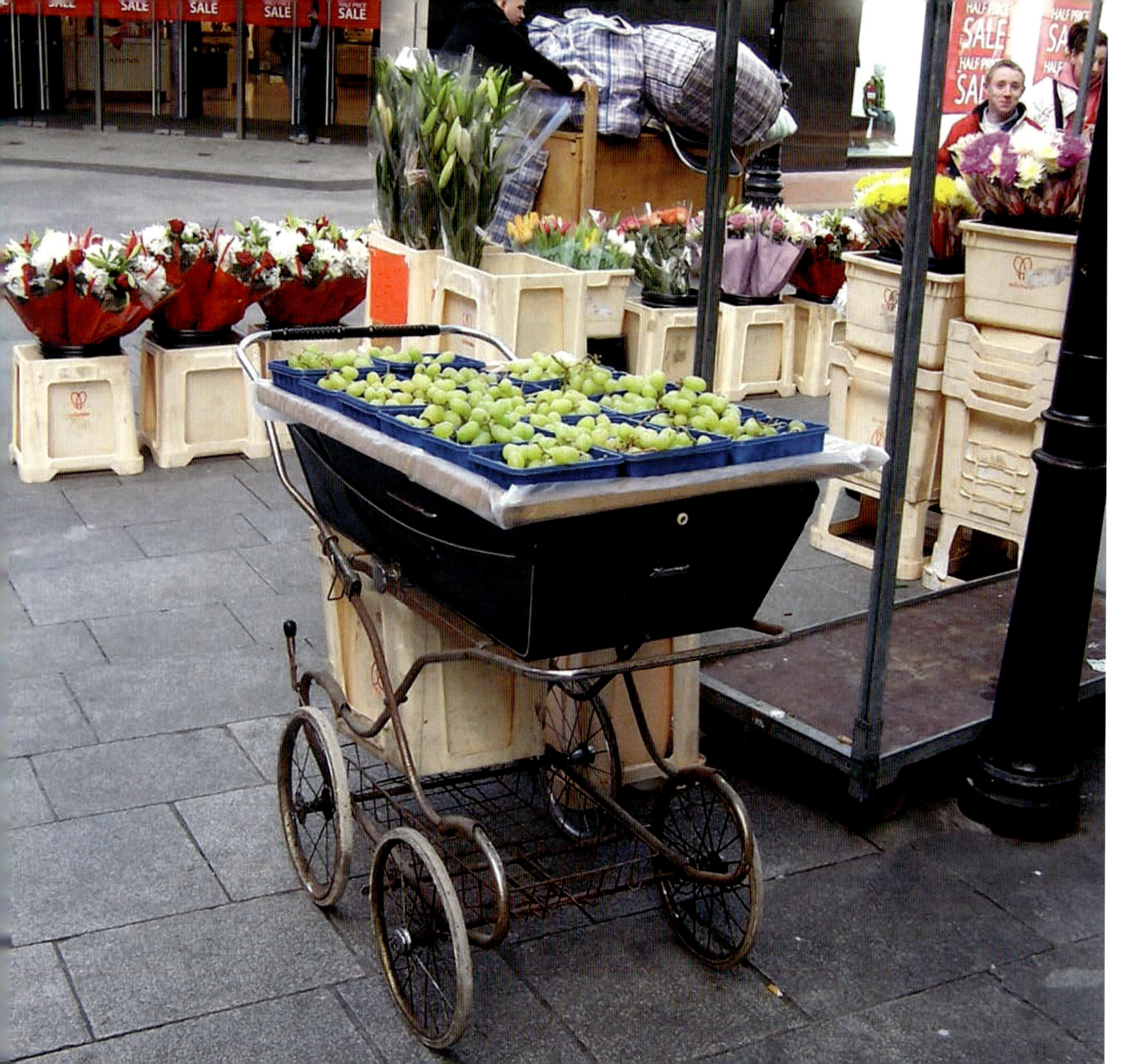
SALE
SALE
SALE
SALE
SALE
HALF PRICE
SALE

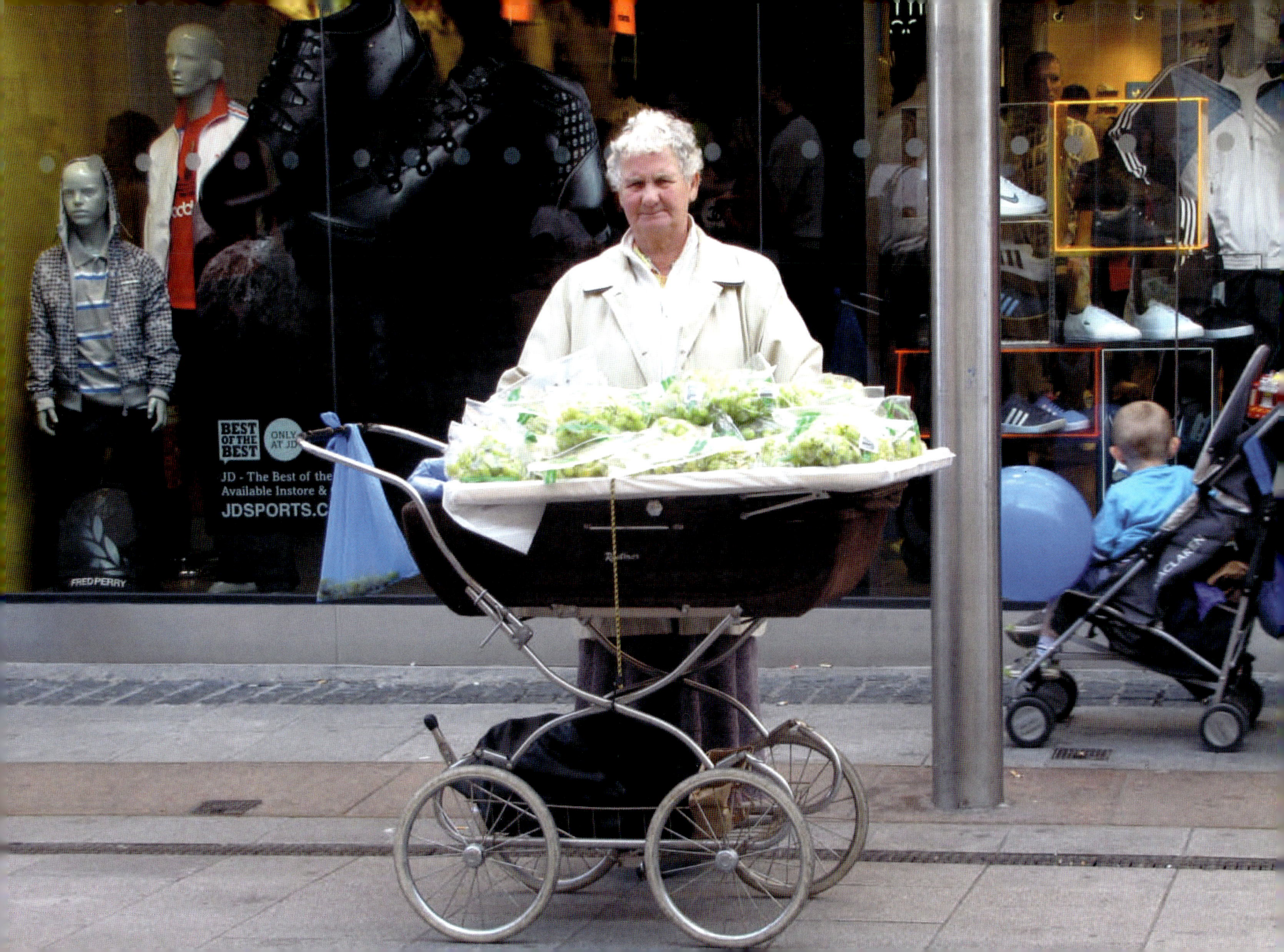
BEST OF THE BEST
ONLY AT JD
JD - The Best of the
Available Instore &
JDSPORTS.C
FRED PERRY

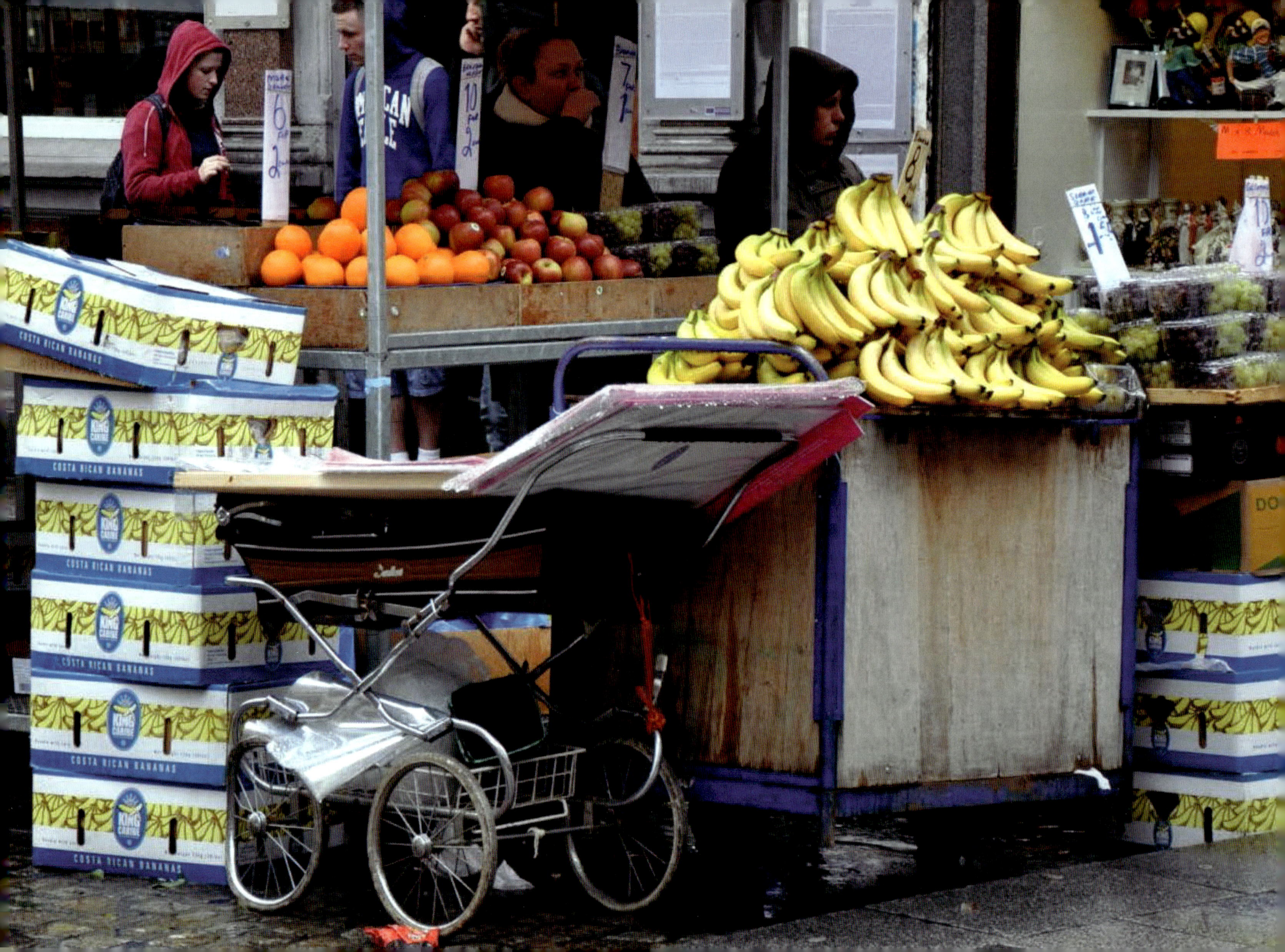
KING CARIBE
COSTA RICAN BANANAS

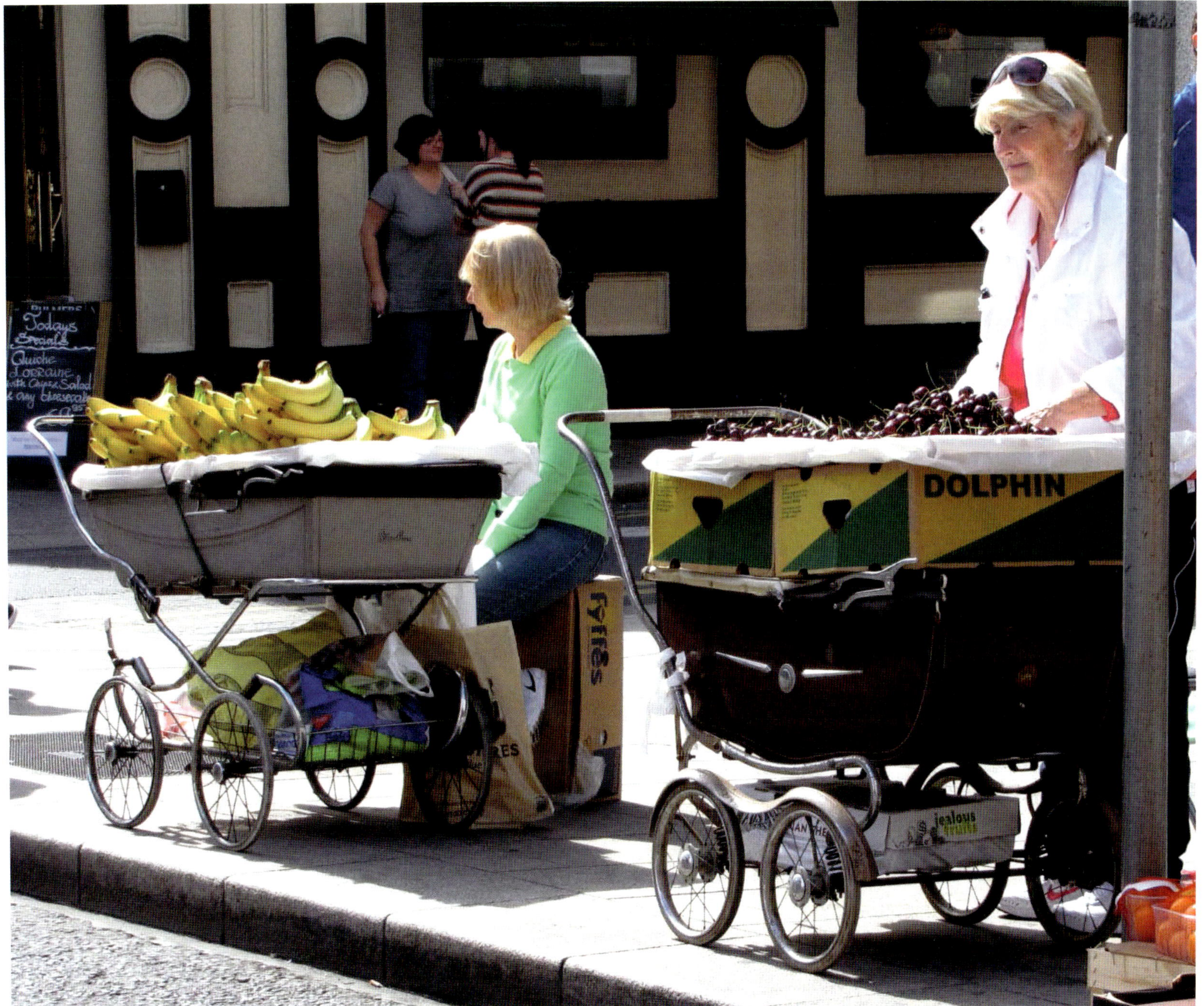
Todays
Specials
Quiche
Lorraine
DOLPHIN
fyffes

Calla's Story

Calla (Kathleen) Duffy, one of Dublin's best known and longest serving street traders, passed away in 2008. Her daughter Marion, who is also a street trader, told me a little about her mother's life.

Calla's mother was a street trader and Calla herself began street trading when she was still a child. Before school, Calla like many children of street traders, went out selling fruit and chocolate from a basket to customers waiting for the trams. She would then return home, change into her school clothes, and set off for school in George's Hill Convent in the markets area of the city. In the circumstances it is not surprising that street trading was to become her life-long occupation.

She mainly sold fruit, but like many traders, sold other goods as the seasons dictated. Calla was known for her resourcefulness. When the shamrock she had acquired to sell on St Patrick's Day was deemed not to be green enough, she gave nature a helping hand and dyed the bunches a deeper green! Other traders were inspired by this move and did likewise.

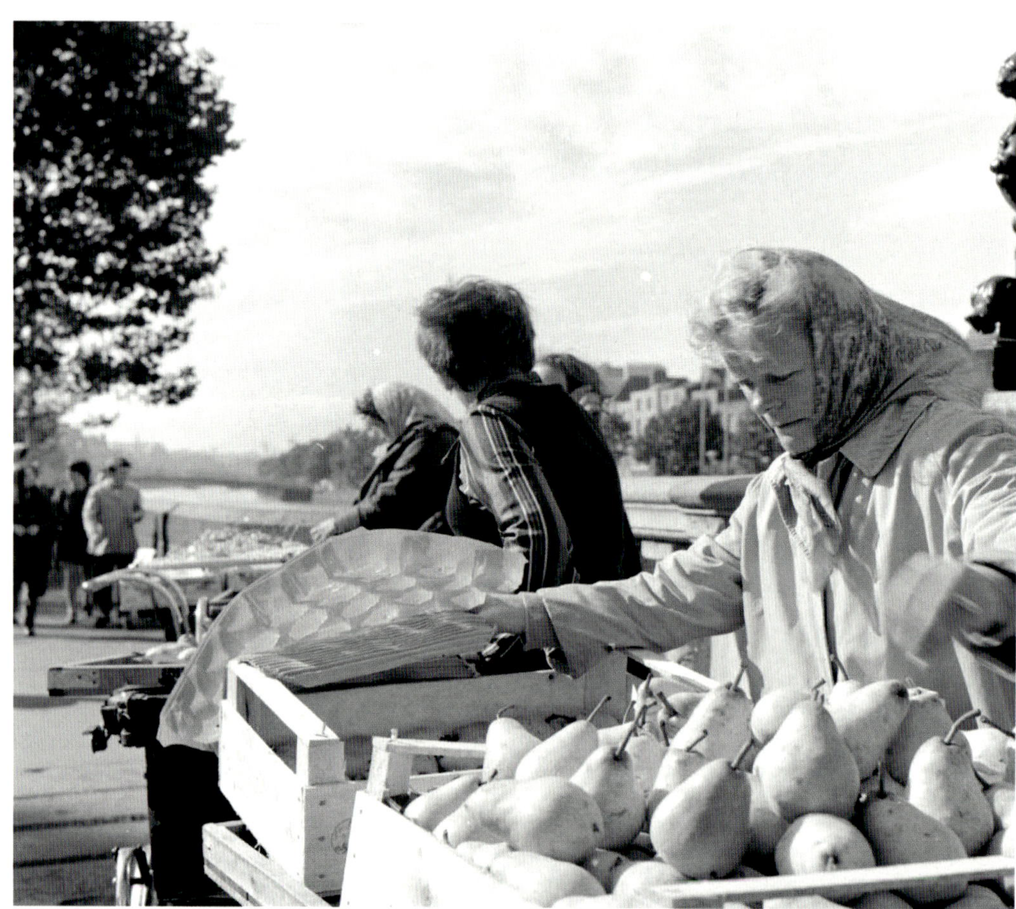

Above Right: Calla selling pears from her pram at Aston Quay, Dublin, in 1969. Sometimes one of her babies could be found asleep in a banana box under the pram as she worked! *(Courtesy of the National Library of Ireland)*

Calla and her childhood friend Tricia Hand (who features later in this book) worked side-by-side for many of the sixty years or so that they were street traders. They were born six weeks apart and passed away within a few months of each other. The banter between the women was so entertaining that the comedian Brendan O'Carroll used to go into town to pick up tips for his shows by listening to the two of them sparking off each other.

On one occasion, when Calla and Tricia wanted a break from trading to go for a cup of tea, they asked two schoolgirls to look after their prams. However, they were gone so long that when they returned, the girls had sold all the fruit, pocketed the proceeds, and abandoned the two empty prams. The two women were philosophical about such things. Although they earned a living as street traders, it was not all about the money. It was more about a way of life, and, although it was a hard life, they really enjoyed the lifestyle and the interaction they had with the people of the city. Often, they would give an extra bag of fruit to someone they knew was in need. Other times they would see mothers with children that they knew had very little, or notice some poor children looking at the fruit. It was not unknown for Calla or Tricia to hand a five-pound note to one of the children and say 'here – put that in your sock and make sure you all have your dinner tonight'. These gestures had a simple basis – while Calla and the other traders did not have much money, they realised that the people that they helped out had even less. At her pitch in O'Connell Street, Calla often came to the rescue of women who had had their handbags snatched, encouraging them to sit with her while they recovered from the shock, before giving them the price of their bus fare home.

Kindnesses like these worked both ways. One staff member in Arnott's shop in Henry Street was particularly kind to Calla. When Calla picked out clothes for her children, he would carefully wrap them and set them aside for collection later during the sale, when she would be allowed to purchase them at a reduced price.

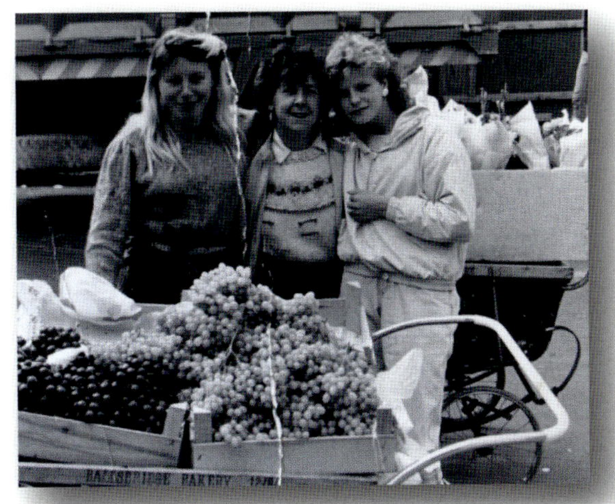

Above: Calla's daughter Marion (extreme right) as a young teenager with her friends who were also street traders and their prams. Every year Calla wrote a letter to Marion's primary school asking that she be excused from school for the month of December so she could help with the Christmas trade. *(Courtesy of Marion White)*

Although she was small woman, Calla had a fighting spirit when it came to insisting on her rights to trade in her native city. 'We are not pushing drugs, we are pushing prams' she would say. 'We are the poor and we are working for the poor'. When Calla was required to pay fines for so-called breaches of the laws on street trading, the 'warrant man' called to the house to collect the money in instalments. These instalments would eventually pay off the fines and offset any prospect of a prison sentence. However, the warrant man was a reluctant money collector, and had great sympathy for some of those from whom he collected. The warmth of the relationship between him and Calla was reflected in the fact that he was always invited inside for a cup of tea and almost always accepted.

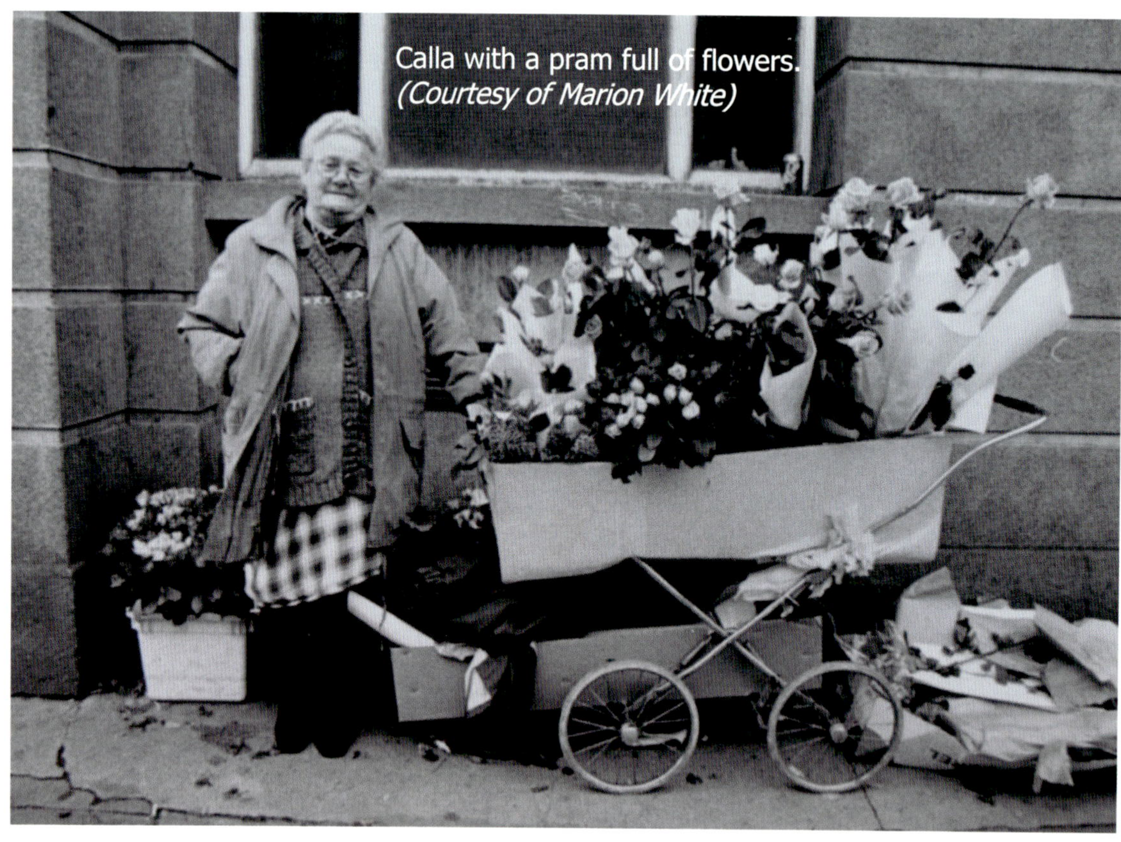

Calla with a pram full of flowers.
(Courtesy of Marion White)

When the long-standing street traders were offered permanent pitches by the authorities, Calla was allocated an official spot at the junction of Abbey Street and O'Connell Street just outside Clark's shoe shop. She gladly accepted the site, but refused a proper stall, preferring instead to continue selling off her little pram. Calla remained a street trader right up to the end of her life. It was the only life that she knew. Her mother's pram is now one of Marion's most treasured possessions. However, Marion also inherited a priceless legacy: The rights to remain trading on that pitch in the heart of Dublin city that her mother fought so hard to win.

In the last weeks of her life Calla, uncharacteristically, made an unexpected statement to Marion,

> 'I have no regrets', she suddenly announced.
>
> 'What about?' asked Marion.
>
> 'About life', she replied. 'I enjoyed every minute of my life. I wouldn't change a thing'.

It seems appropriate to leave the last word to one of Calla's regular customers, the writer Pat Ingoldsby, who wrote a poem in her honour shortly after she passed away. The following is an extract from that poem, and it speaks volumes about how highly Calla Duffy was thought of in her native city.

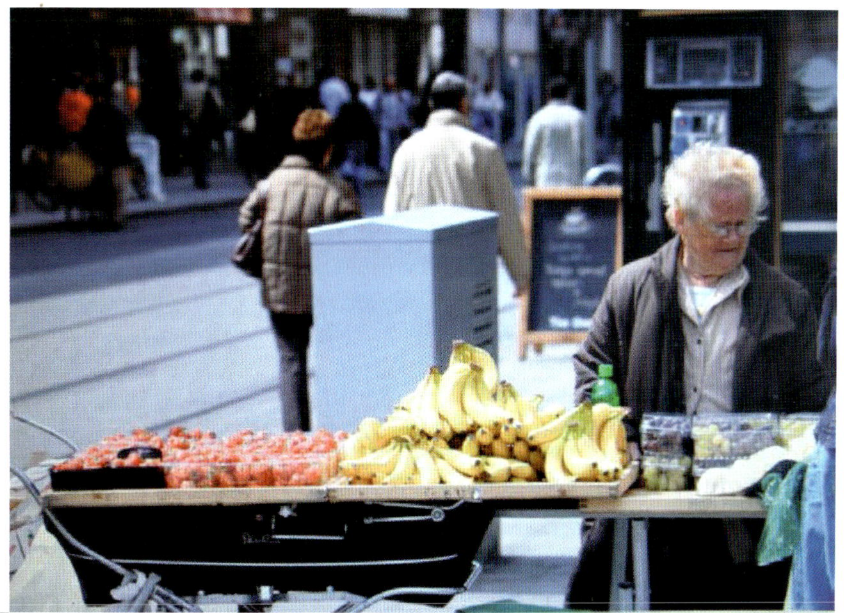

Above: Calla at her pitch on the corner of Abbey Street and O'Connell Street. *(Courtesy of Gary McMurray)*

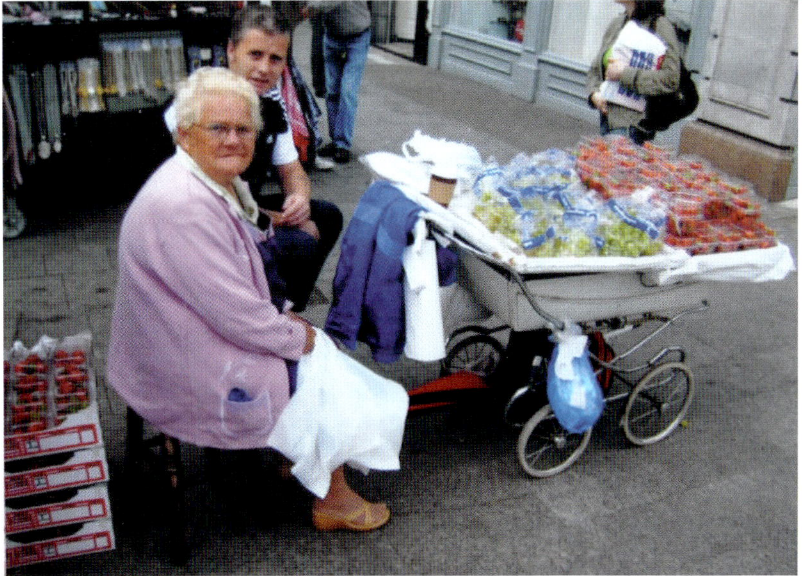

From: ***'A poem for Kathleen'***

... She was everything about this town I love and respect.
Sometimes I would be going down with my books
and she would handsel me with a Euro or two.
Sometimes I would be going home at night
and she would speed me on my way
with a bag of grapes or some bananas and pears.
Always she would have the good word.
...it was her city and it is much the poorer now without her.

by Pat Ingoldsby

Photo Gallery 2: Full Prams and Empty Prams

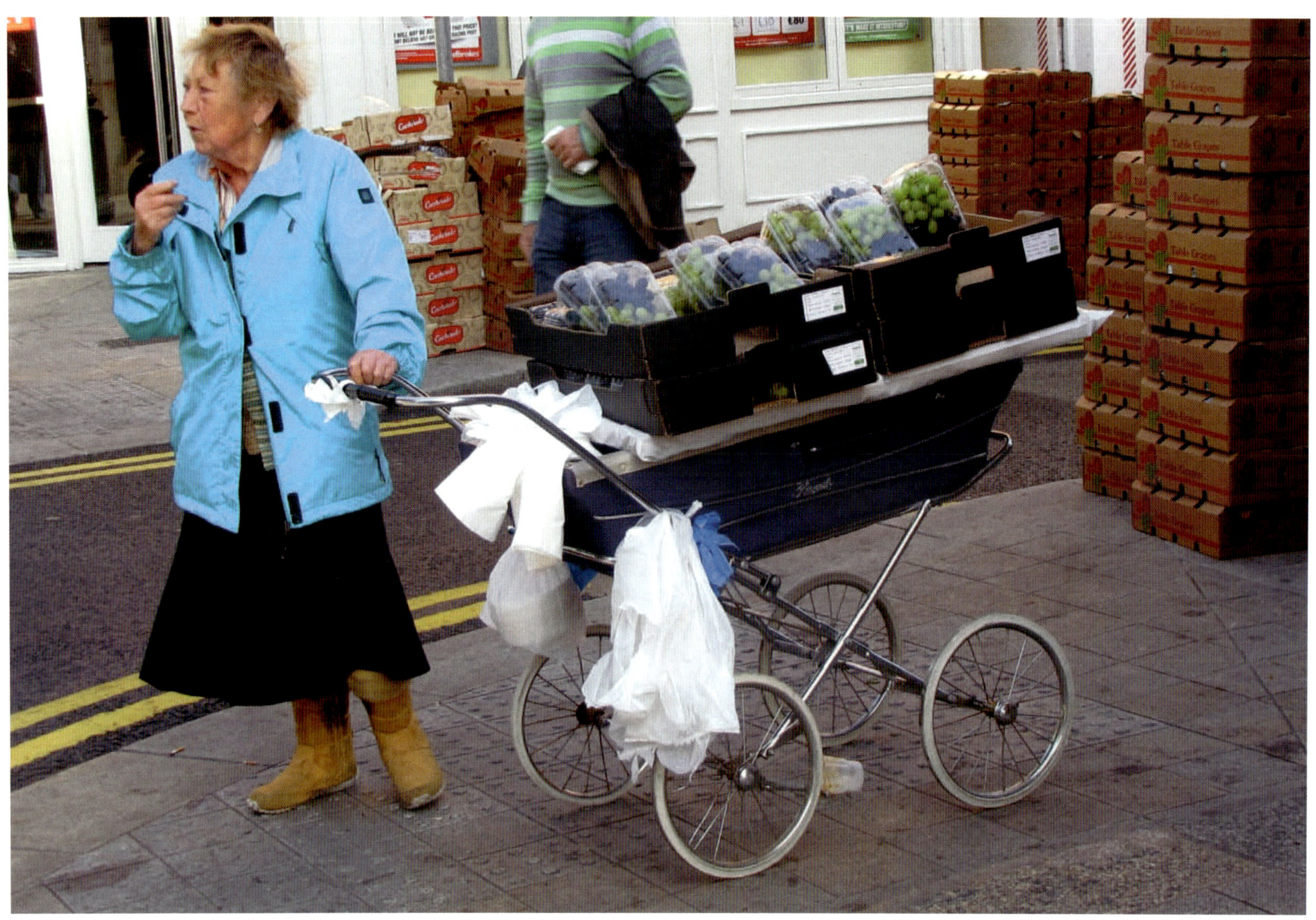

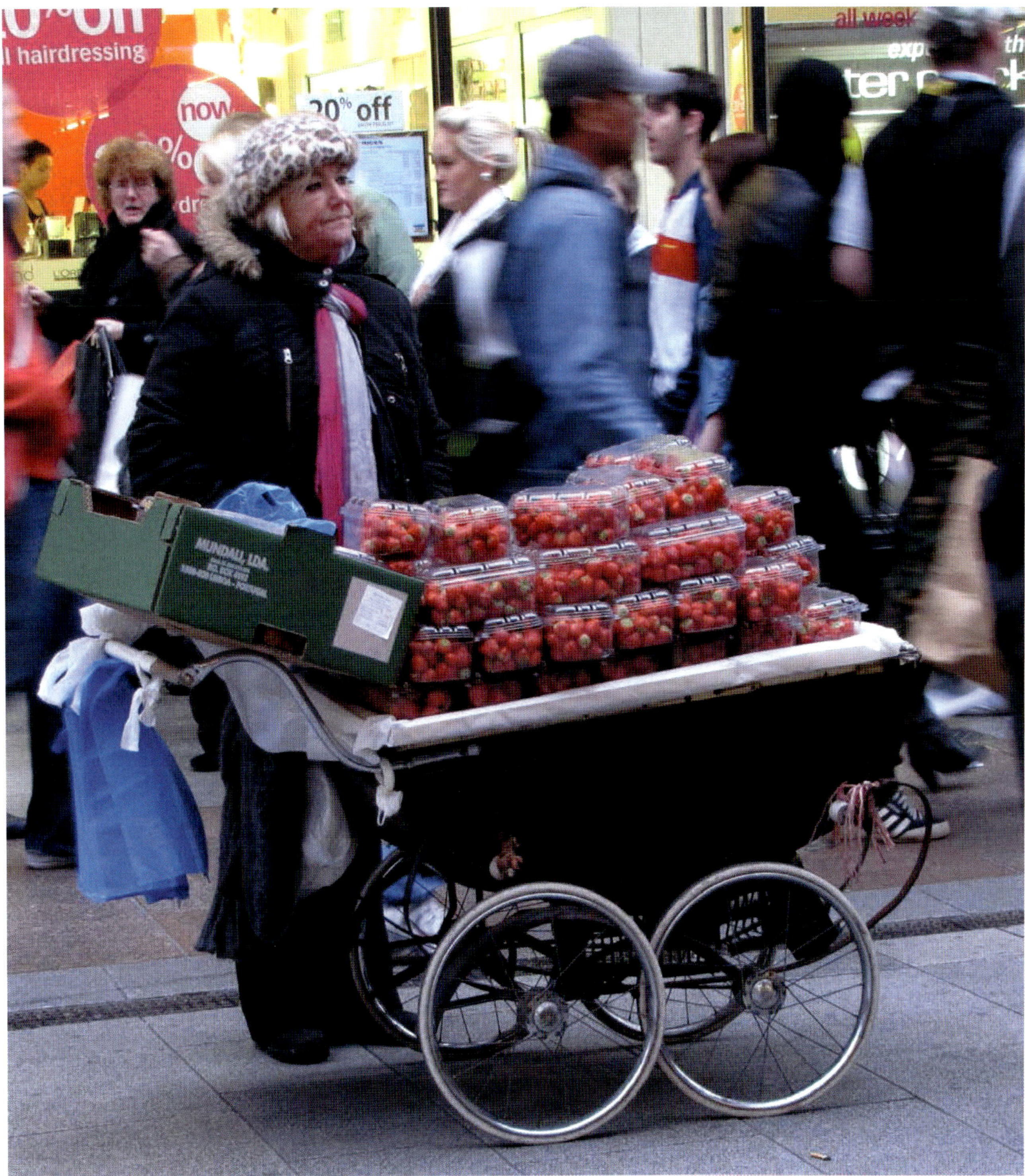
hairdressing
now
20% off
all week

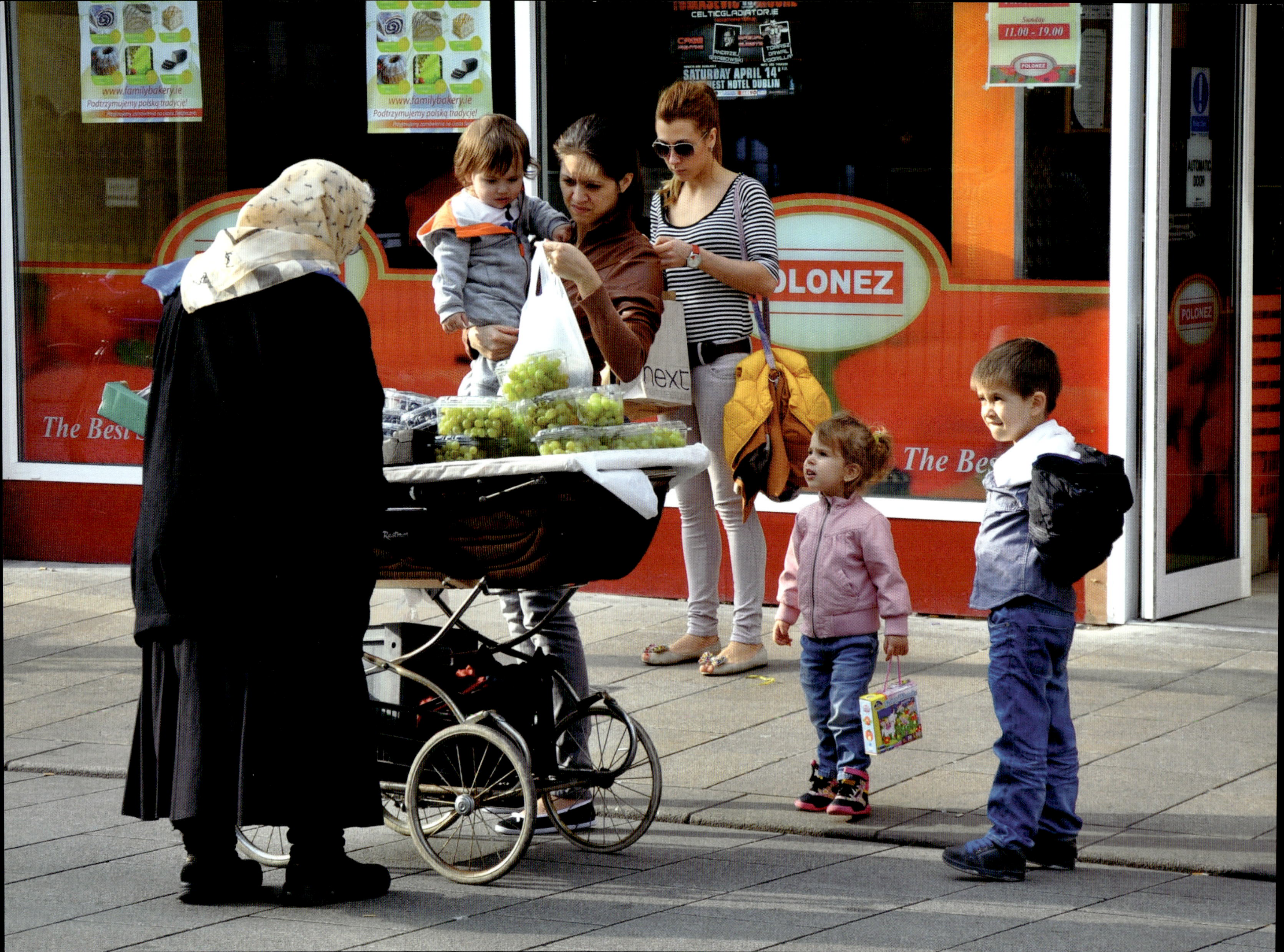
www.familybakery.ie
Podtrzymujemy polską tradycję!
www.familybakery.ie
Podtrzymujemy polską tradycję!
CELTICGLADIATOR.IE
SATURDAY APRIL 14
Sunday
11.00 - 19.00
POLONEZ
POLONEZ
The Best
The Best
next

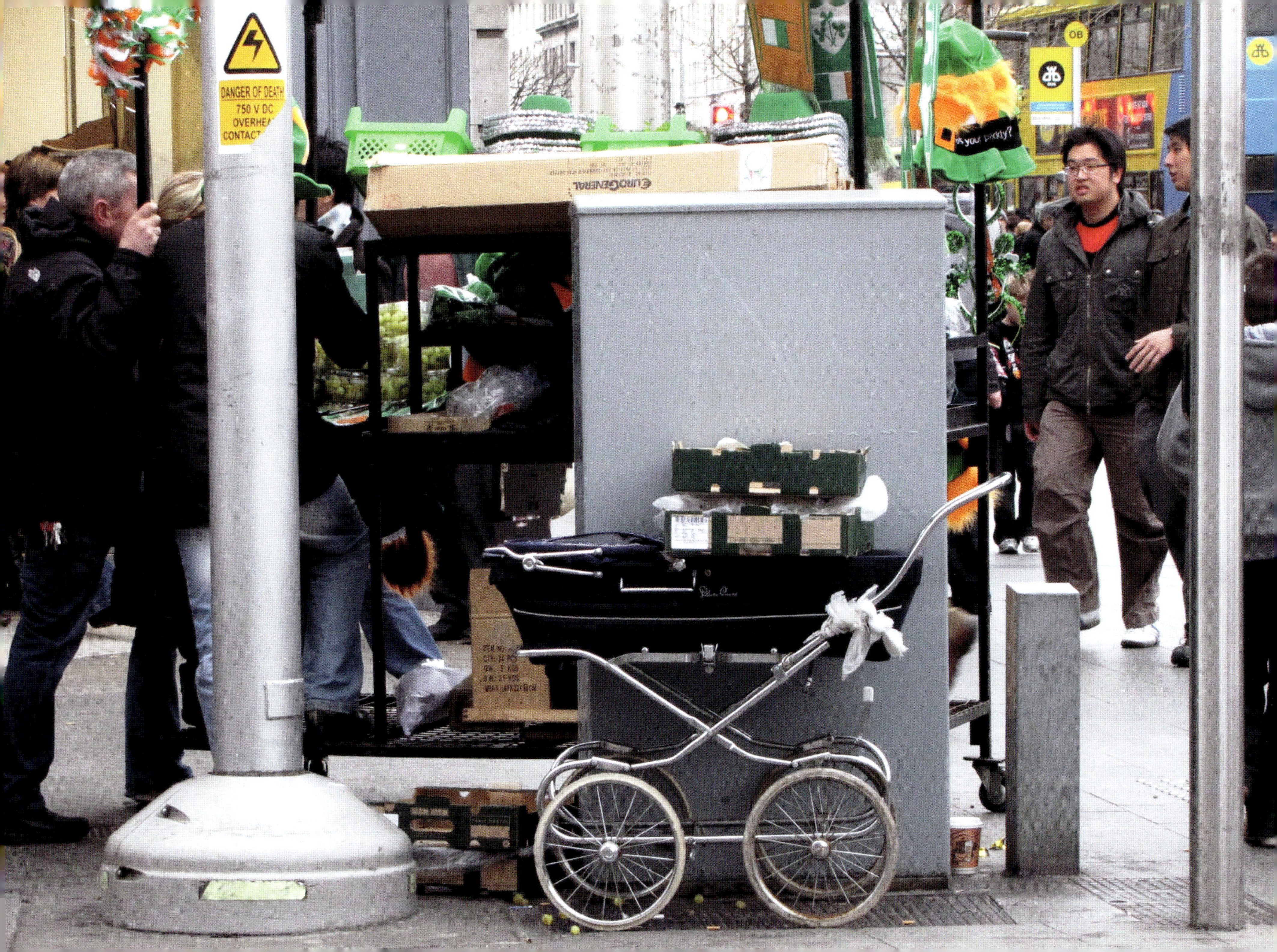
DANGER OF DEATH
750 V DC
EUROGENERAL

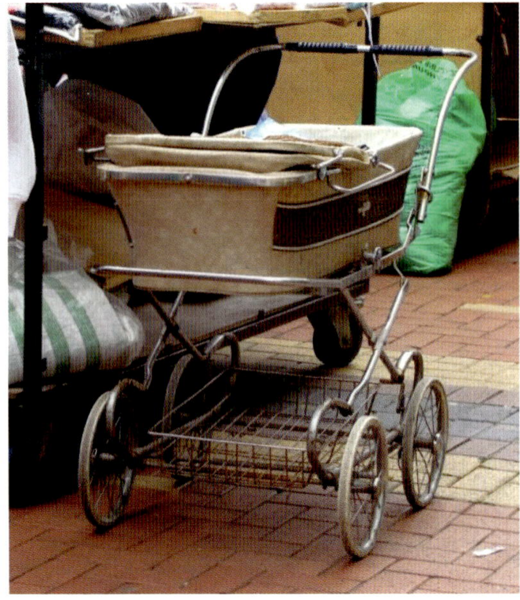

It sometimes seems as if traders' prams have been abandoned, but the owner is usually not far away. All photographs taken at Cole's Lane, opposite Arnott's shop.

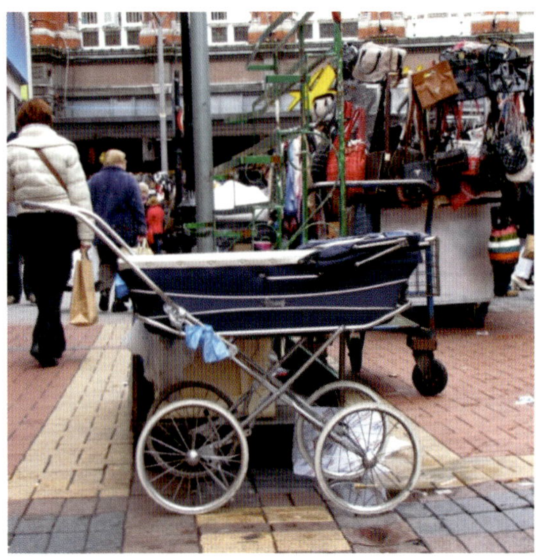

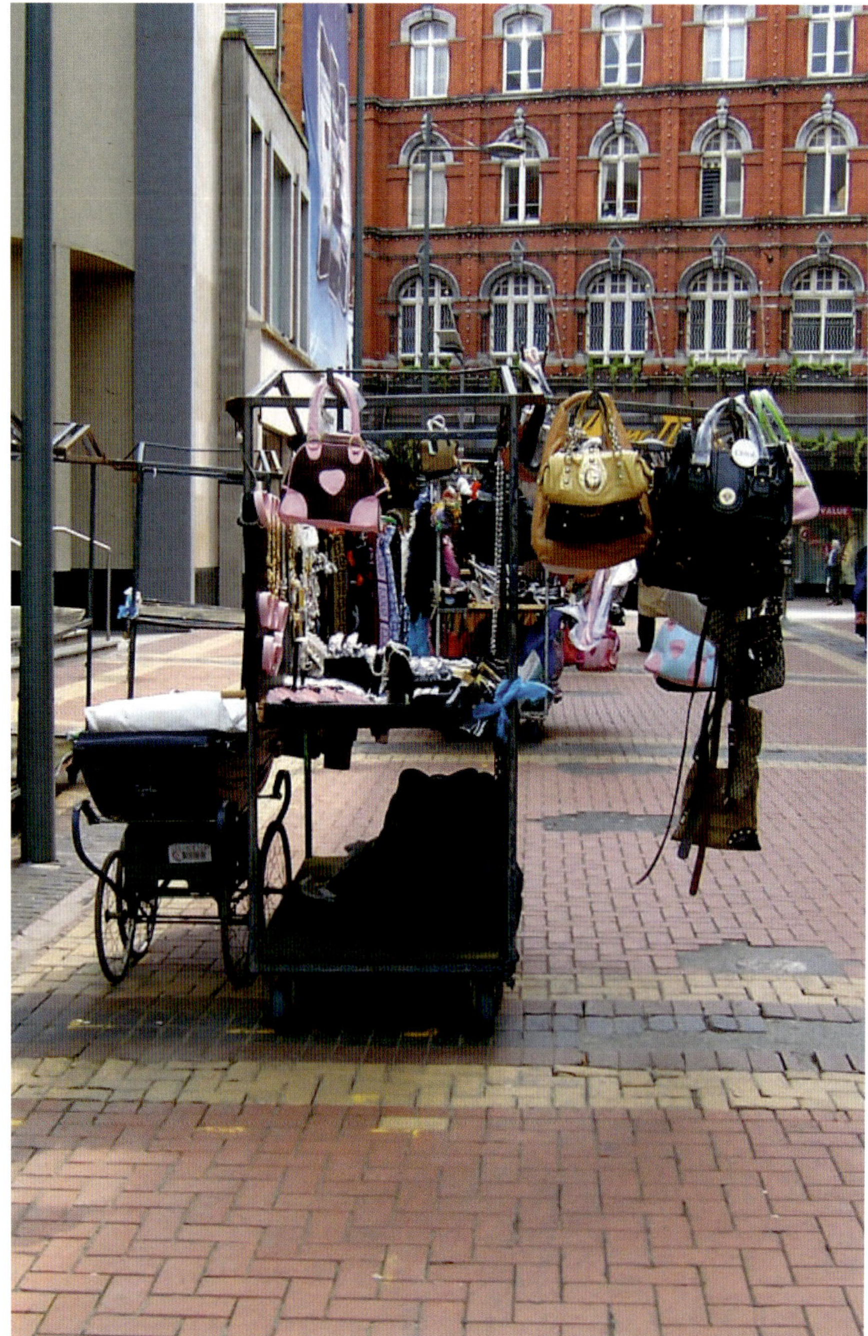

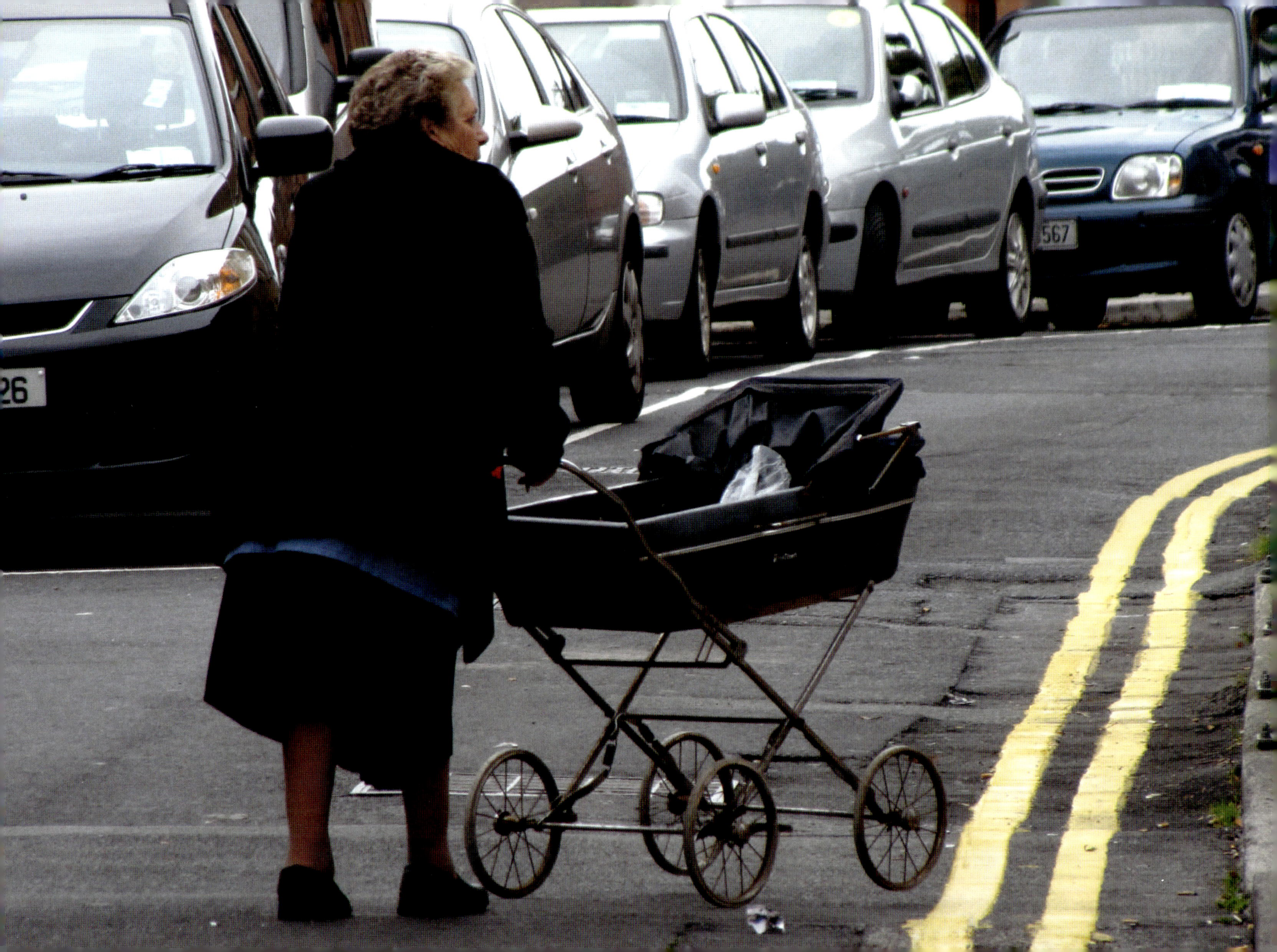

Vera's Story

Dun Laoghaire, a coastal town in south county Dublin, is home to a very special street trader. Vera Shortall is something of an institution in the locality, as she has been selling fish from her stall in the same little spot in the centre of Dun Laoghaire for over seventy years. All of Vera's family were in the fishing business. In fact, she was part of the sixth generation to be involved in the industry. She grew up in Dun Laoghaire, one of a large family of five brothers and nine sisters. As a young child, instead of going to school, she helped her father to fish for herring. She also assisted her mother in running her fish stall.

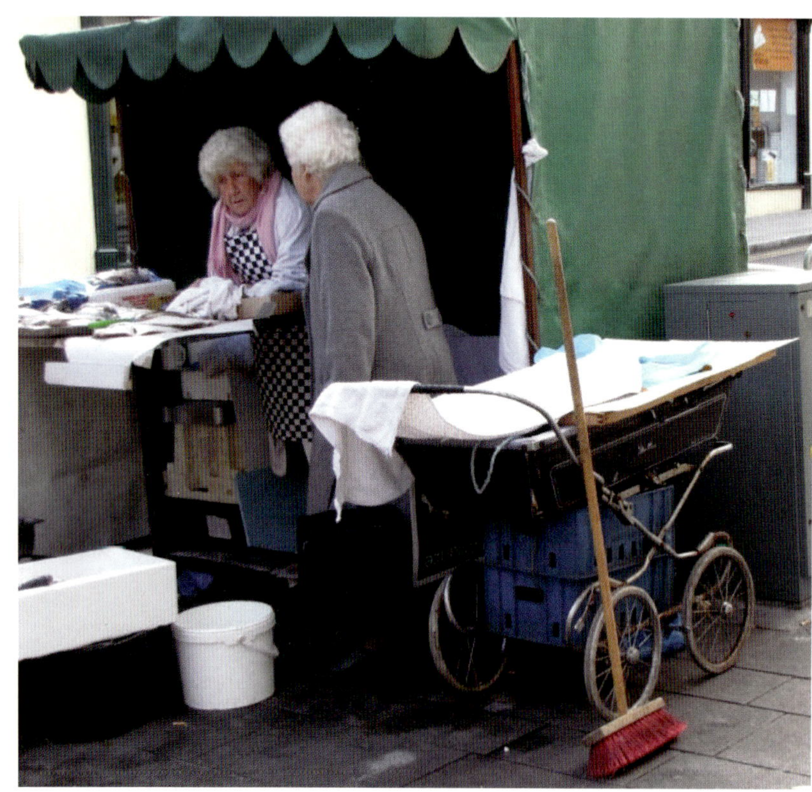

Above: Vera chats with a customer at her stall at Convent Road, Dun Laoghaire.

Tragically, in 1934, when Vera was about four years old, two of her older brothers, Richard and Henry, died at sea. They were just 20 and 19 years old, respectively. They had been returning in their boat to Dun Laoghaire from Dublin's North Wall where they had earlier earned money for tying up an incoming collier ship. As a mark of sympathy to the well-known Shortall family, the municipal flag was flown at half-mast in the town of Dun Laoghaire.

On a sunny day in October 2009, I went to Dun Laoghaire to take some photographs of Vera. As usual, she chatted with customers who stopped to buy fish, and busied herself filleting huge pieces of fish in the intervals. It was immediately apparent to me that, while Vera is valued for providing the locals with fresh fish, she is also valued socially. Many people stopped to chat with her, and she happily chatted back. While Vera has a loyal clientele of locals, she at times has counted some less than ordinary clients among her customers. In the 1980s, the Italian ambassador to Ireland would pull up in his chauffeur-driven car on Fridays to buy fish for his supper!

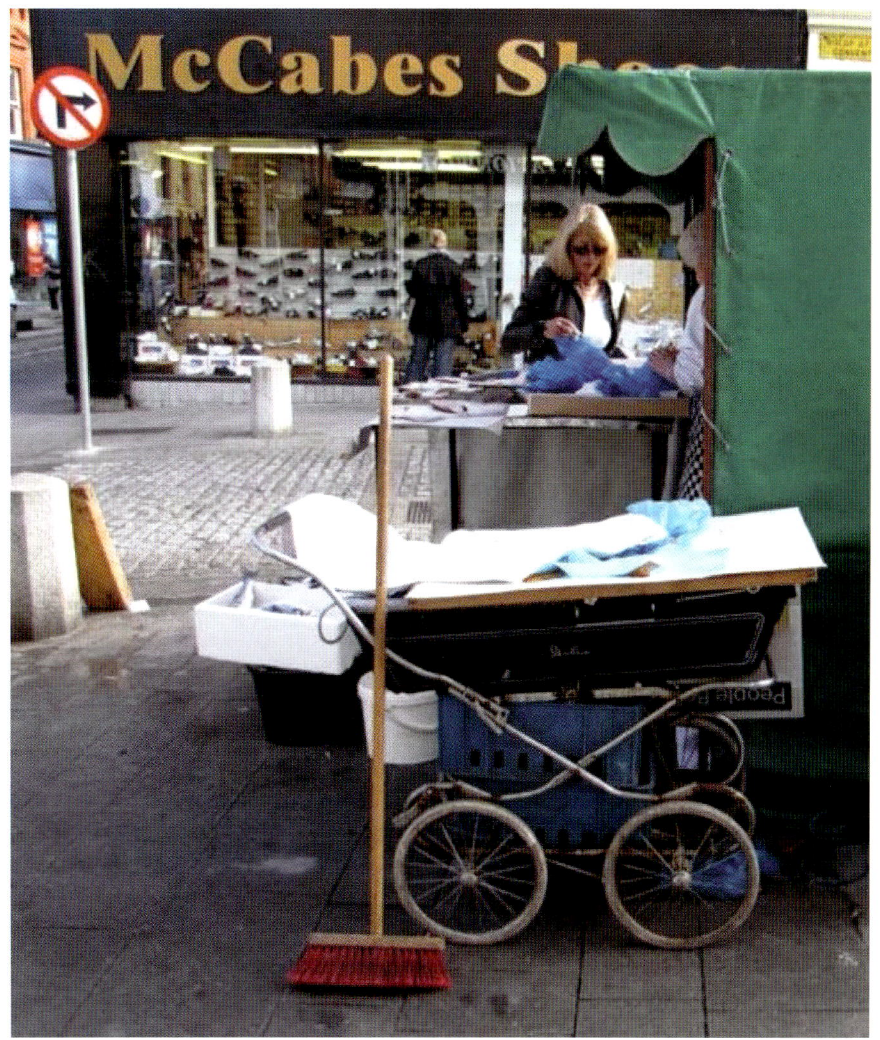

When business was quiet, I approached her and asked if I could talk to her for a few minutes. I told her I was collecting information on street traders who use prams as part of their business.

'I've been here seventy years,' she told me.

I asked her about her pram.

'I used to have a beautiful Silver Cross pram, but it was stolen,' she said.

She told me that she had been photographed years before with that very pram and that the resulting piece of work had won an award. I was intrigued by this, and greatly regretted not being able to see it.

She went on to tell me that she had several prams housed in a shed, along with spare wheels and other parts. Some of them are fabric covered models, and not so good for being out in all weathers or transporting the fish. She told me her current pram (the navy Silver Cross shown here) was bought years ago in Buckley's Auction House in Sandycove, but she bemoaned the fact that it was beginning to corrode and pointed out some rust on the base.

She said that it was impossible to get prams like it anymore. The pram, she assured me, is well looked after, and she gives it a thorough valeting once a week. However, the best prams, she claimed, are the older types that had foot-wells that allowed the babies to lower their feet when they sat up. My mother would remember them, she assured me.

Some time later, when I was researching historical material to include in this book, I came across a wonderful article about Dublin's *pram women* written by Tim Magennis a quarter of a century ago. It was, in fact, done as part of the Dublin millennium celebrations in 1988. And there, much to my delight – beaming out from the page – was Vera at her fish stall, complete with the old Silver Cross pram that she had told me about!

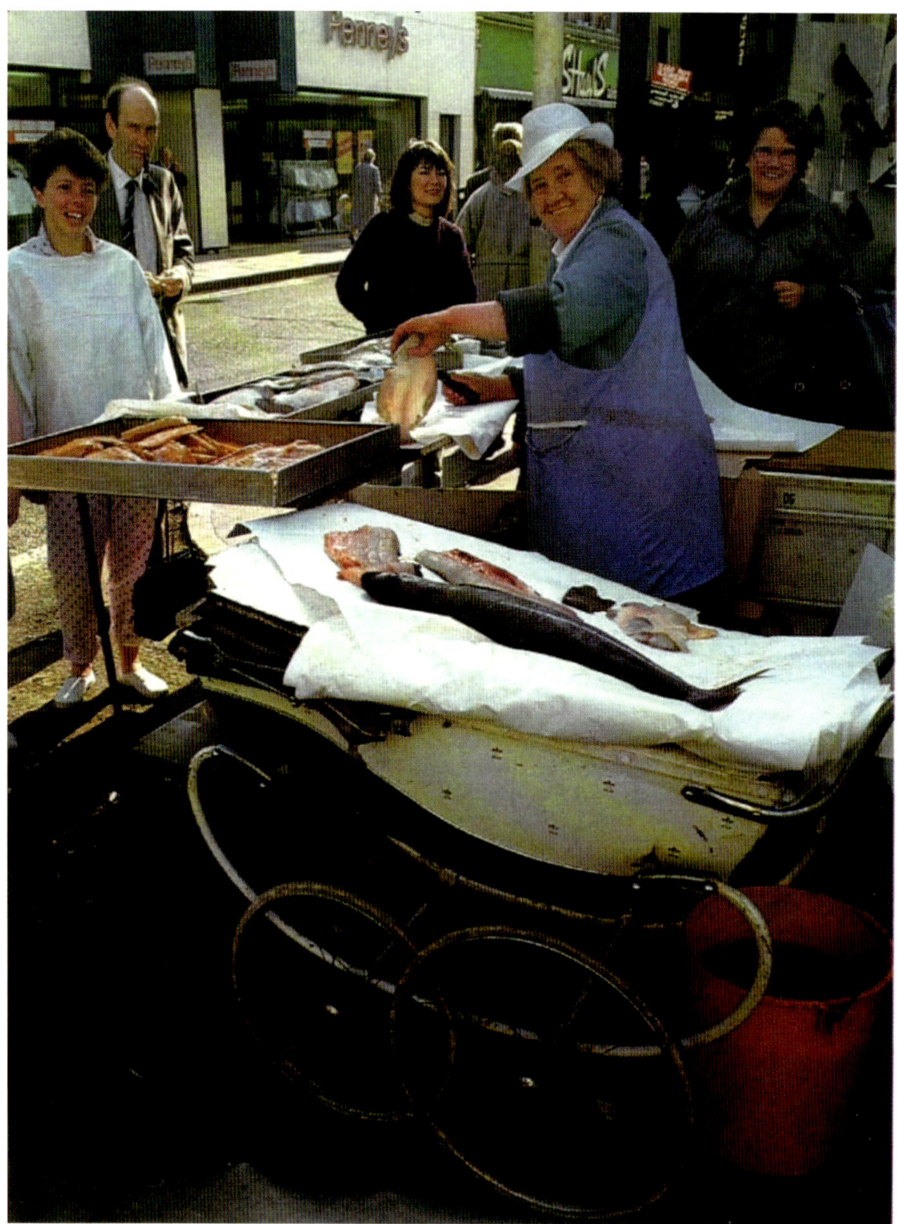

Right: Vera photographed in 1988 at her fish stall in Dun Laoghaire.
(Courtesy of Ireland of the Welcomes)

Photo Gallery 3: Prams with Eye-Catching Fruit

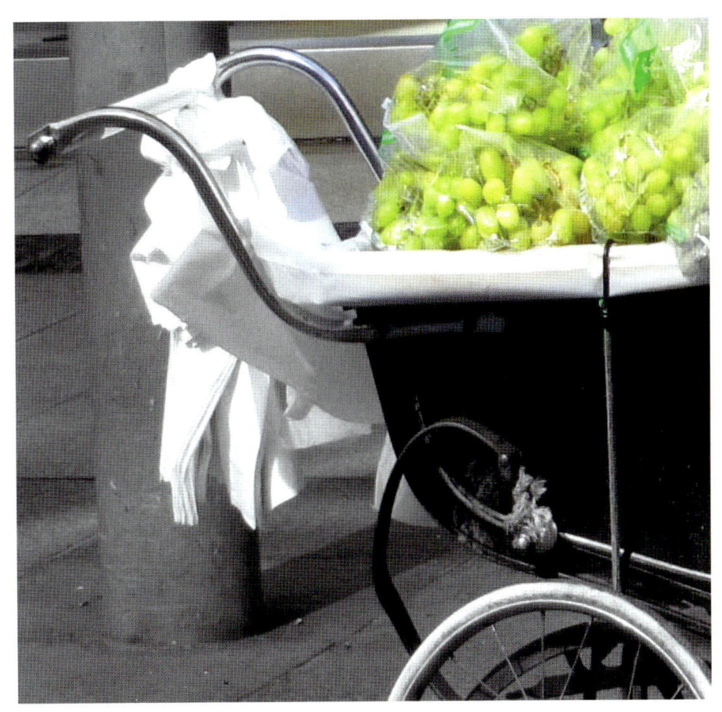

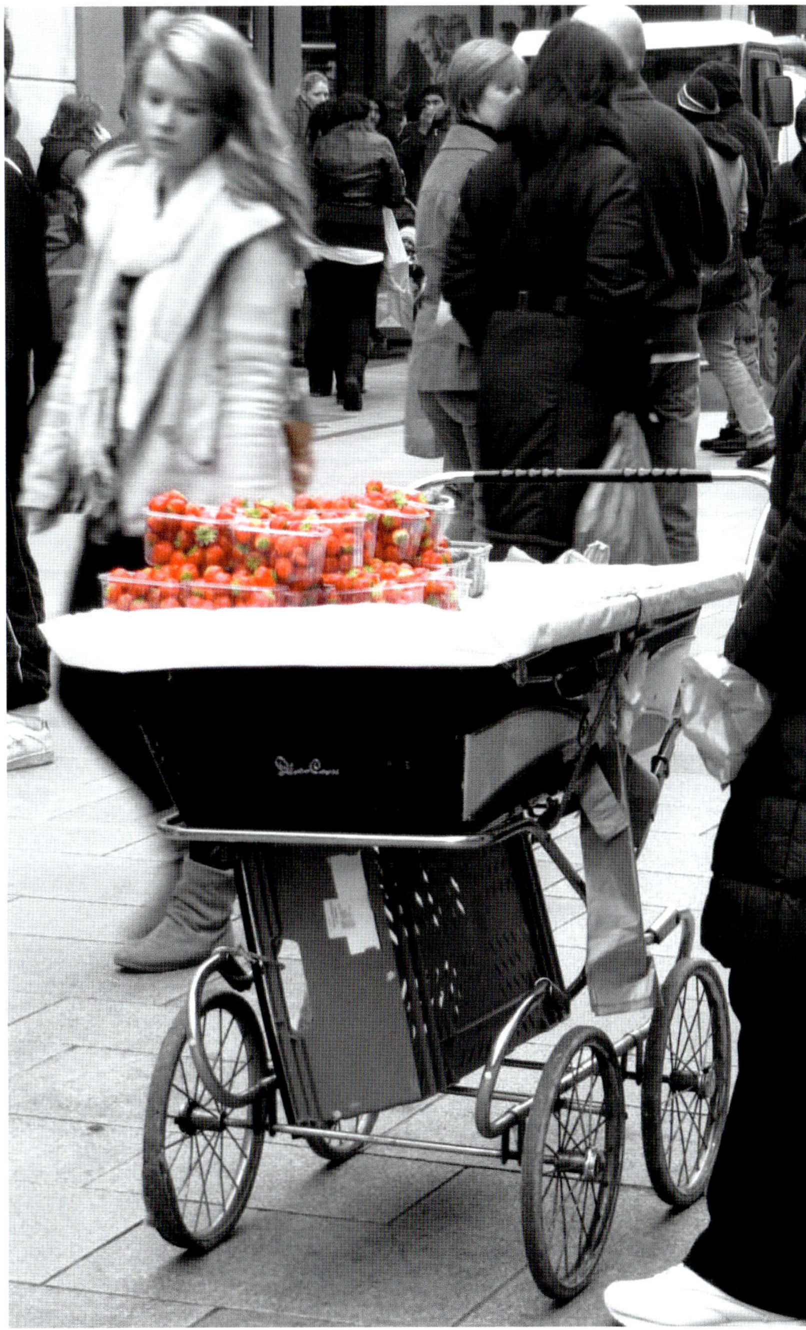

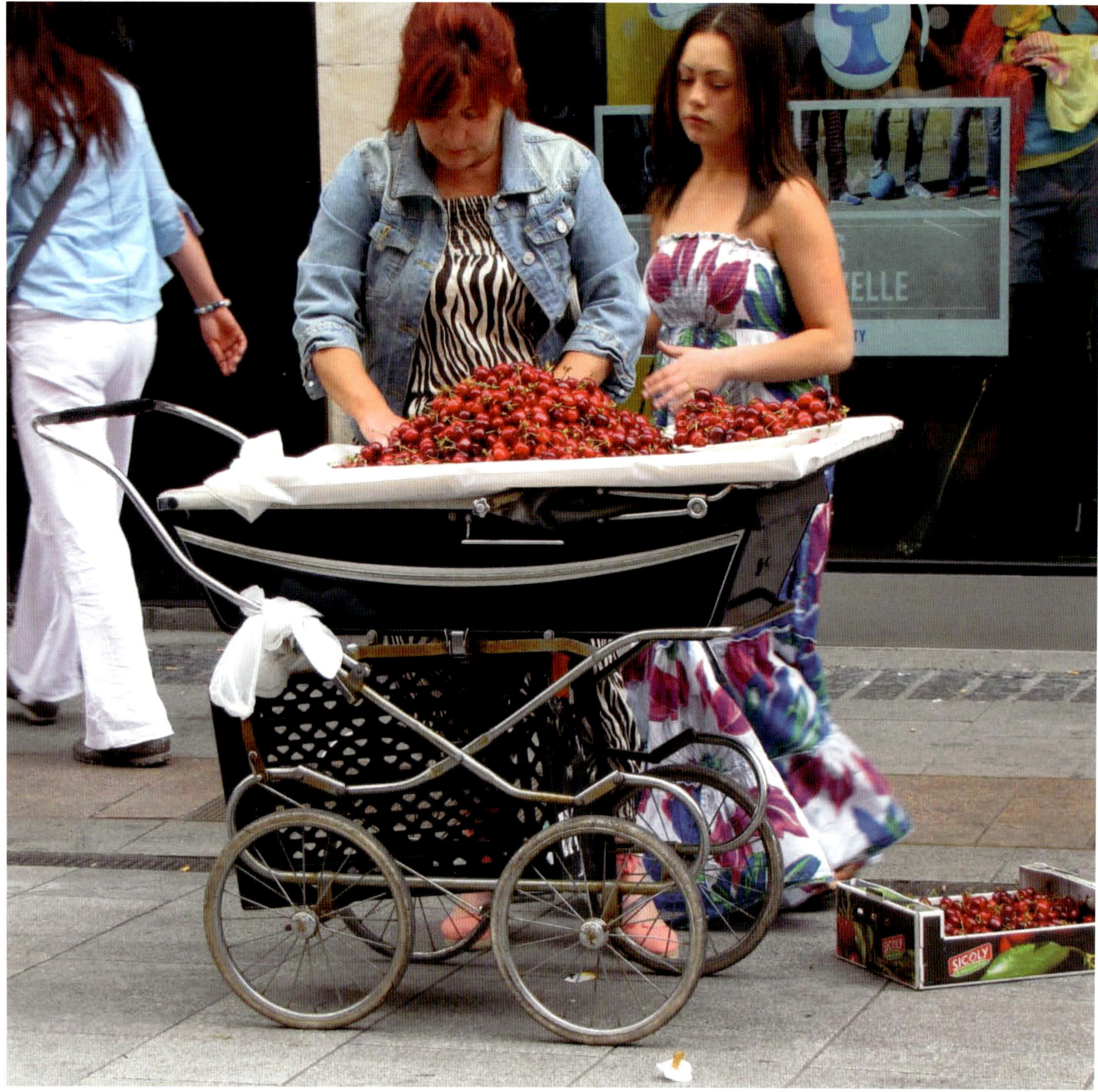
SICOLY

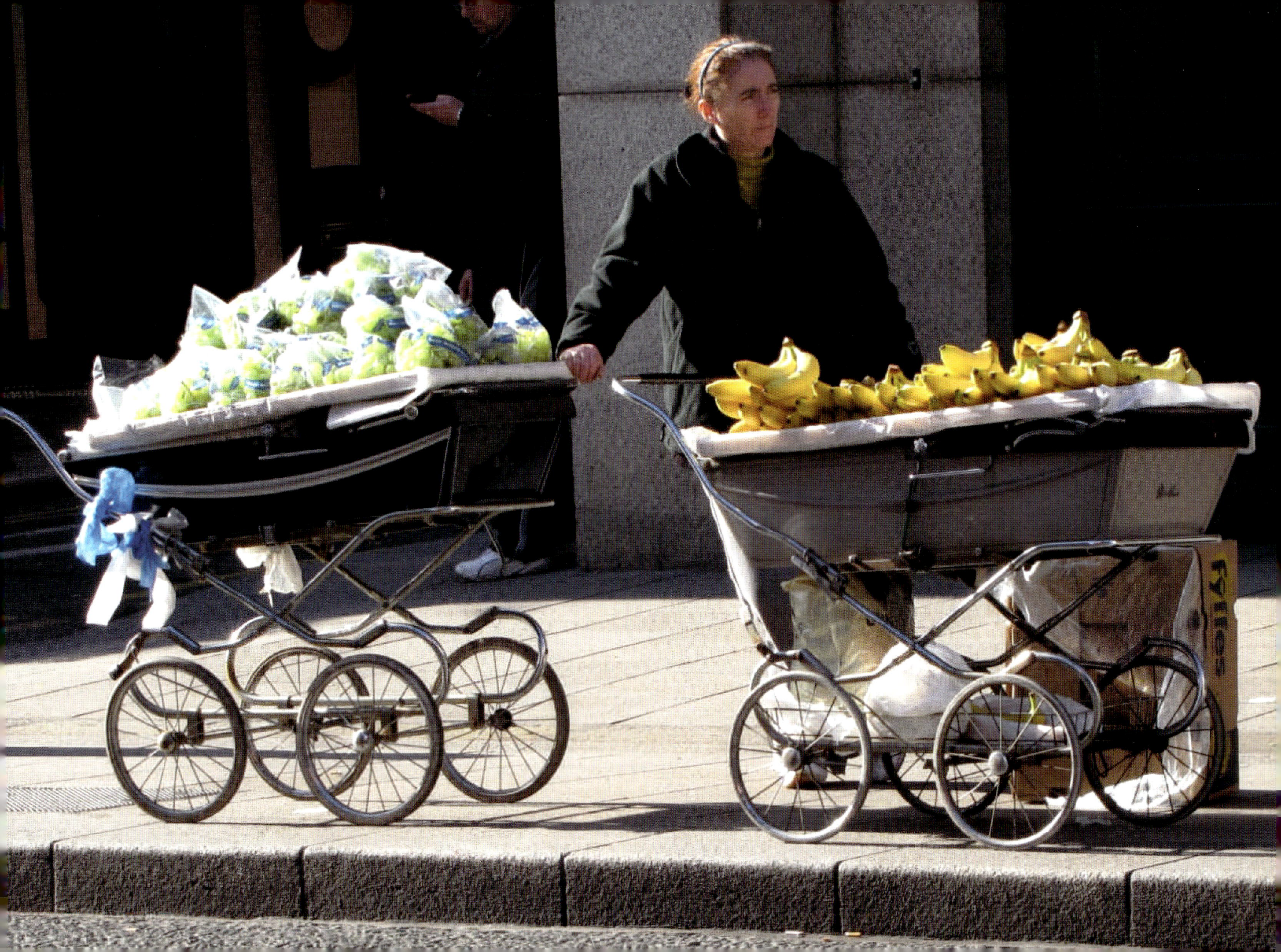
fyffes

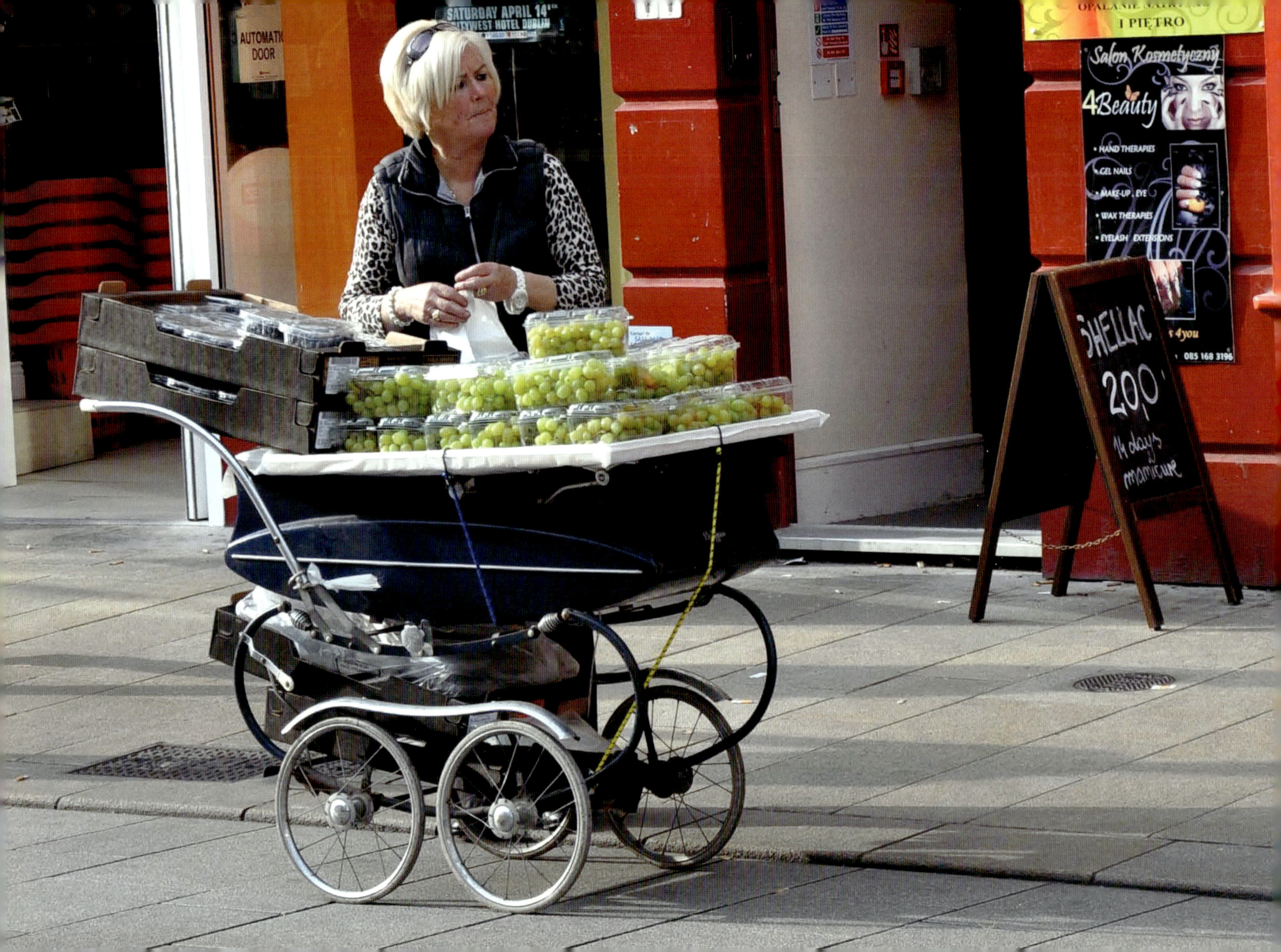

SATURDAY APRIL 14th
I PIĘTRO
Salon Kosmetyczny
4Beauty
HAND THERAPIES
GEL NAILS
MAKE-UP , EYE
WAX THERAPIES
EYELASH EXTENSIONS
085 168 3196
SHELLAC
20,0
14 days
manicure

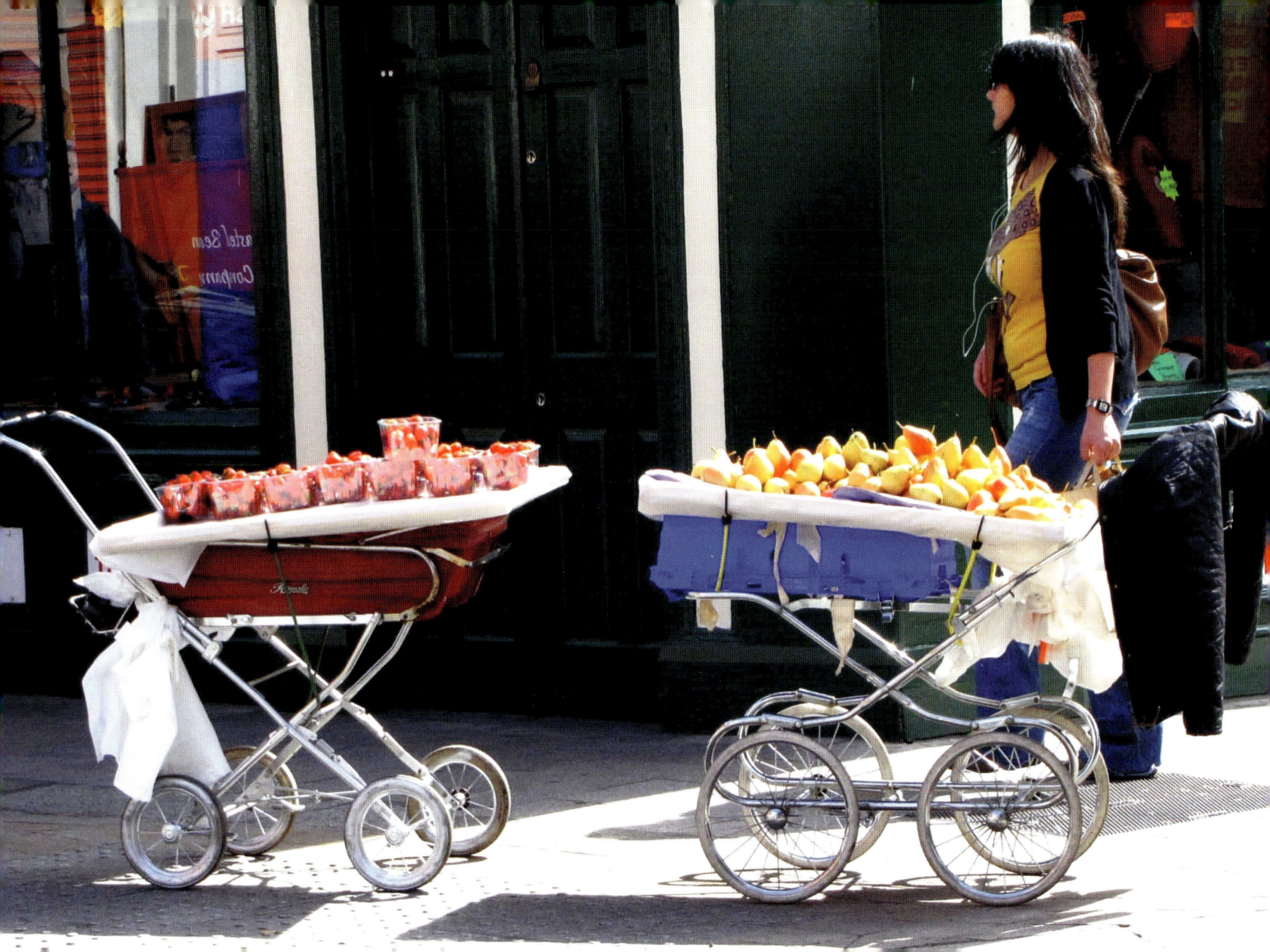

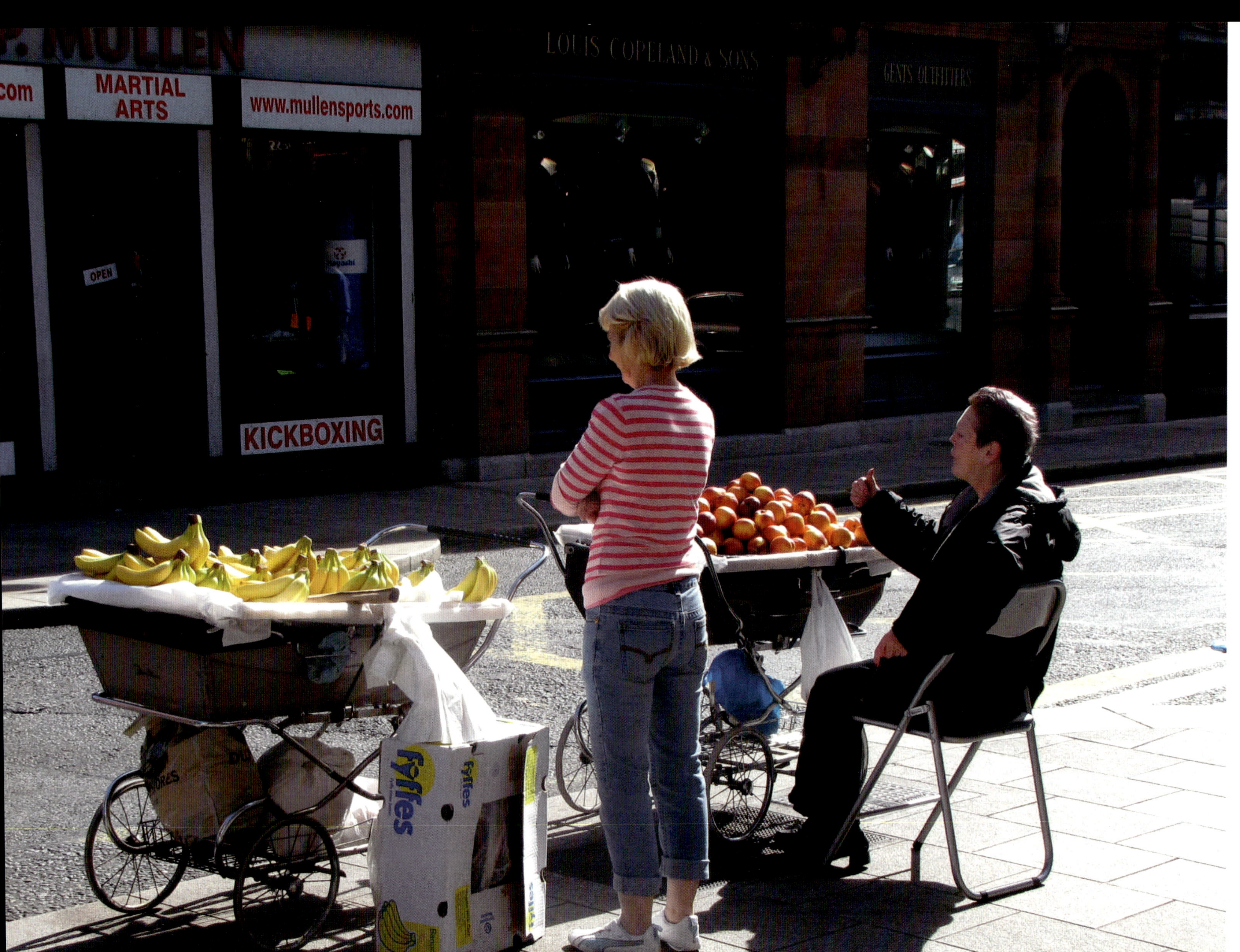
MARTIAL ARTS
www.mullensports.com
OPEN
KICKBOXING
LOUIS COPELAND & SONS
GENTS OUTFITTERS
fyffes

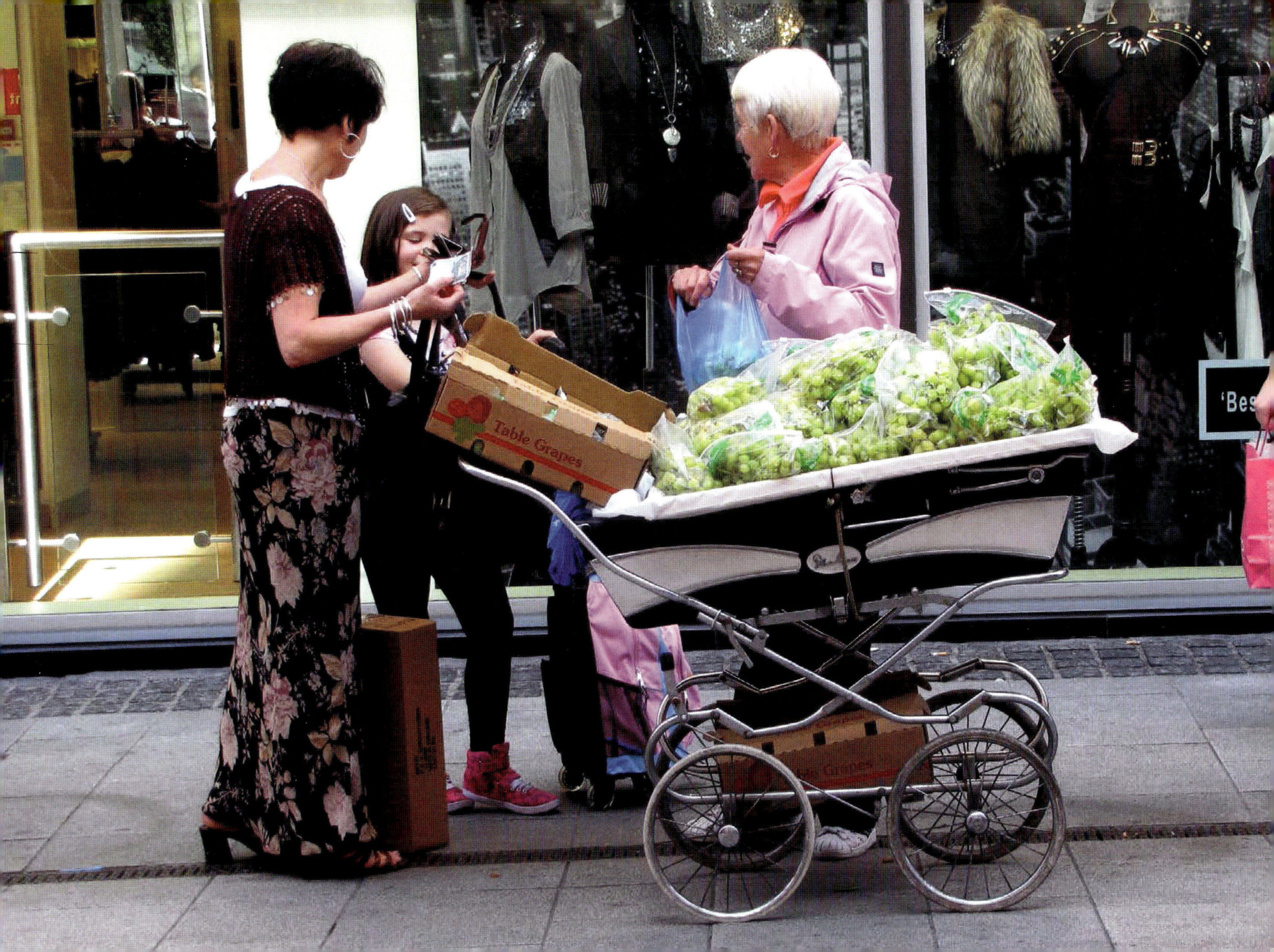
Table Grapes

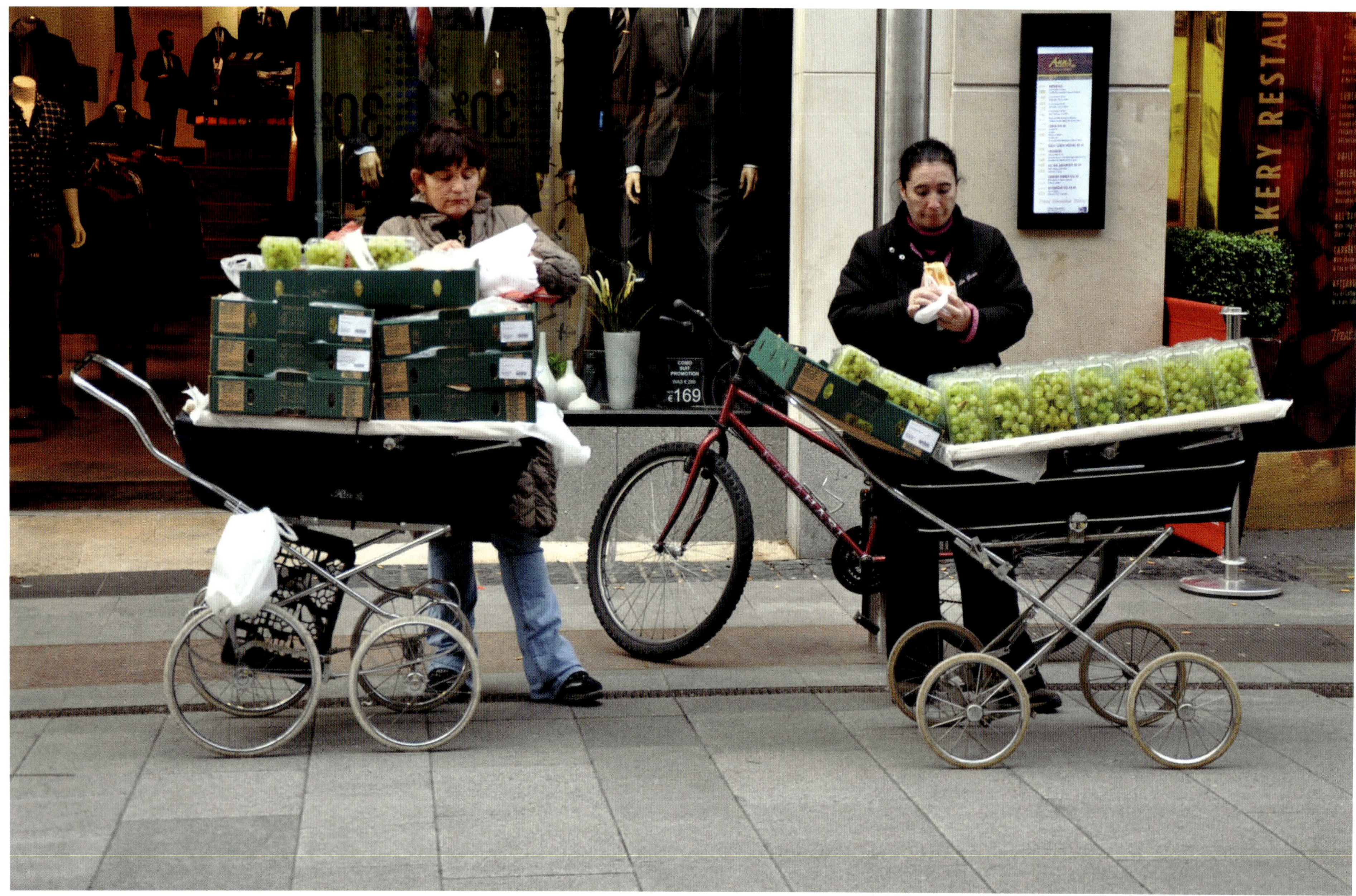
AKERY RESTAU
COMO SUIT PROMOTION
€169

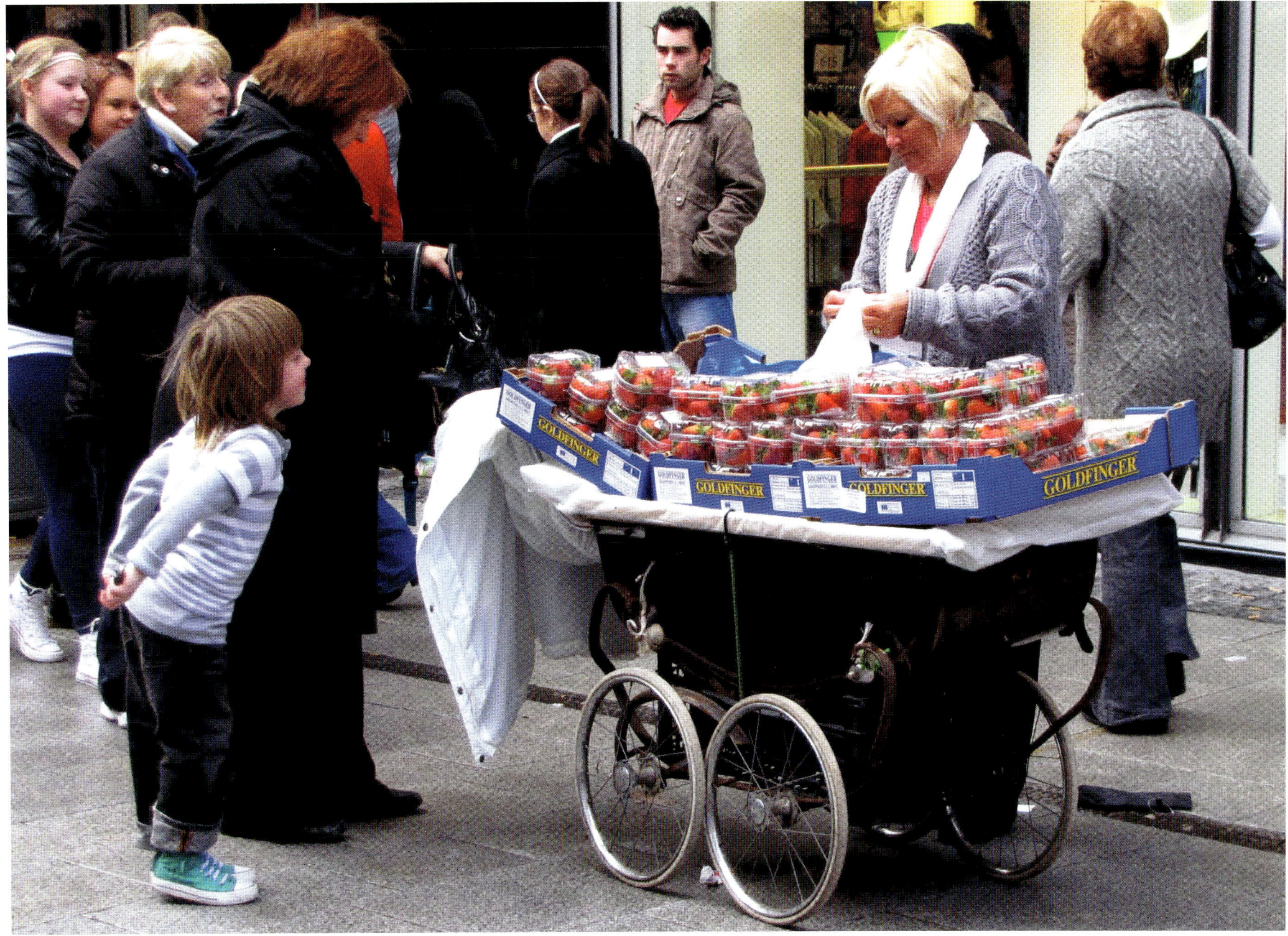
GOLDFINGER
GOLDFINGER
GOLDFINGER
GOLDFINGER

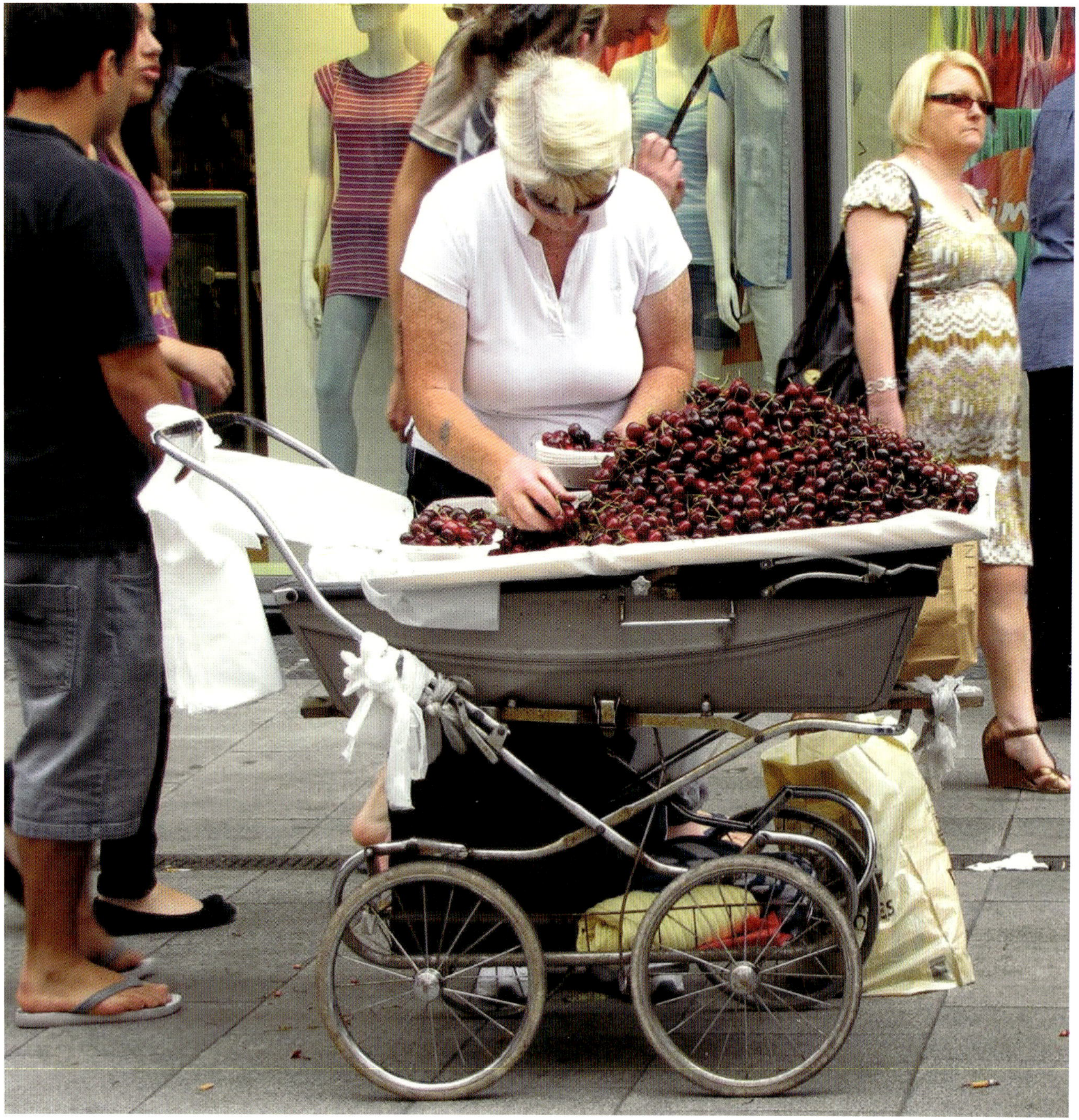

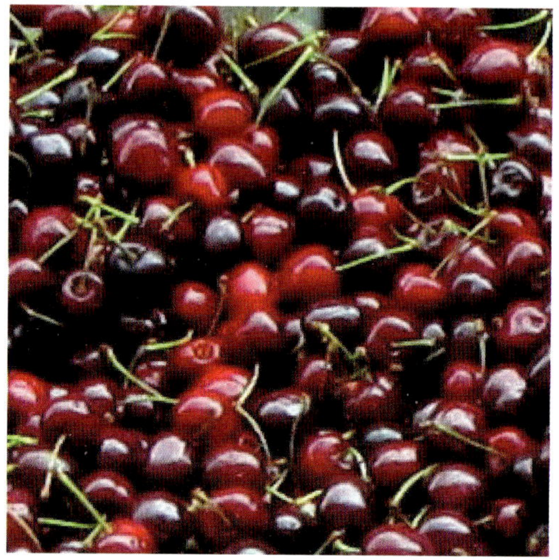

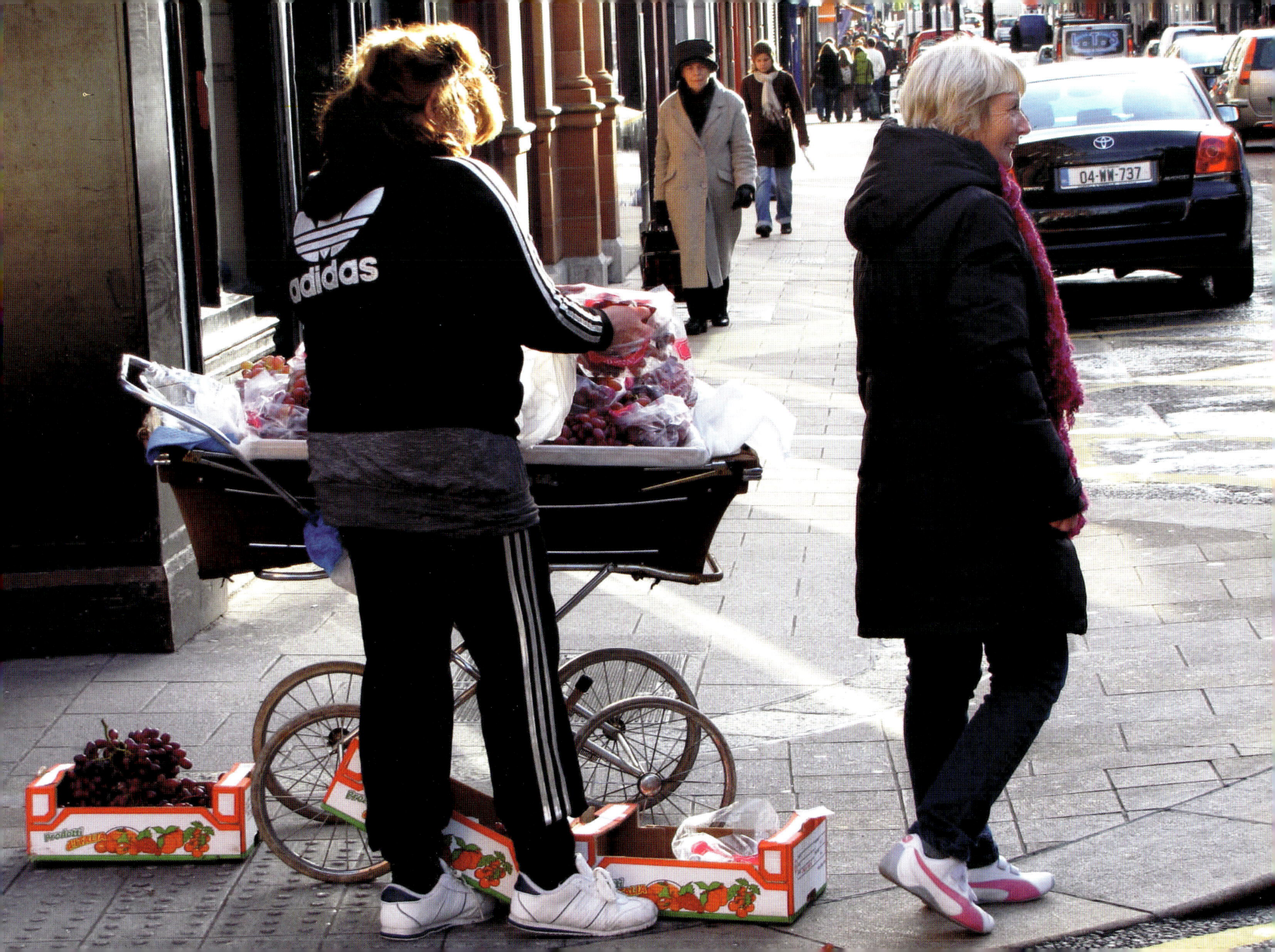
adidas
04-WW-737

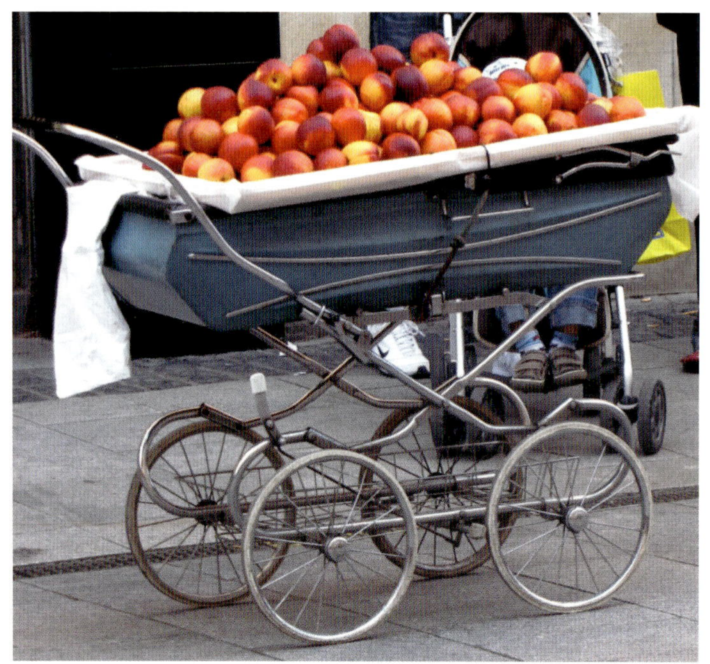

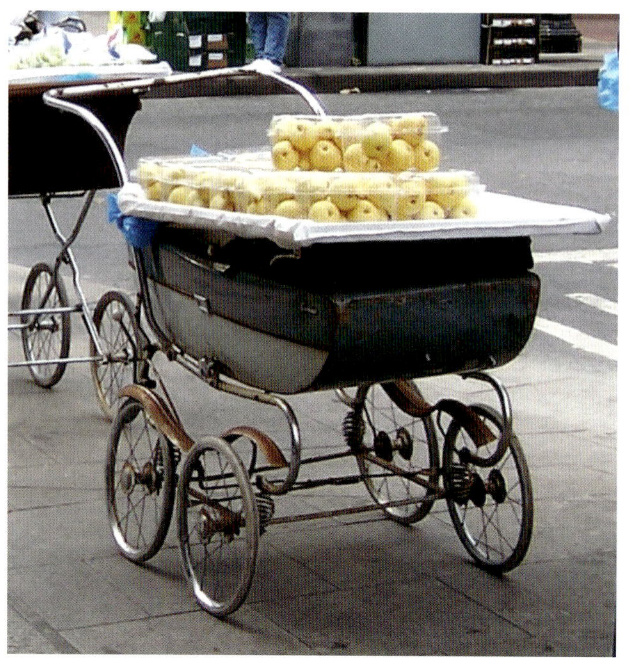

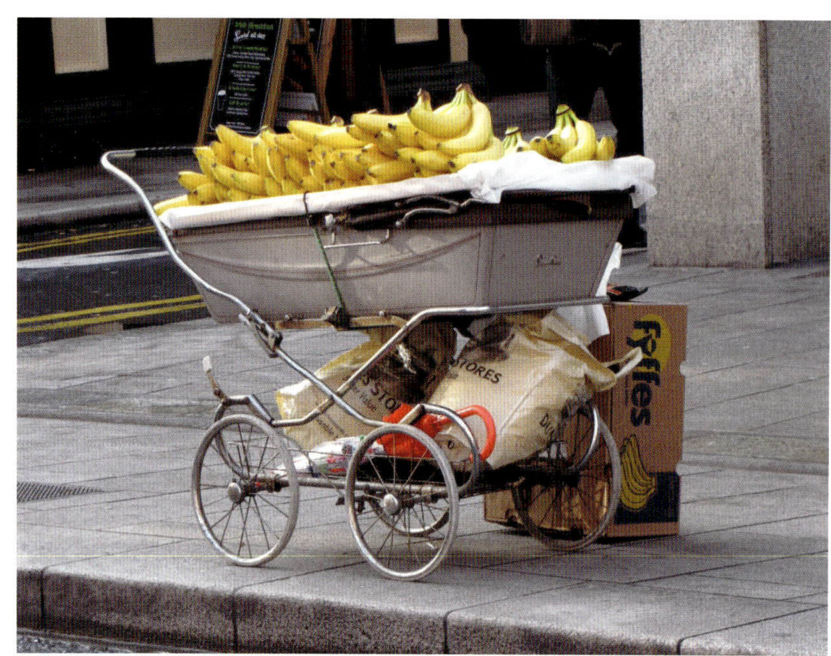
fyffes

Tricia's Story

Tricia Hand was a woman whose warmth and generosity touched many people over the course of her lifetime. The mere mention of her name to those who knew her is guaranteed to unleash a flood of tributes. Ellen Preston, interviewed earlier, described Tricia as 'one of a kind'. Sadly, Tricia passed away in 2009, but she will be remembered with great fondness by those who knew and loved her. She spent her entire life as a street trader, right up to a few weeks before she died. Tricia's only child, Carol, offered to tell me about her mother.

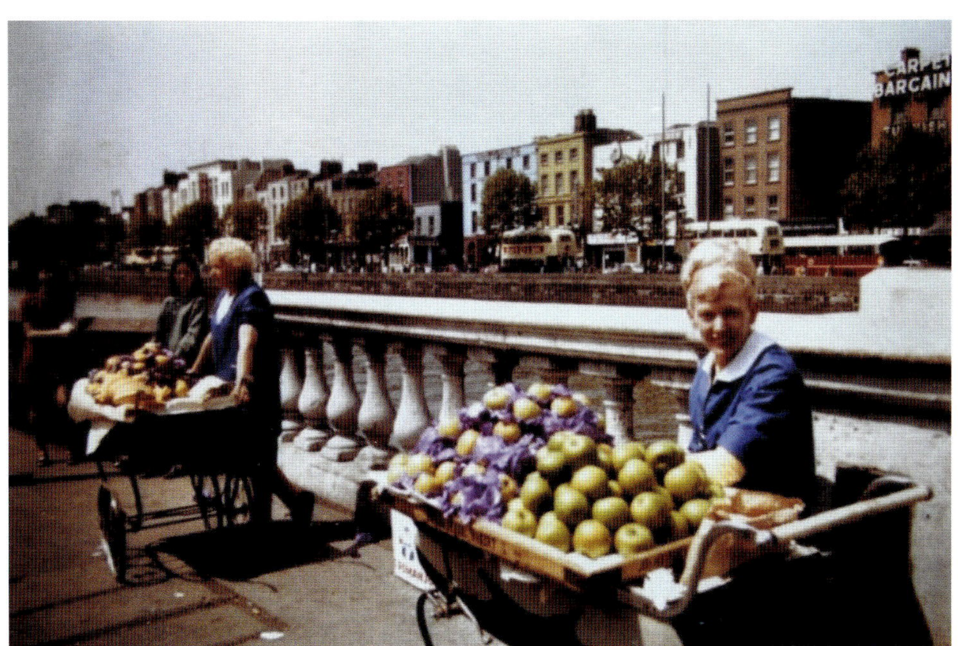

Above: A young Tricia Hand selling fruit from her pram at Aston Quay, beside O'Connell Bridge, in the 1960s. *(Courtesy of Carol Foley)*

Tricia Hand was born into a large family that lived a stone's throw away from Dublin's city centre in Granby Lane. Unlike the other traders described here, there was no tradition of street trading in Tricia's family. She began street trading at the age of ten or eleven as a means of helping to support her large family. She started by selling fruit after school from a basket hung around her neck. She and some friends would stand on the quays with baskets of apples or pears, and not return home until all their stock was sold. Even though she was still a child herself, she became the breadwinner of the family.

Tricia eventually got a pram and started selling in Henry Street and Moore Street. At that time there were only about six women in the area regularly selling from prams. Despite the fact that she was younger than some of the other traders, Tricia became like a mother figure to them. She would often take charge of buying the stock, and see that everyone had their share. She would go to the market at 6am to get the best of the strawberries and share them out. If one of the women was short of money, Tricia would buy the stock for her and get repaid only when it was resold.

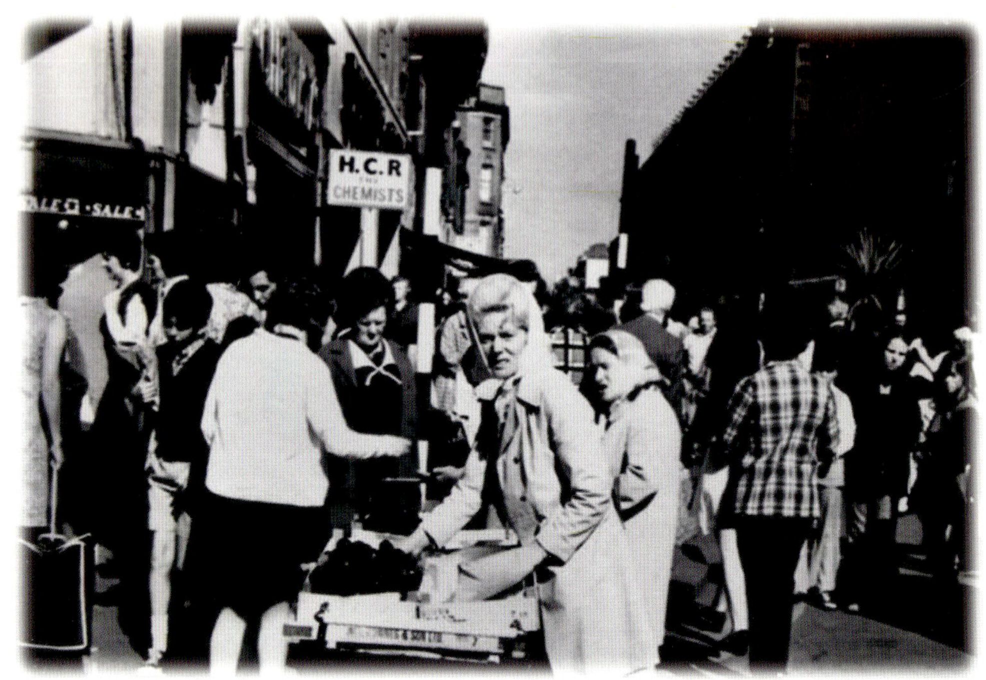

At Easter time, she bought small chocolate eggs which she and the other women would arrange in little baskets for sale off the prams. Anything that was required by the shoppers in the area was sold, including fruit, chocolate, flowers, and novelties. Those who traded alongside her recall her extraordinary generosity to others and her concern that everyone was doing okay. In effect, she had unofficially assumed the role of manager of their little group. Her daughter Carol noted how, in later life, Tricia's caring nature was evident in her devotion to her own mother and father. It was as though she felt it was always her place to look after other people.

Above: Tricia selling fruit from her pram in a busy Henry Street. *(Courtesy of Carol Foley)*

Of course, she encountered the same problems as everyone else involved in street trading, and this included being pursued by the Gardaí for trading without a permit. She, like the others, was sometimes apprehended by the so-called 'snatch squads' – Gardaí that swooped on the pram traders and loaded them and their prams into vans to be taken to Store Street station. She was not one to be taken easily though, and many a Garda was treated to an earful of invective as a result of Tricia's displeasure at being thus apprehended! True to character, however, when Garda Paddy Boylan who had spent a lot of his life arresting the street traders retired, it was Tricia who organised a collection for him so he had a good send-off.

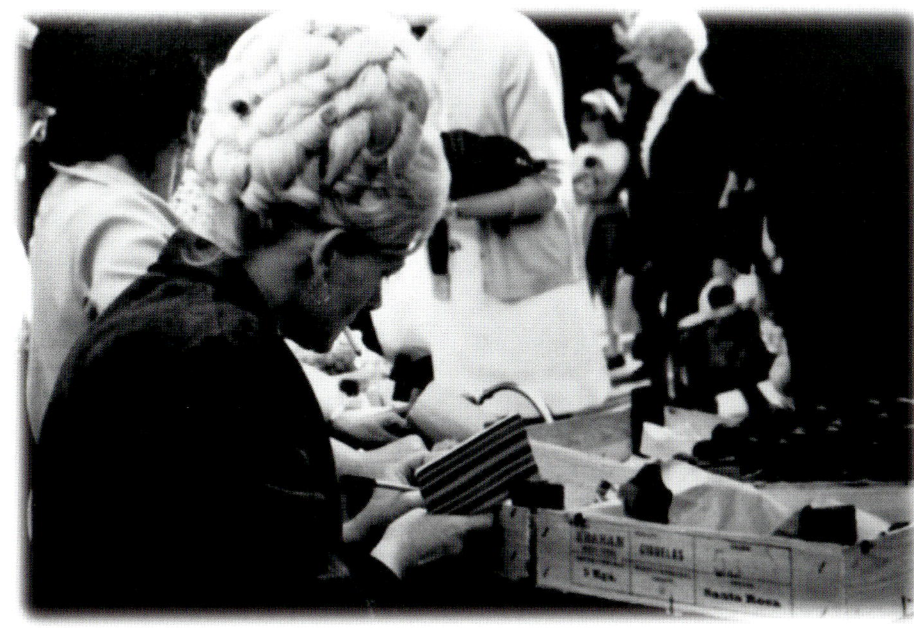

The other enemy of the street trader was the weather. Her daughter Carol recalls joining Tricia at Christmas time at her stall in Henry Street and not being able to cope with more than ten or fifteen minutes of standing outside in the icy conditions. Yet, Tricia and the others did just that that all day long, warmed only by a constant supply of tea bought from the local cafe. The prams that played so important a role in the maintenance of street traders' livelihoods were treated like gold-dust. In the early days, Tricia kept her pram in a friend's flat in Ormond Square. The family that lived there spent most of their time in the kitchen at the back of the flat, and the front room – or 'parlour', as it was known – was rarely used. So each day after work, Tricia would wheel the pram from Henry Street up to the flat where it stood overnight, to be retrieved and brought to the markets again the next morning. In later years, a weekly charge ensured that the pram could be safely stored overnight in a more convenient location at the rear of Moore Street.

Above: Tricia, with her striking blonde hair, doing some paperwork beside her pram. *(Courtesy of Carol Foley)*

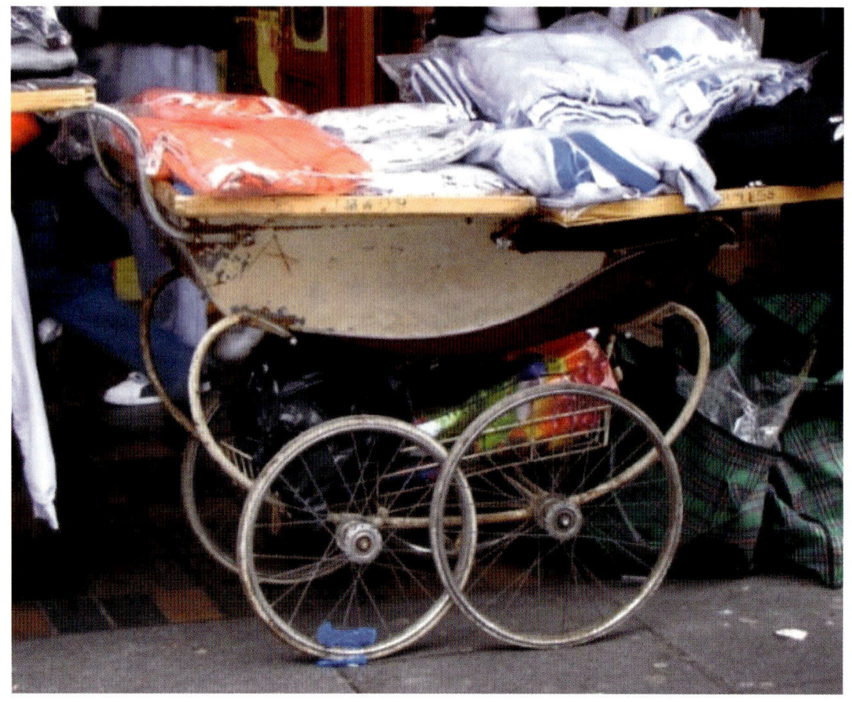

While it is generally acknowledged that the life of a street trader is challenging at the best of times, Tricia never complained about going to work. She loved the life she had created for herself. When the Dublin Corporation offered the traders financial compensation to revoke their pitches a few years ago, one might have expected Tricia, then aged about seventy, to accept such an offer. However, while most people her age and younger would have been delighted to retire and accept the offer, she refused. What else would she do except carry on trading? Even towards the end of her life when she became ill, all she wanted was to get better so she could get back out to her stall. That stall, and all the people surrounding it, were her life.

She is missed by all who knew her, and none more so than by her daughter. Among Carol's most precious keepsakes are her mother's trader's smock and her *lucky* 'pocket' (her favourite belted purse for keeping the takings), both of which she showed me at the end of our meeting. Tricia kept that special pocket wrapped up under her pillow every night, saying defiantly: 'If there is a break-in, they will have to move my head to get it'. Being close to that pocket, and appreciating its symbolism, provided an incredibly moving end to our meeting. Her pram is equally treasured, and stands in the family's garden. It has been painted and planted up with shrubs and bulbs. On the side is a little plaque that simply reads 'Tricia's garden'.

Above: Tricia's old Silver Cross pram in its usual spot outside the Ilac shopping centre on Moore Street.

Opposite page: Tricia's pram as it is now, painted and planted, and aptly named "Tricia's Garden".

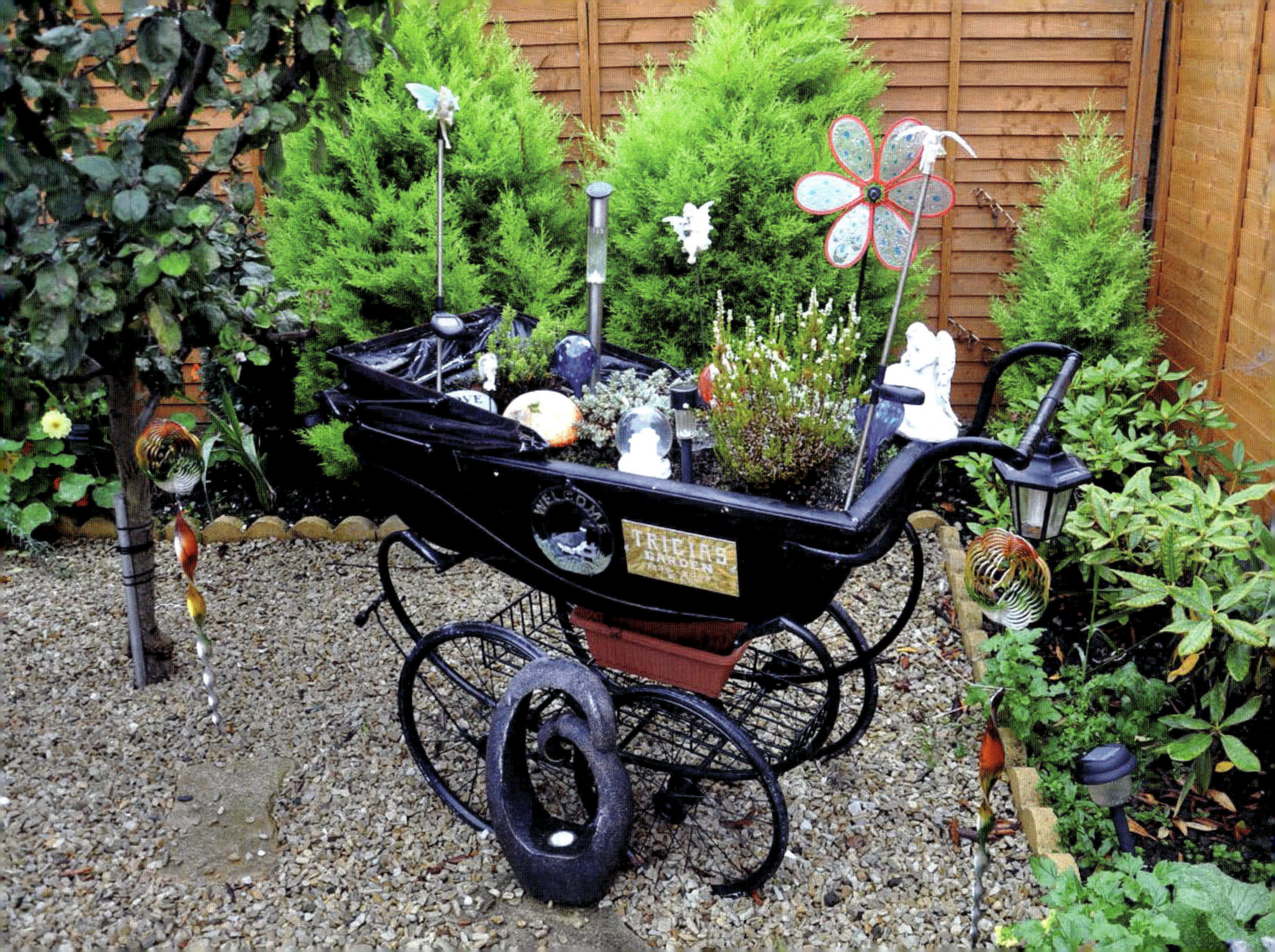
WELCOME
GARDEN

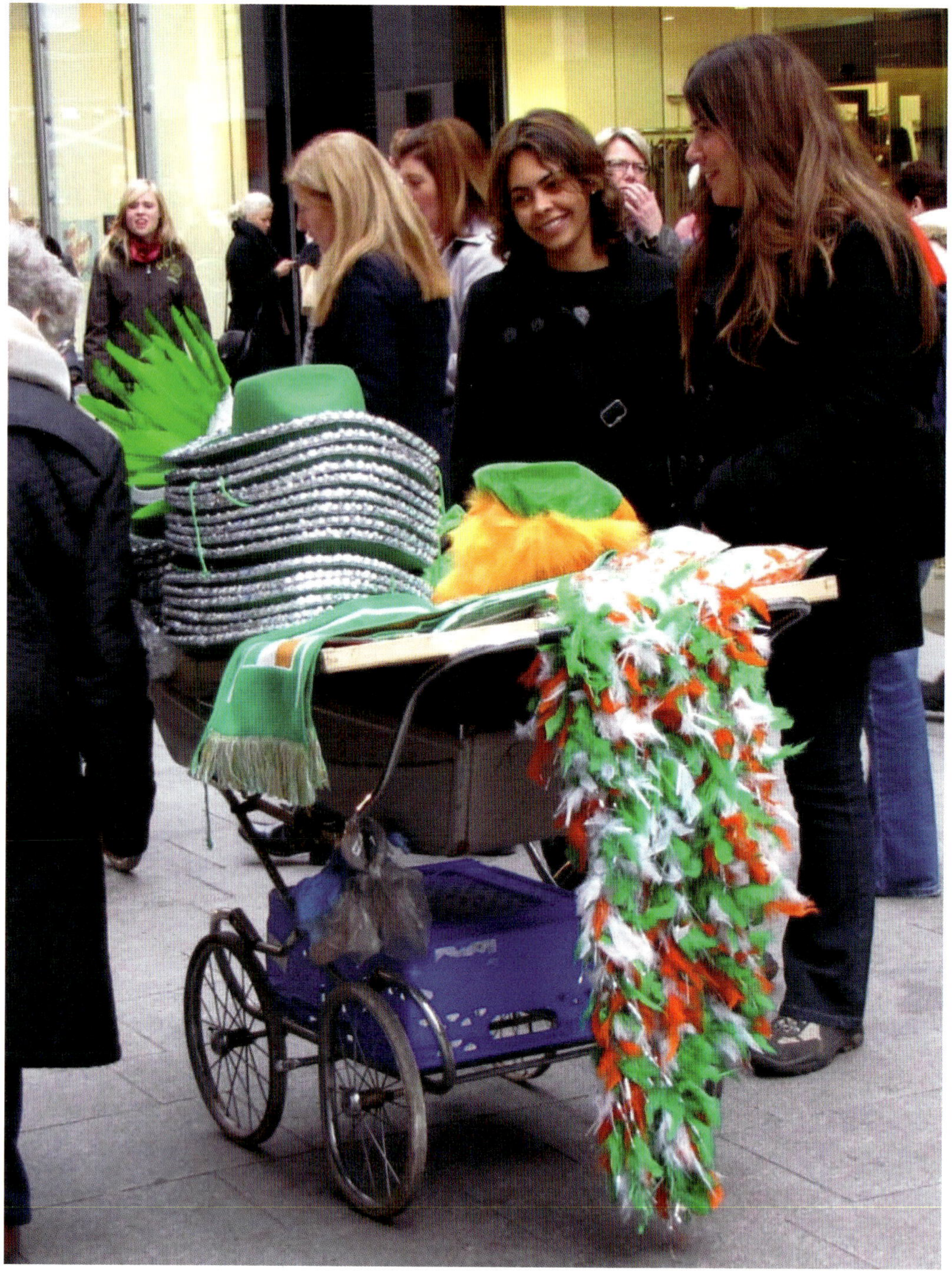

PHOTO GALLERY 4: PRAMS WITH THINGS ALL IRISH

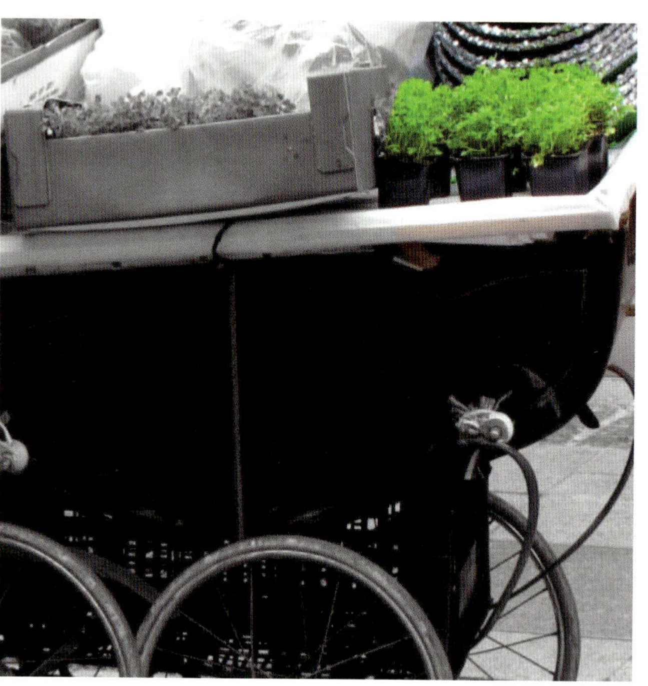

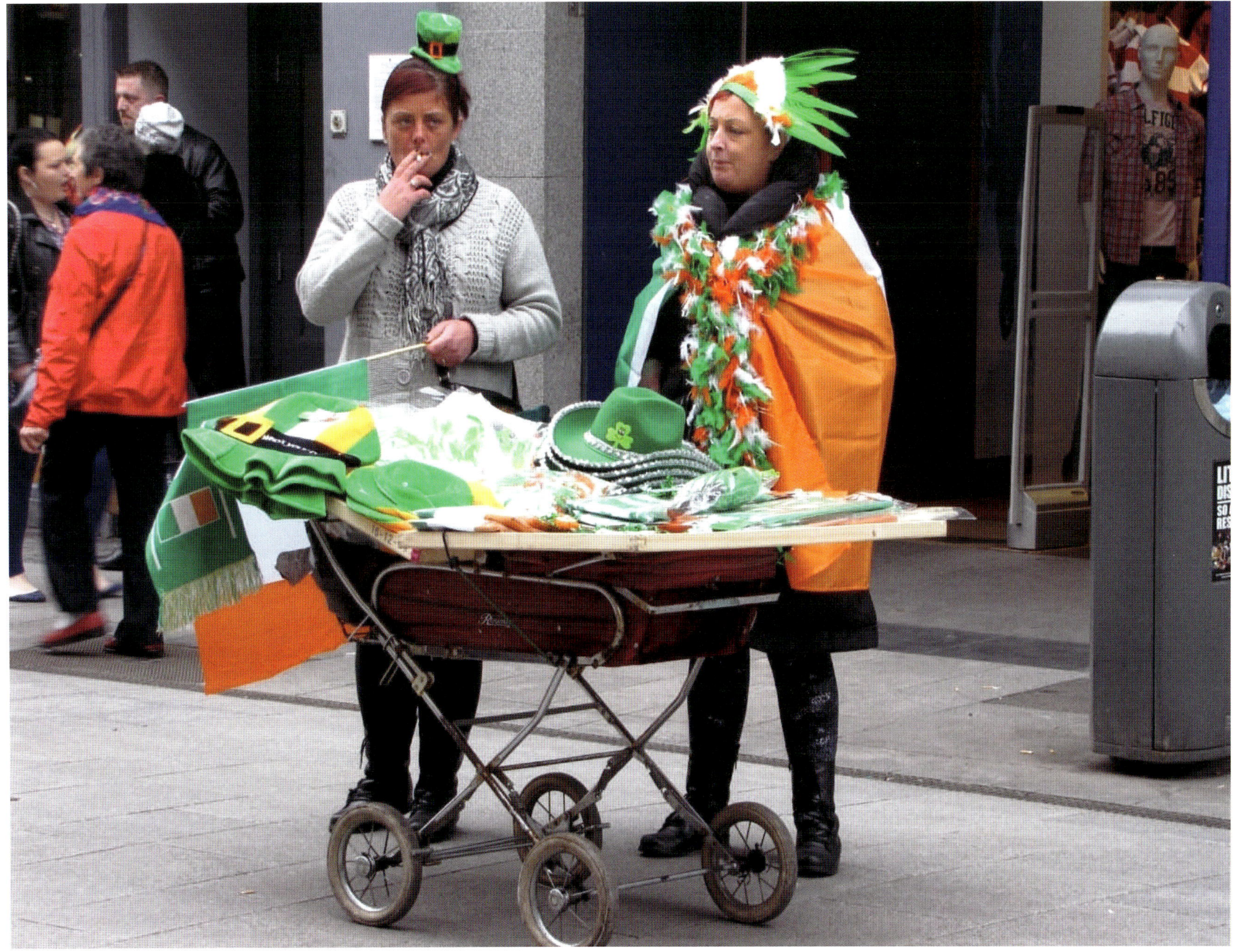

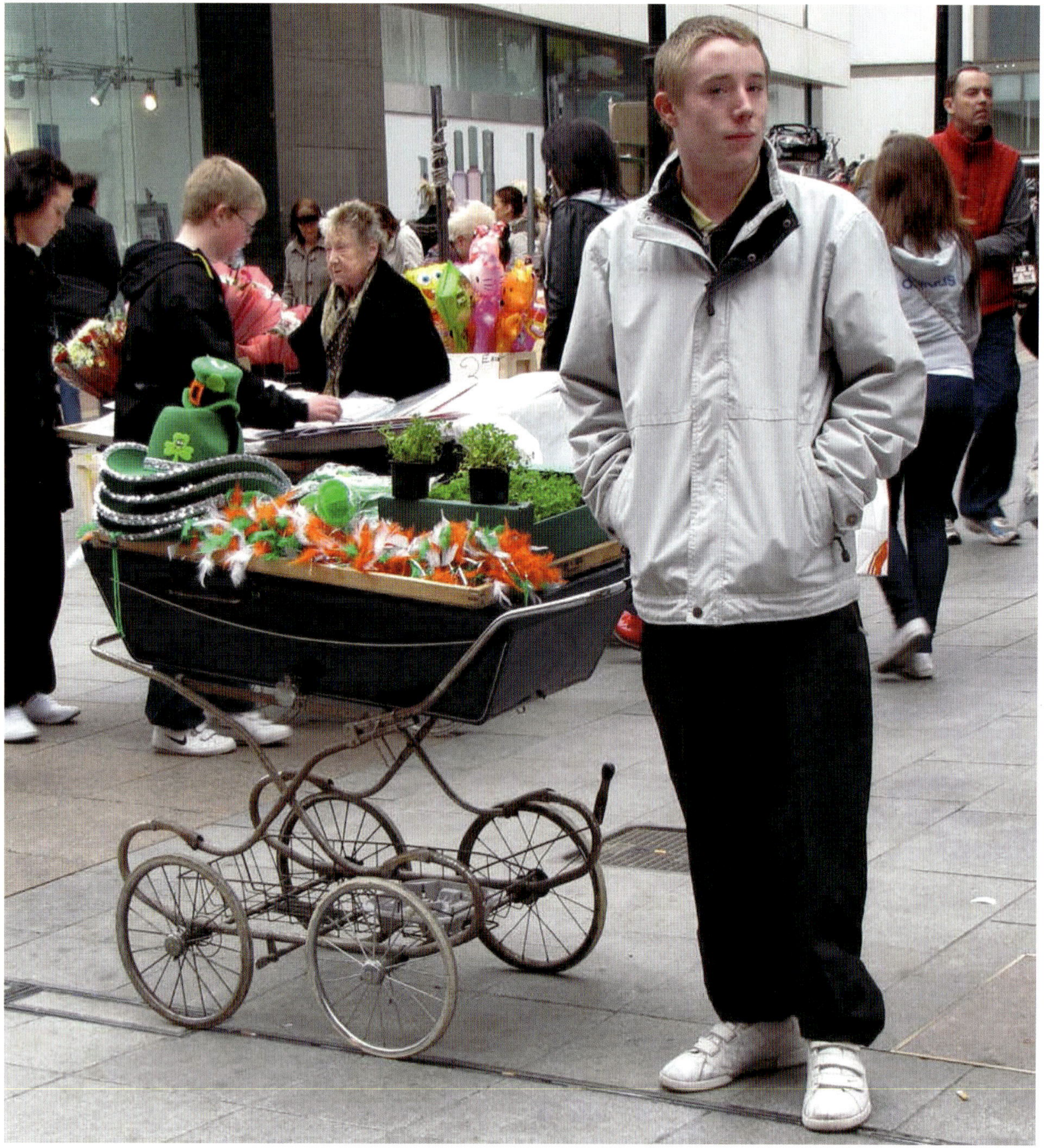

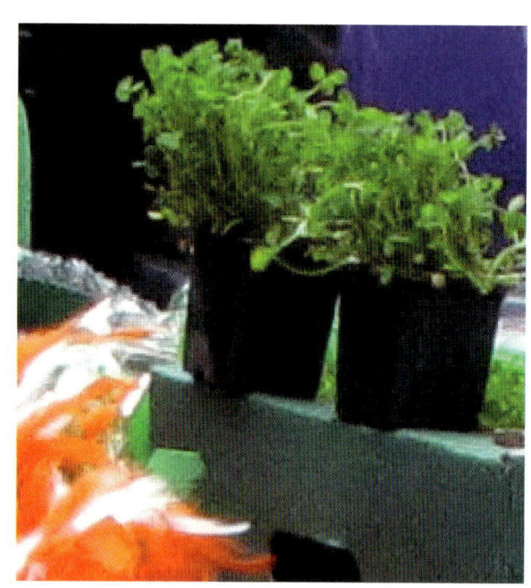

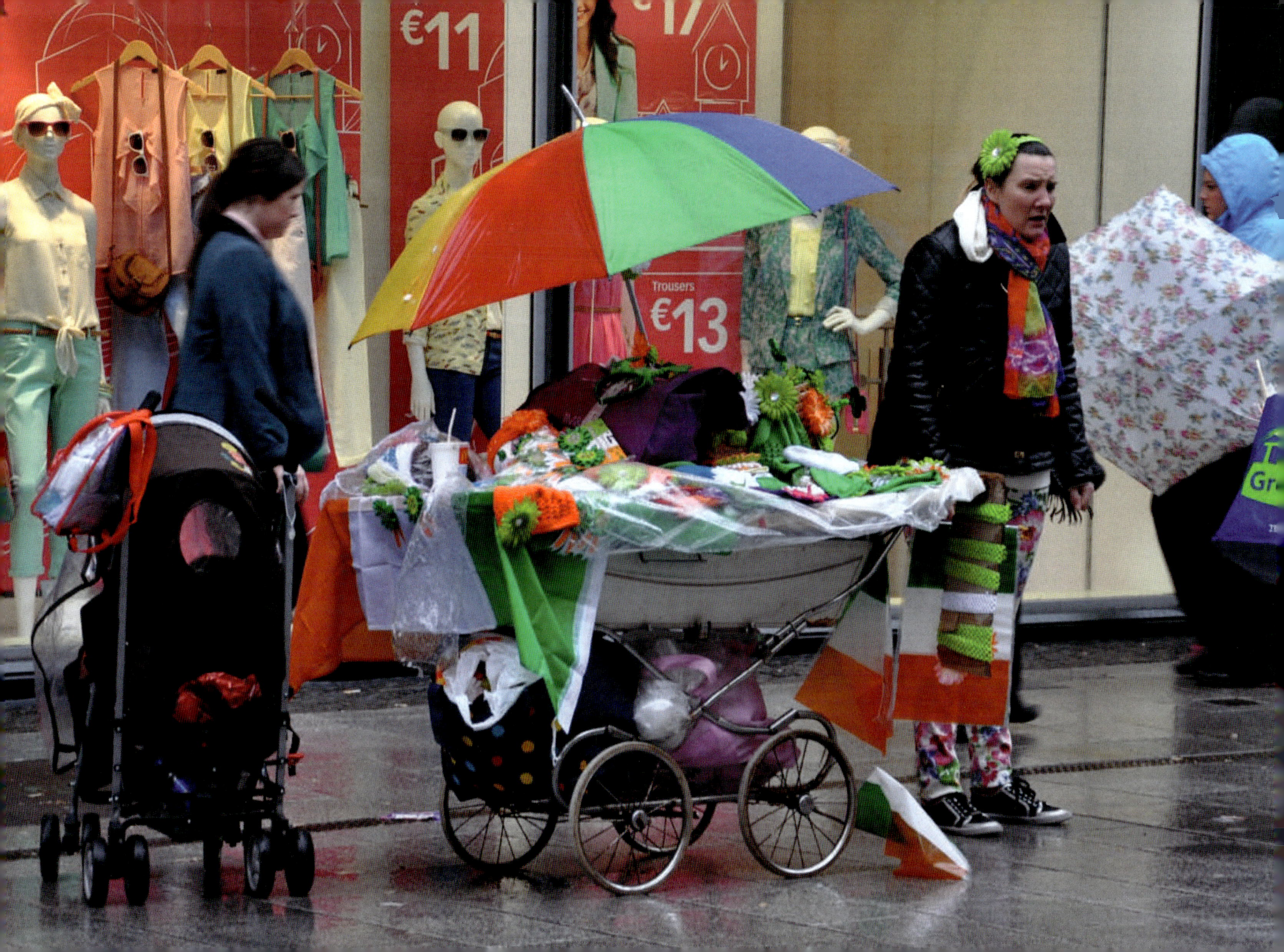
€11
Trousers
€13

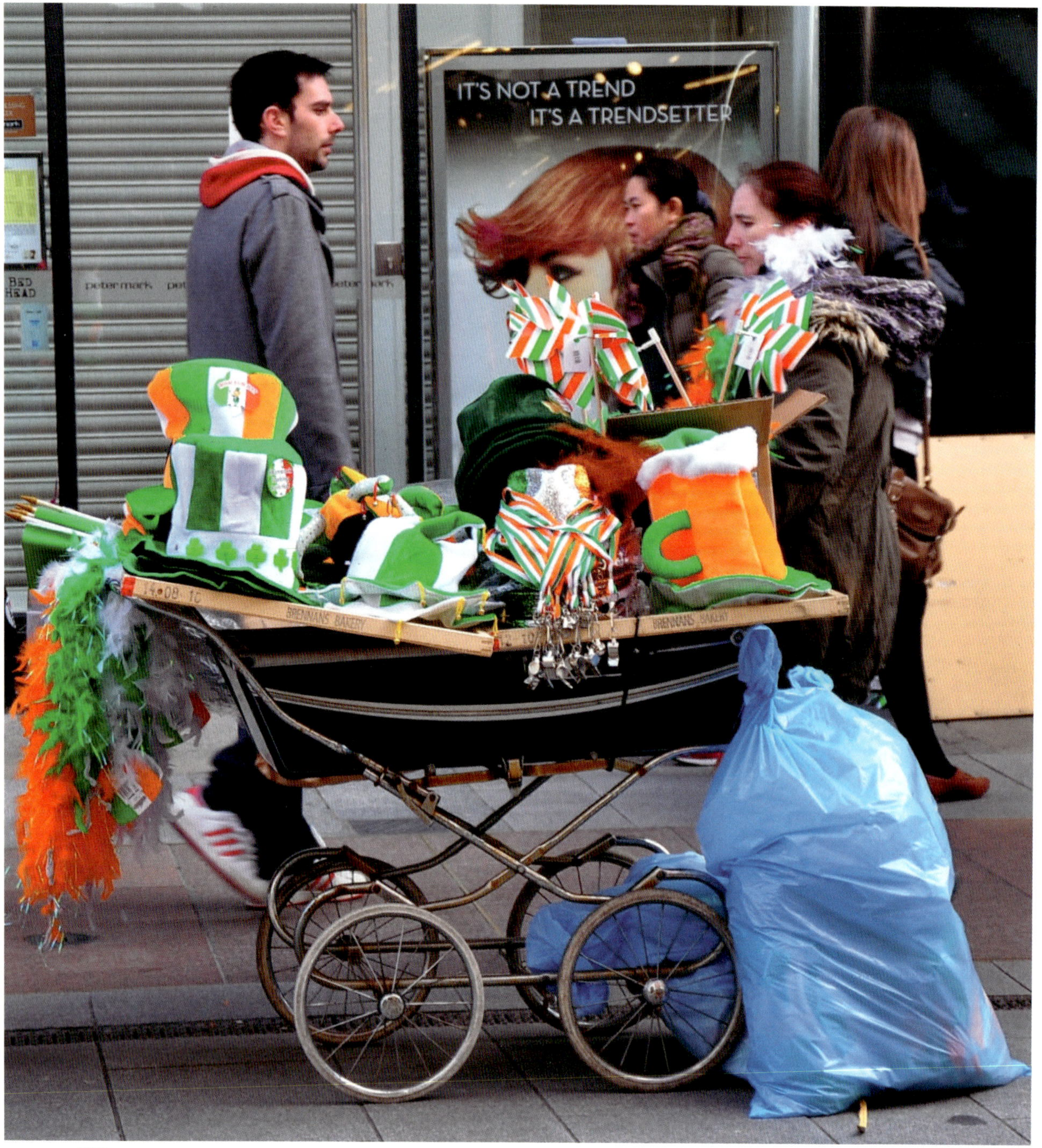

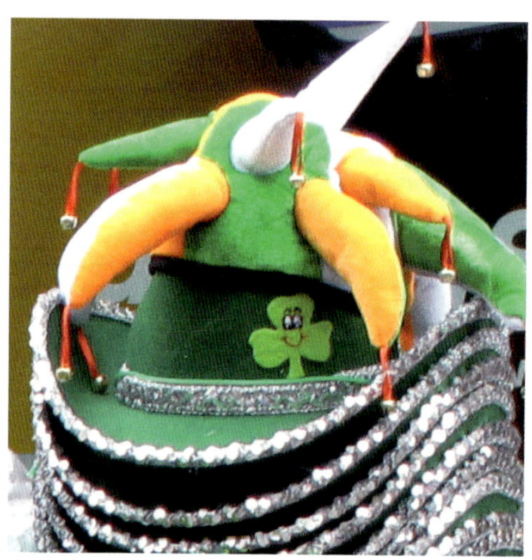

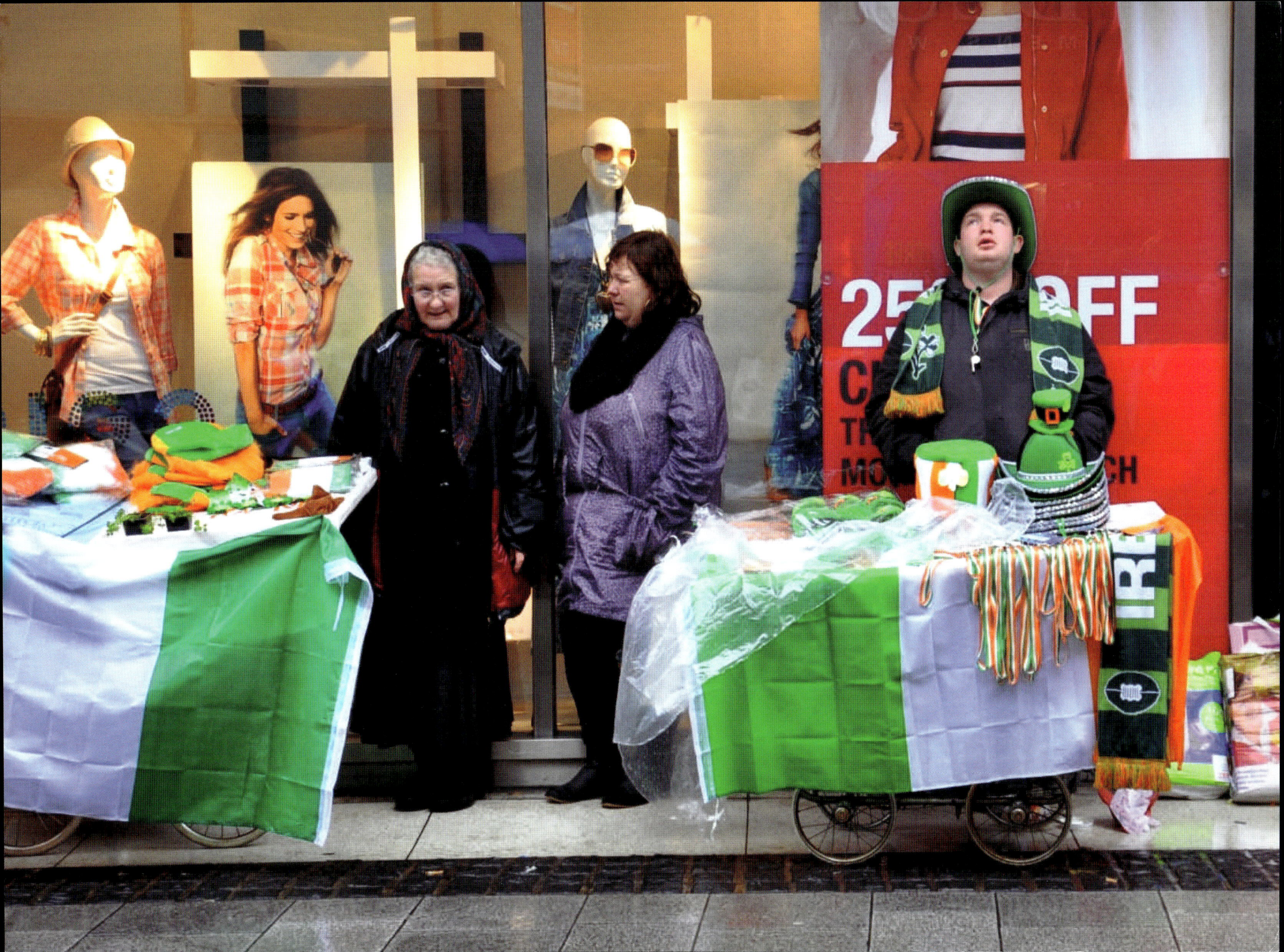
25
IRE

Lily's Story

Lily Kearns was born in Dublin, the fifth child in a family of ten children. Her father worked on the docks and her mother was a street trader. Lily married at seventeen and gave birth to the first of her two children, Karen, when she was only eighteen. After her son, Alan, was born, she began street trading – selling fruit from a pram in Henry Street – to support her family. Several traders would club together to buy a pallet of fruit, and two would wash the fruit while two sold off the prams. At first, things went well, although it was hard work. However, life was made increasingly difficult by the Gardaí, who constantly moved the traders on. Lily, like the other traders at the time was regularly arrested and fined for operating without a proper licence. Initially, the fine was £5, but in 1985, as part of what is now considered a deliberate attempt to get the traders off the streets, the fines were increased to £700 or £800. The traders could not afford to pay these huge fines, and Lily's failure to pay resulted in her being sent to Mountjoy prison. Her three friends Mary Holmes, Rita Murphy and Dolly Mangan had been sent to the same prison earlier that day.

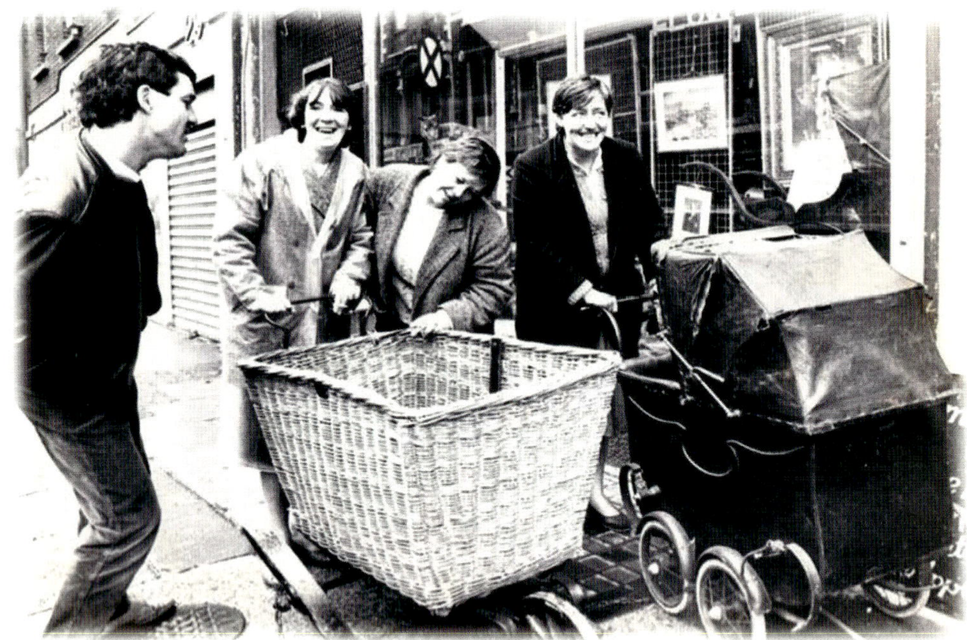

Left: Lily (second from left), with two other street traders Chrissy Mangan and Lily Flood in 1985. The three women were on their way to appear in court, and stopped to pose with some old prams outside an antique shop on the quays in Dublin. The photo opportunity was seized by Mick Rafferty (left) who handed his camera to a bystander to capture the moment. *(Courtesy of Lily Kearns)*

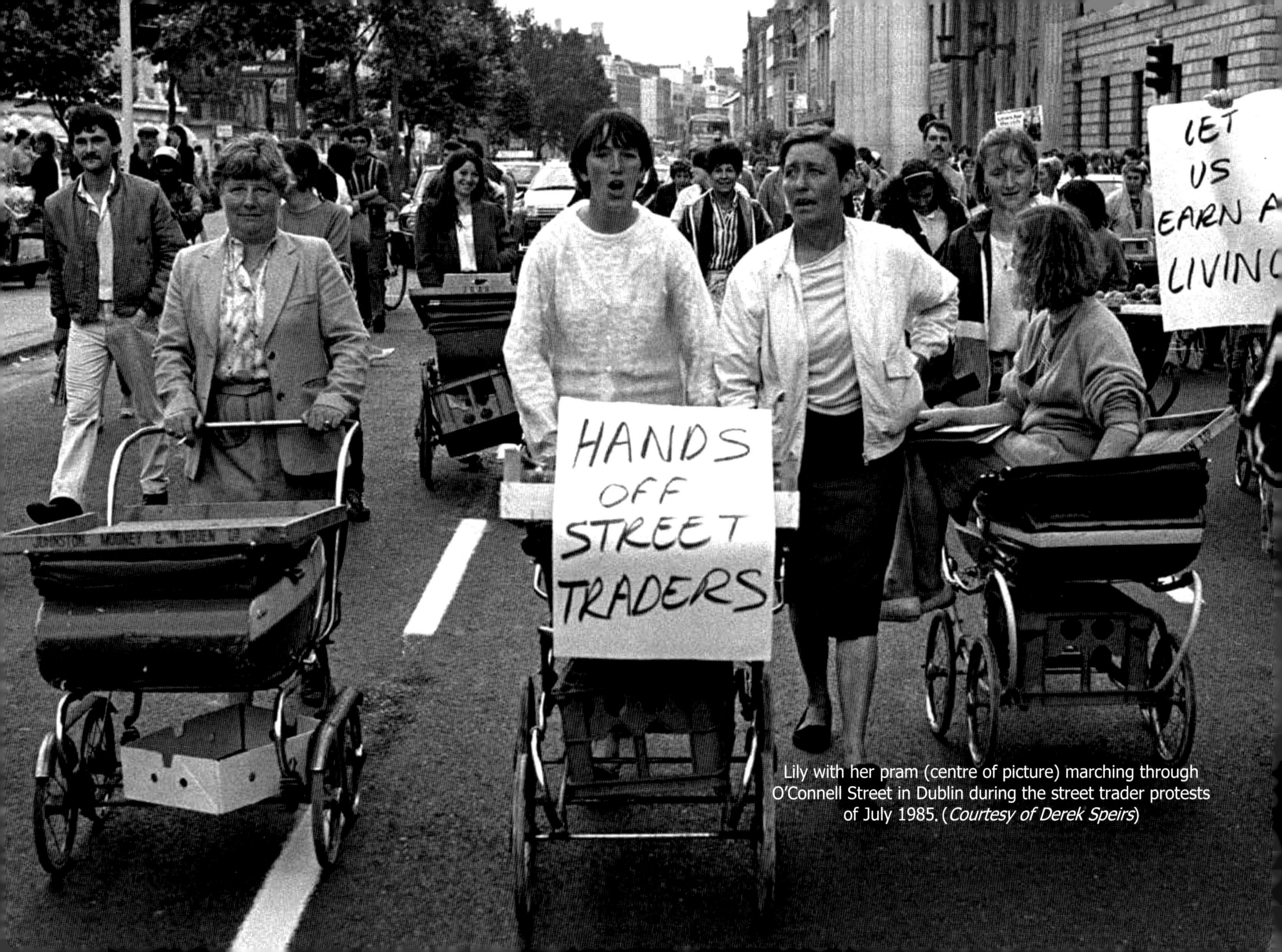

Lily with her pram (centre of picture) marching through O'Connell Street in Dublin during the street trader protests of July 1985. (*Courtesy of Derek Speirs*)

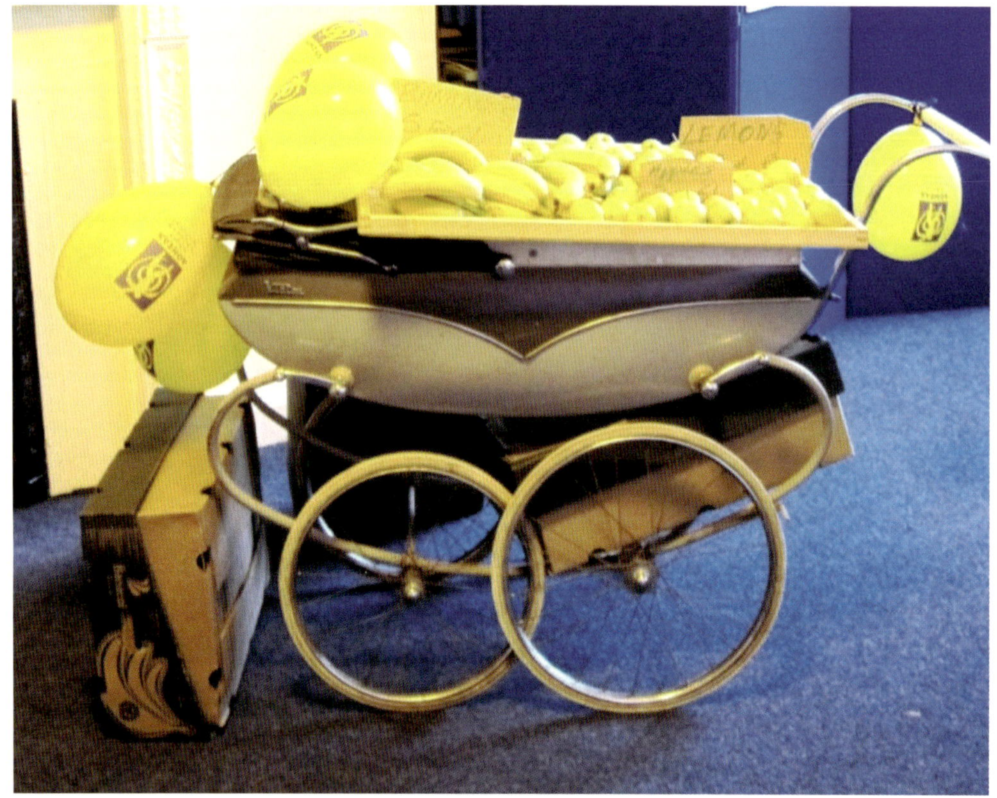

Above: Lily's Pedigree pram which she brought to an exhibition in 2012 of photographs of street traders taken by the author. It was the undisputed star of the show!

Lily recalls being very well looked after in prison. In fact, in honour of Mary's 30th birthday (which she had the misfortune to spend in jail), one of the wardens brought plates of chicken wings, with matchsticks for candles, to the women to mark the occasion. (Mary herself features later in the book). The women were released eight days later, their fines having been paid in some cases by money borrowed from family and friends. There was great support for the plight of the street traders from the ordinary people of Dublin. The sense of community among the traders themselves was also wonderful. While Lily and the others served their sentences, crowds of traders gathered outside the prison in the evening, shouting for their release.

Tragically, Lily's husband died at the age of 42, a loss she found extremely difficult to overcome. She stopped trading altogether for a time, but eventually with the support of a close circle of friends, she began trading again. She was to give up completely in 1999, when she felt the enterprise was no longer profitable. However, like many of the traders featured here, Lily kept her pram. It is a beautiful Pedigree *Victor* pram which would have cost a considerable sum in its day. She would never part with that pram.

Photo Gallery 5: Prams With Cards and Chocolates

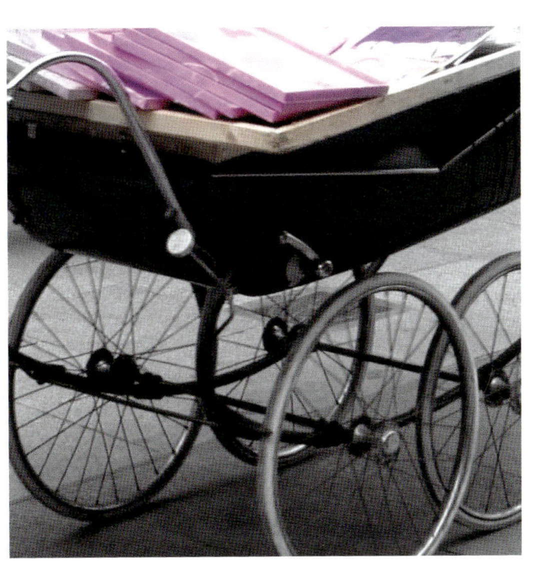

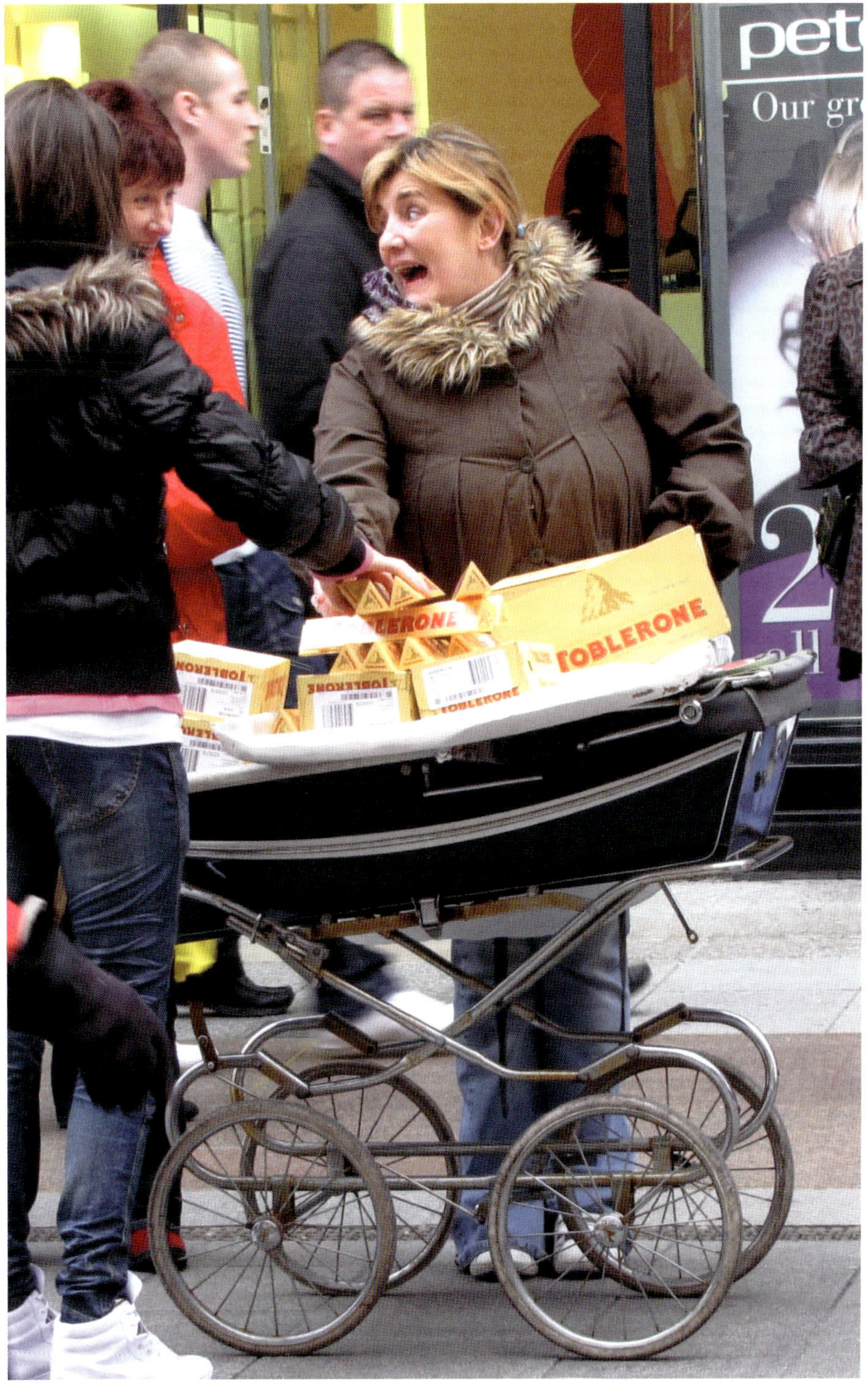

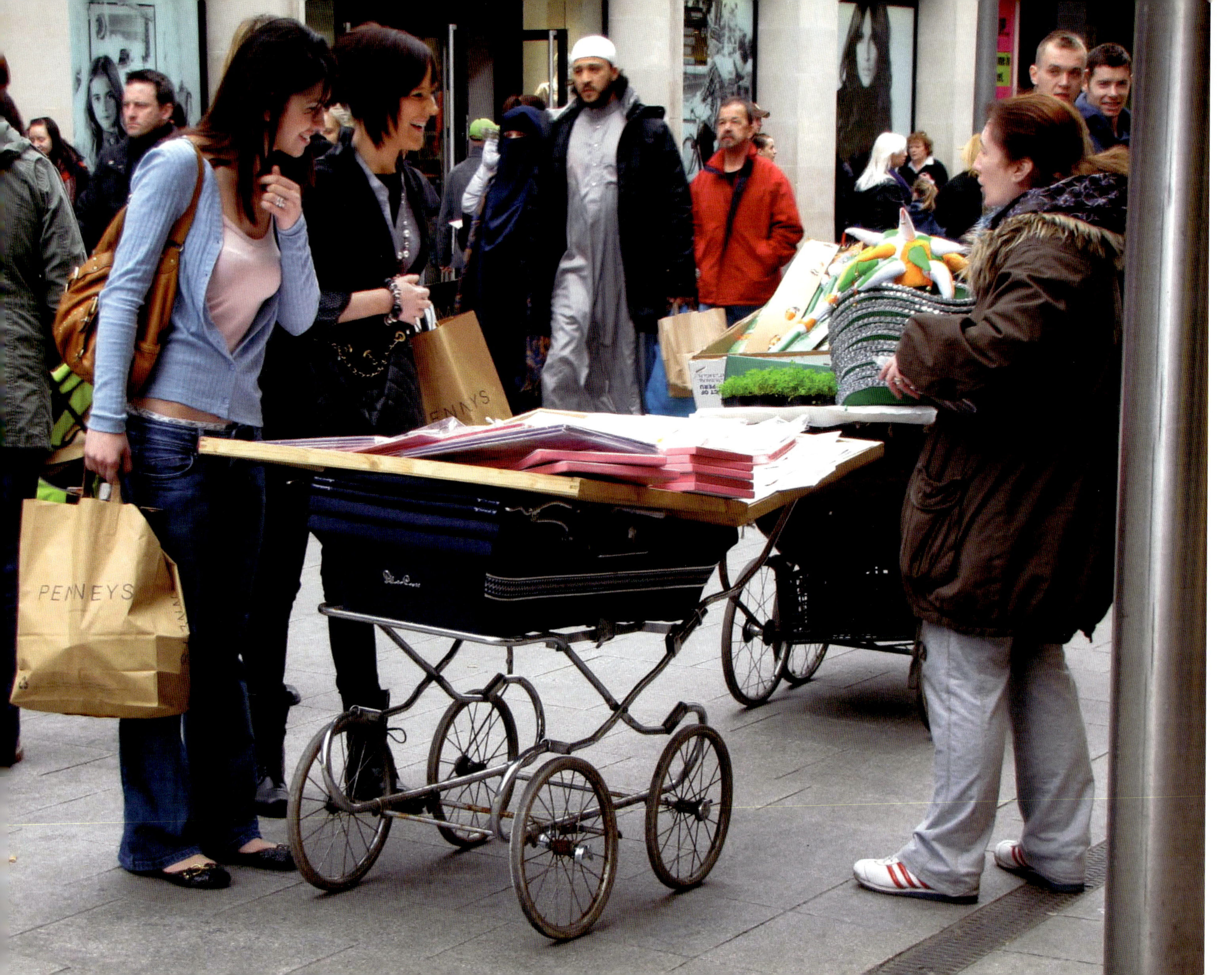
PENNEYS

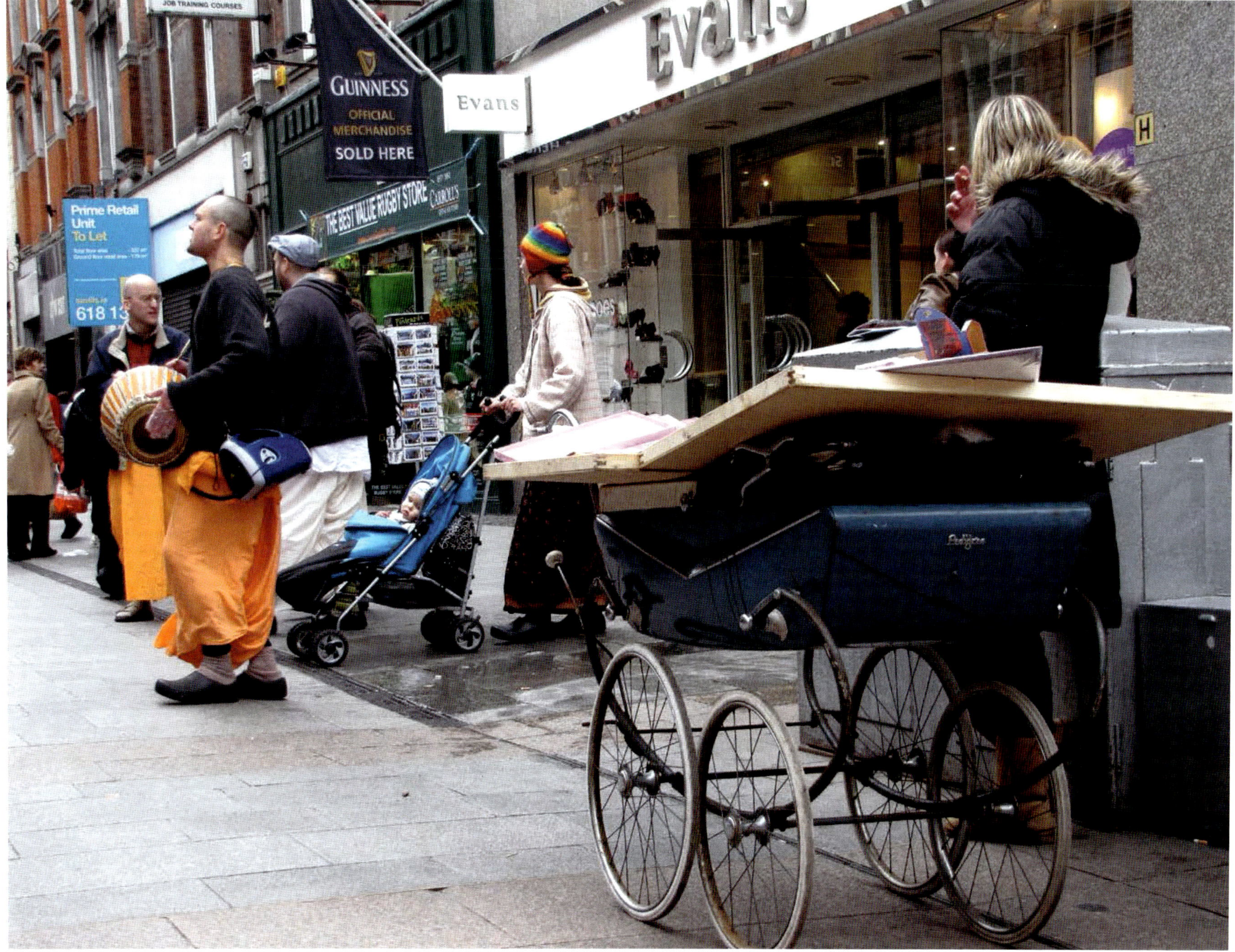

JOB TRAINING COURSES
GUINNESS
OFFICIAL MERCHANDISE
SOLD HERE
Evans
Evans
Prime Retail Unit
To Let
THE BEST VALUE RUGBY STORE
H

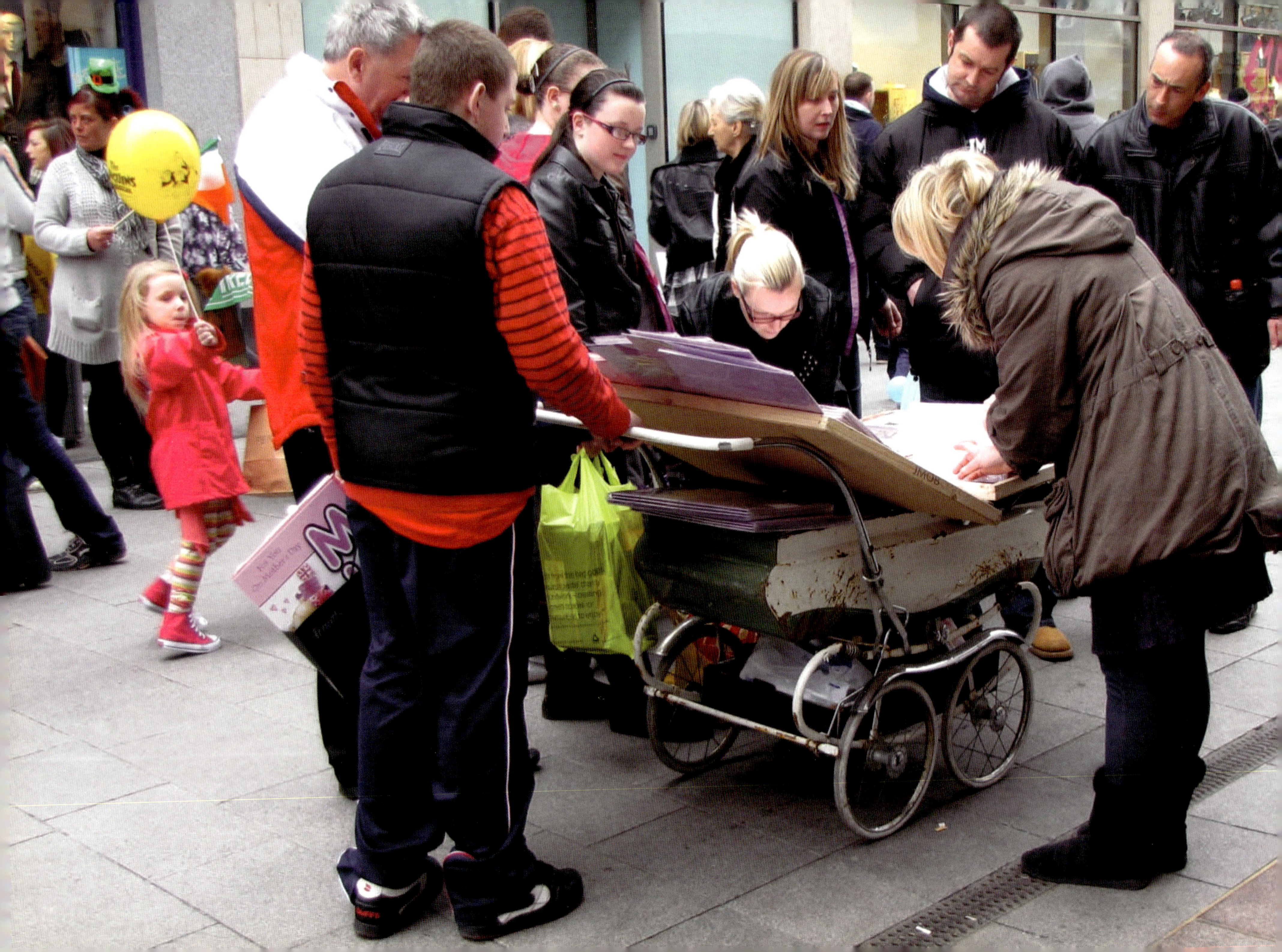

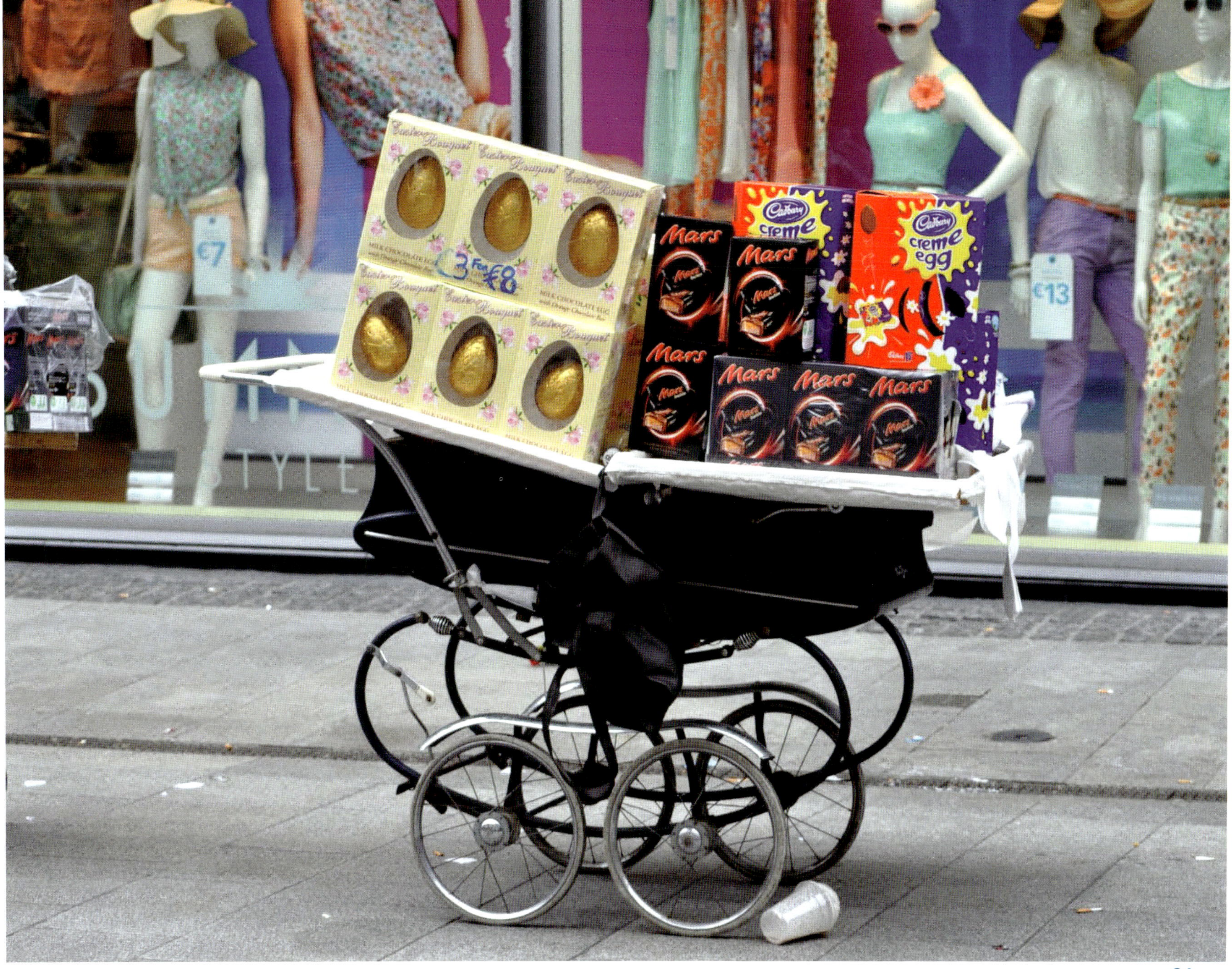
€7
3 For €8
Mars
Cadbury
creme egg
€13
STYLE

Mary's Story

Mary Holmes has been a street trader all her adult life. Unlike most of the other traders featured here, trading was not a tradition in her family, but rather in the family she married into. At the age of 17 she got married, and, within a short time, her mother-in-law presented her with a pram and told her to 'get down to that market and start selling!'. Mary did as she was told and headed for the market with her sisters-in-law, one of whom loaded up her pram with tomatoes. Back on the street she was instructed to stand in a particular spot, put the tomatoes in bags, and shout out '20 pence a bag of tomatoes!' The next morning, her sister-in-law called for her again and off they went to the market. Mary's life as a street trader had started.

As well as selling fruit, Mary sold seasonal produce at Halloween, and the extra money earned would dress her two boys for Christmas. When December came, Mary took a stall on Henry Street selling wrapping paper, cards, and Christmas gift sets. The profits paid for toys for her boys, as well as her other Christmas expenses and food. Mary traded like this for about a decade. Then she started attending the strawberry auctions at 6 o'clock in the morning, where she placed bids for the pick of the fruit.

The other traders began to depend on Mary to go to the auctions and secure the best produce. Eventually, the practice earned her the nickname 'Mary Pallet', as she would arrive in the street with a pram so full that she was obscured from view by stacks of strawberries, pears, or whatever else was good that day. The whole pallet was meticulously checked for bad fruit, and the fruit was washed before being arranged on top of the prams. Selling only the best fruit ensured repeat trade from customers. In handing out the stock, Mary made sure that no-one was ever left standing with nothing to sell – everybody got a share, and that way everybody earned some money. The older traders were helpful to the younger ones too. Mary recalls Ellen Preston being very good to her and lending her the money to buy stock in the market. There was a great sense of community among the traders, young and old.

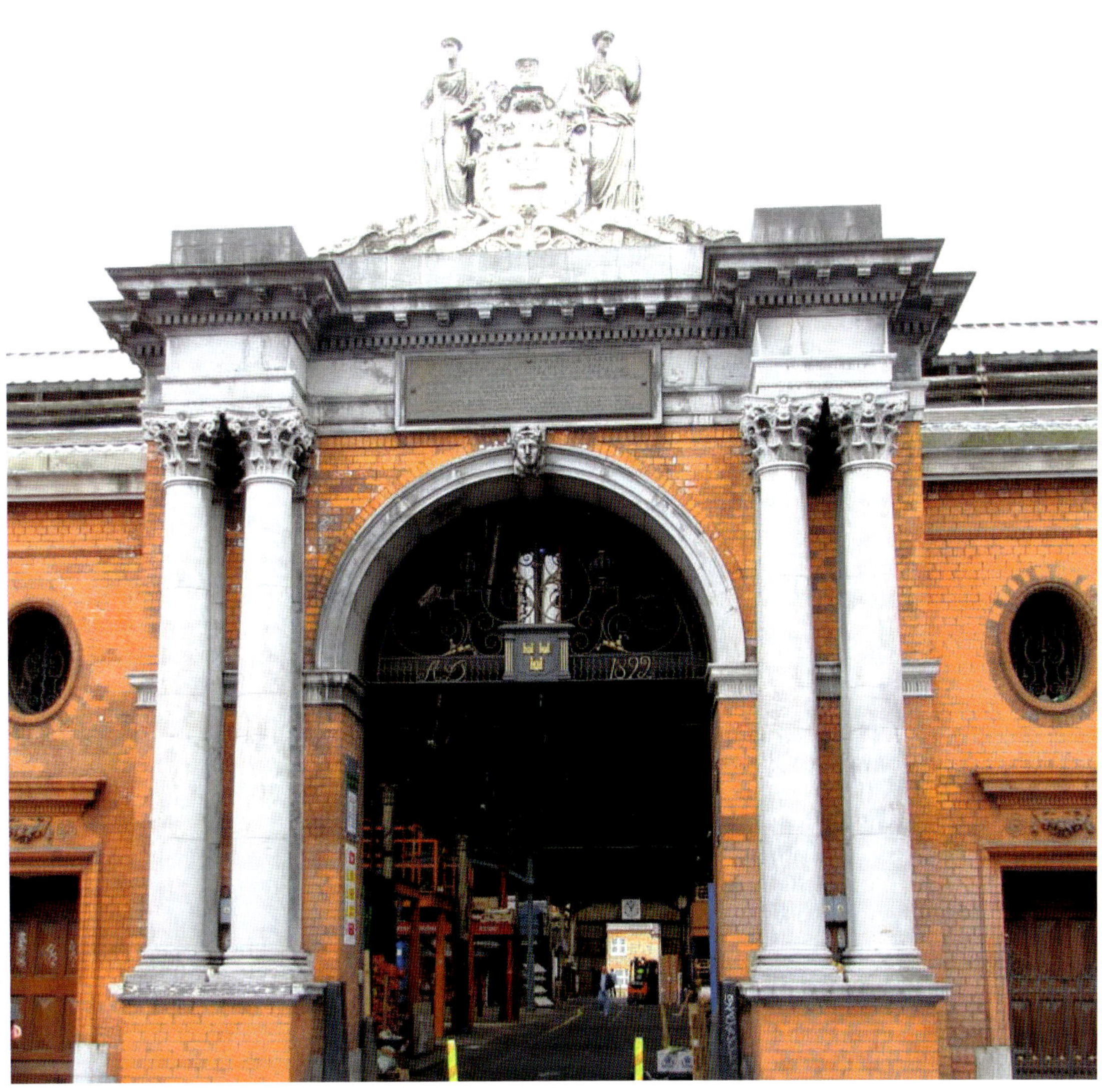

One year there was an unexpected bonanza for the pram traders with the arrival of a boatload of very special pears. These bright yellow pears, that were twice to three times the size of normal pears (and for some reason became known as the *hijacked pears*) arrived in Dublin almost ripe. It was speculated that the boat carrying the shipment had been somehow delayed or diverted and had been at sea longer than intended. The dealers in the fruit market needed to shift the pears quickly, and this was seized as a perfect business opportunity for Mary and the other pram traders. The people of Dublin went mad for the pears! The traders could make £10-12 a night selling them, an amount Mary described as a 'miracle' for the time. The pears were such a success for the pram traders that they raced to the market every morning to stock up on them again until all supplies were exhausted.

Above: The fruit and vegetable market in Smithfield in Dublin. The building dates from 1892, and is considered an architectural landmark on the north side of the city.

Over the years, Mary received her fair share of attention from the Gardaí. Paddy Boylan was the local Garda responsible for the city centre, and he constantly apprehended Mary and the other traders. Mary recalled herself and others being loaded into vans with their prams to the bemusement of American tourists who stood by taking photographs of the spectacle.

Another individual who was often arrested by Gardaí and loaded into the van was the one-man bandsman who earned his living busking around Henry Street and O'Connell Street. (Presumably he was an easy *collar* as a quick getaway would have been impossible with such an extensive assortment of instruments.) As there was often a lot of sitting around and waiting in Store Street station, having a one-man band among those arrested was not without its advantages. When the boredom became too much, someone would say 'Ah c'mon let's have a bit of a sing-song!' and the one-man band would start up, and Mary – who was always up for a song – led the women. Before long, they were all dancing on the tables. The Gardaí manning the station, unable to withstand the noise and the commotion, would come out and shout 'get them all out of here!' leading to all of those arrested being released from the station. Tony Gregory was also regularly called to Store Street to represent the traders and argue the case for returning their goods. Mary recalled that 'He always got our stuff back for us. He was the only one that stood by us – he was the one we could always depend upon.'

Like many others, Mary's trading activities sometimes led to her appearance in court, the outcome of which very much depended on who was on the bench on the day. One judge only ever issued fines in the order of £2 to £5, but fines from others could be astronomical. On one occasion a particular judge had several street traders in front of him. He fined the first woman, Rita Murphy, £700. Rita thought she had misheard the amount and asked 'Excuse me, Your Honour, did you say £7?'. 'I said £700' came the reply. Mary was up next. She too was fined £700. The next woman before the judge had her solicitor present who rose to speak on her behalf. The solicitor explained that his client was in very difficult financial circumstances and had a large family to support.

'How many children have you got?' asked the judge.

'I have nine, Your Honour', she replied.

'Well I am fining you £900 then. That's £100 for each of your children'.

Judges also imposed custodial sentences, often because the fines imposed were so large that they were beyond the capacity of the traders to pay them. On one occasion, Mary found herself in Mountjoy prison with six other traders in one big cell. Among her cell mates were Rita Murphy (mentioned above), and Lily Kearns (who featured earlier in the book). When all was quiet in the prison at night, Mary – who as we already know was given to breaking into song in the face of adversity – decided to liven things up by singing loudly all night long, and in the process, ensured that nobody got any sleep. When the prison governor came around to tell Mary that she should pack up her things because she was going home (not a result of her singing, but because her fine had been paid by her family), the others in the cell decided that, if Mary was getting out, they were not staying inside any longer either. Both Lily and Rita told Mary to go and get their respective husbands and to instruct them to collect up enough money to pay the fines so the women could be released.

Mary headed off to find Rita's husband and she found him in his local bar having a pint.

> 'Rita sent me to get the rest of the money', she told him.
>
> 'Would you like a drink Mary?' He replied.
>
> 'I would', she said, and sat down.

Mary never made it back to Mountjoy prison that night and there was hell to pay the next day.

The friendships between the women were to survive the episode. Mary and Lily are friends to this day. Sadly, Rita Murphy died earlier this year. She and Mary traded alongside each other for 28 years. As Mary looked at some photographs I took of Rita in Mary Street several years ago, she said 'That street was Rita's life. She would have gone out on Sundays if she could. She hated coming home. She didn't care about the cold. Rita was my best pal, I loved her. If I could have those times back again I would'. Rita and her pram are pictured on the cover of this book.

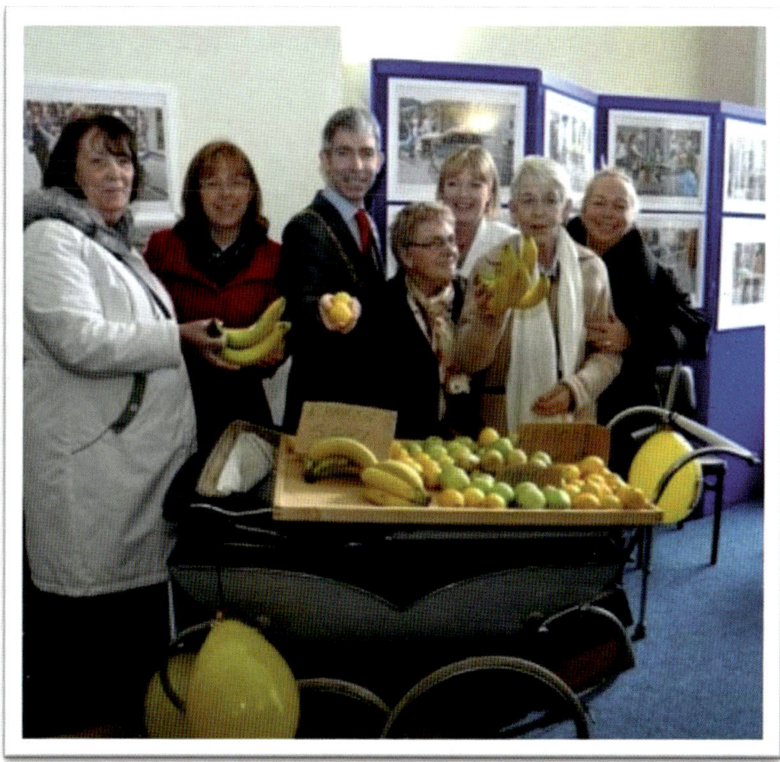

From right: Mary Holmes, Rita Murphy, the author, Ellen Preston, The Lord Mayor of Dublin Councillor Andrew Montague, Councillor Emer Costello, and Lily Kearns. This photograph was taken in February 2012 at the launch of an exhibition of photographs of street traders by the author at the Dublin Adult Learning Centre, Mountjoy Square.

Photo Gallery 6: Prams With Pretty Things

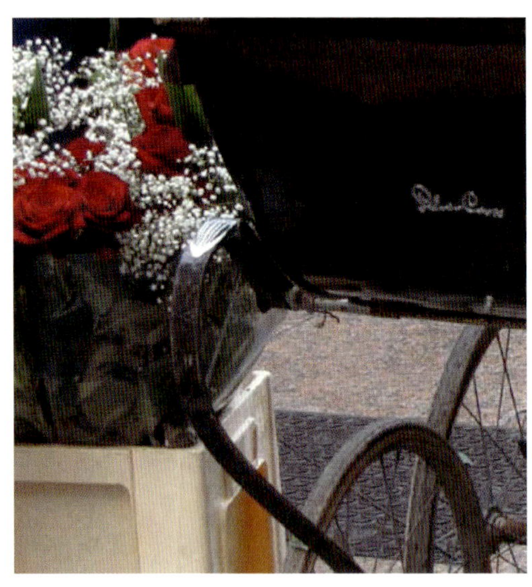

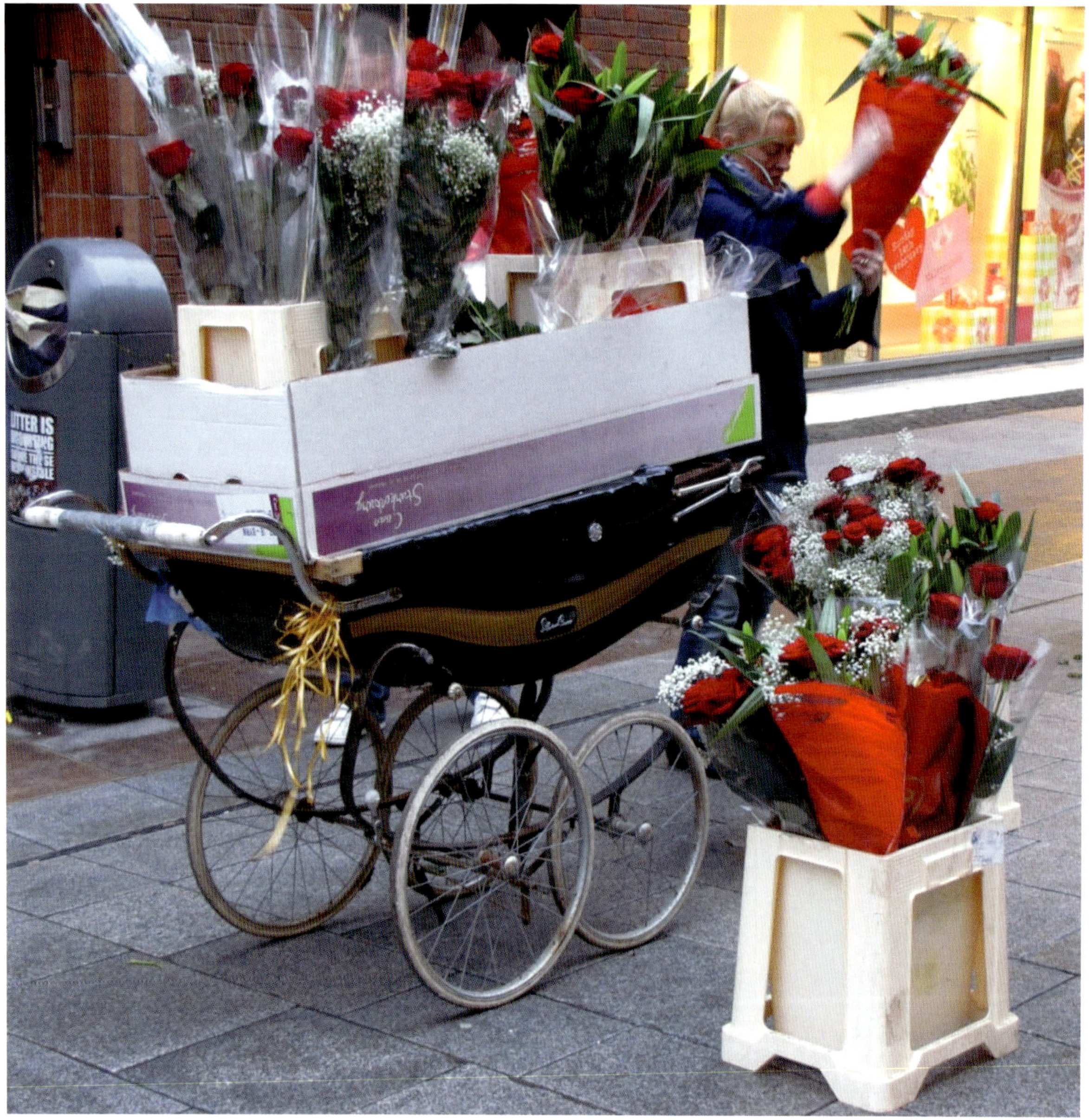

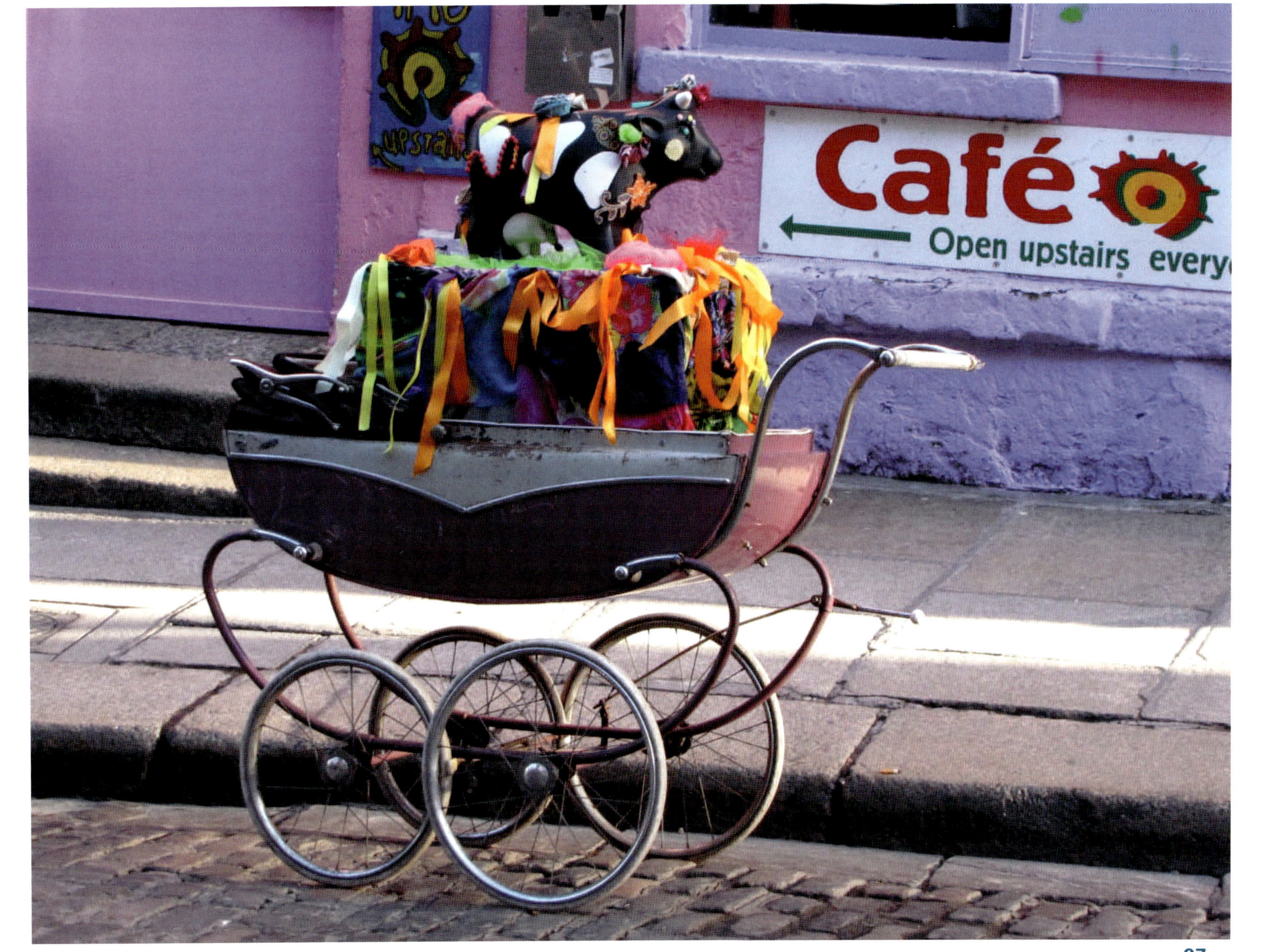
Café
Open upstairs

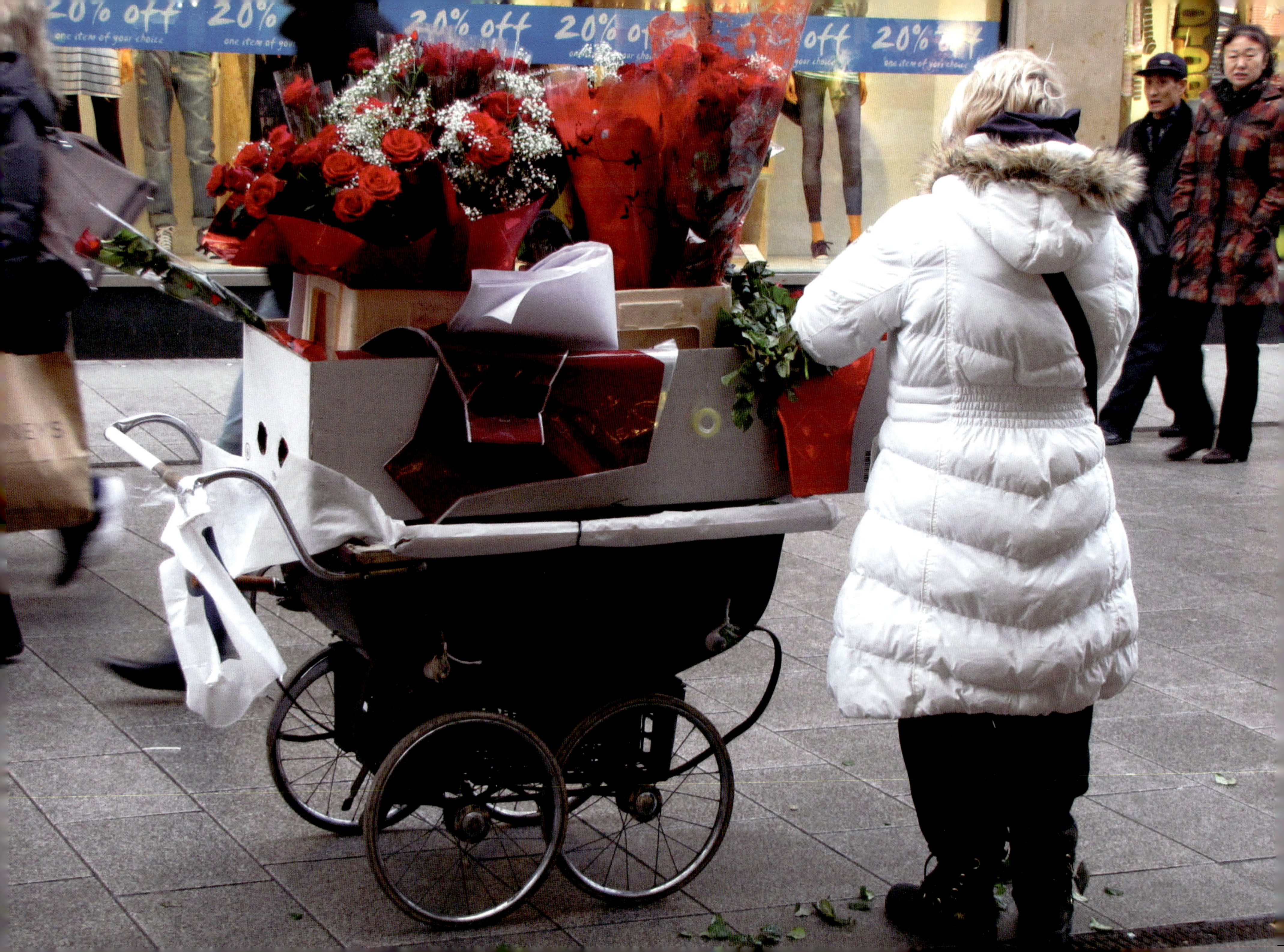
20% off 20%
one item of your choice
20% off 20%
20% off
one item of your choice

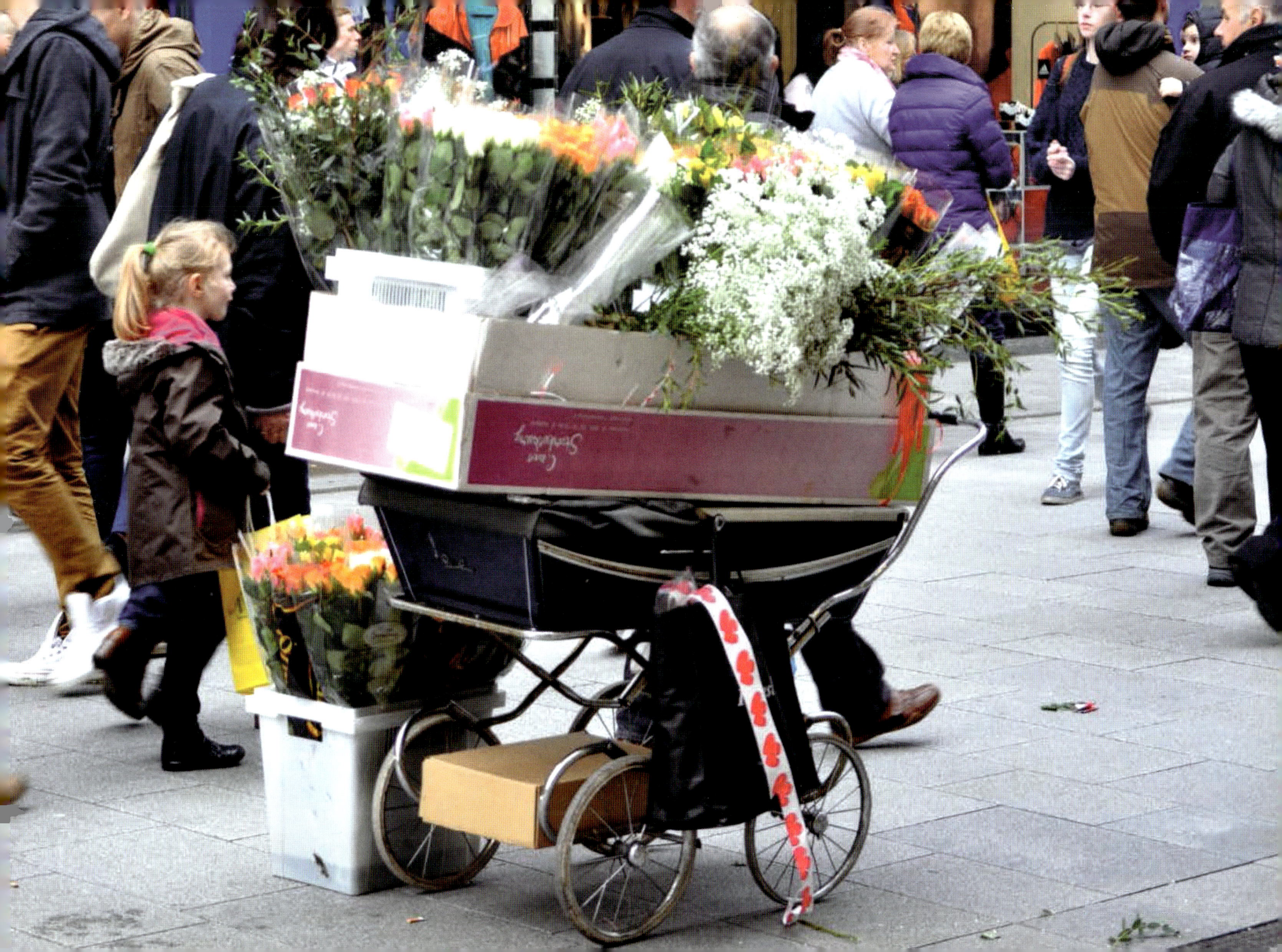

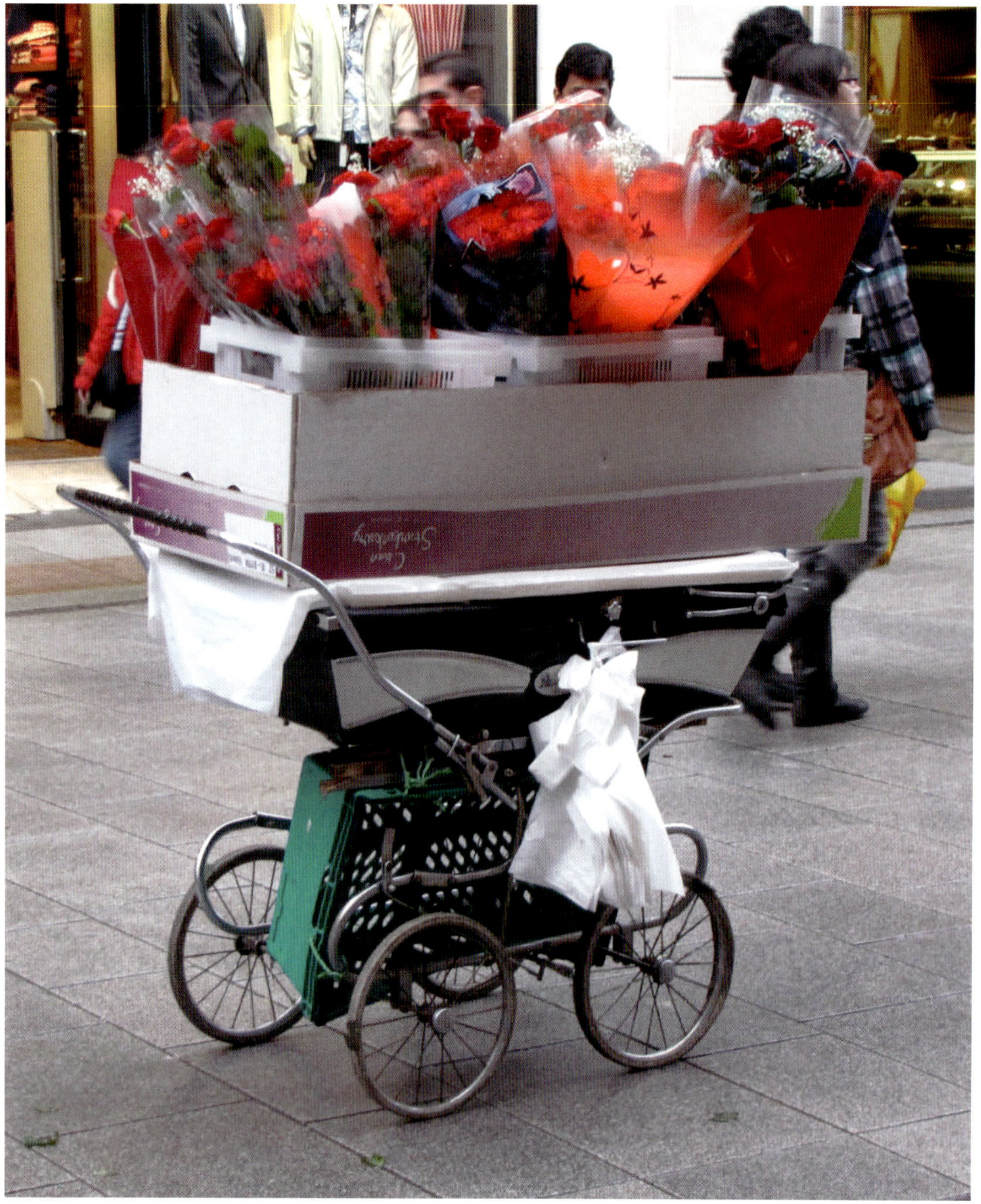

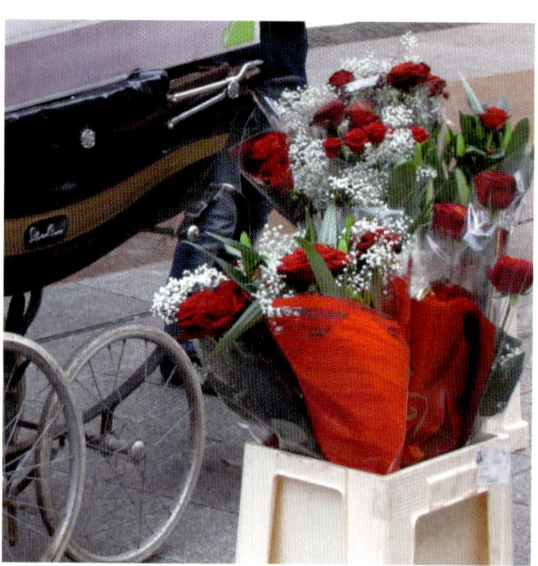

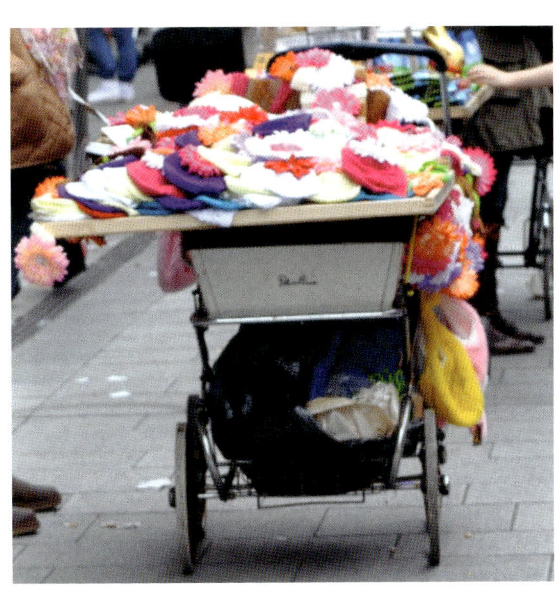

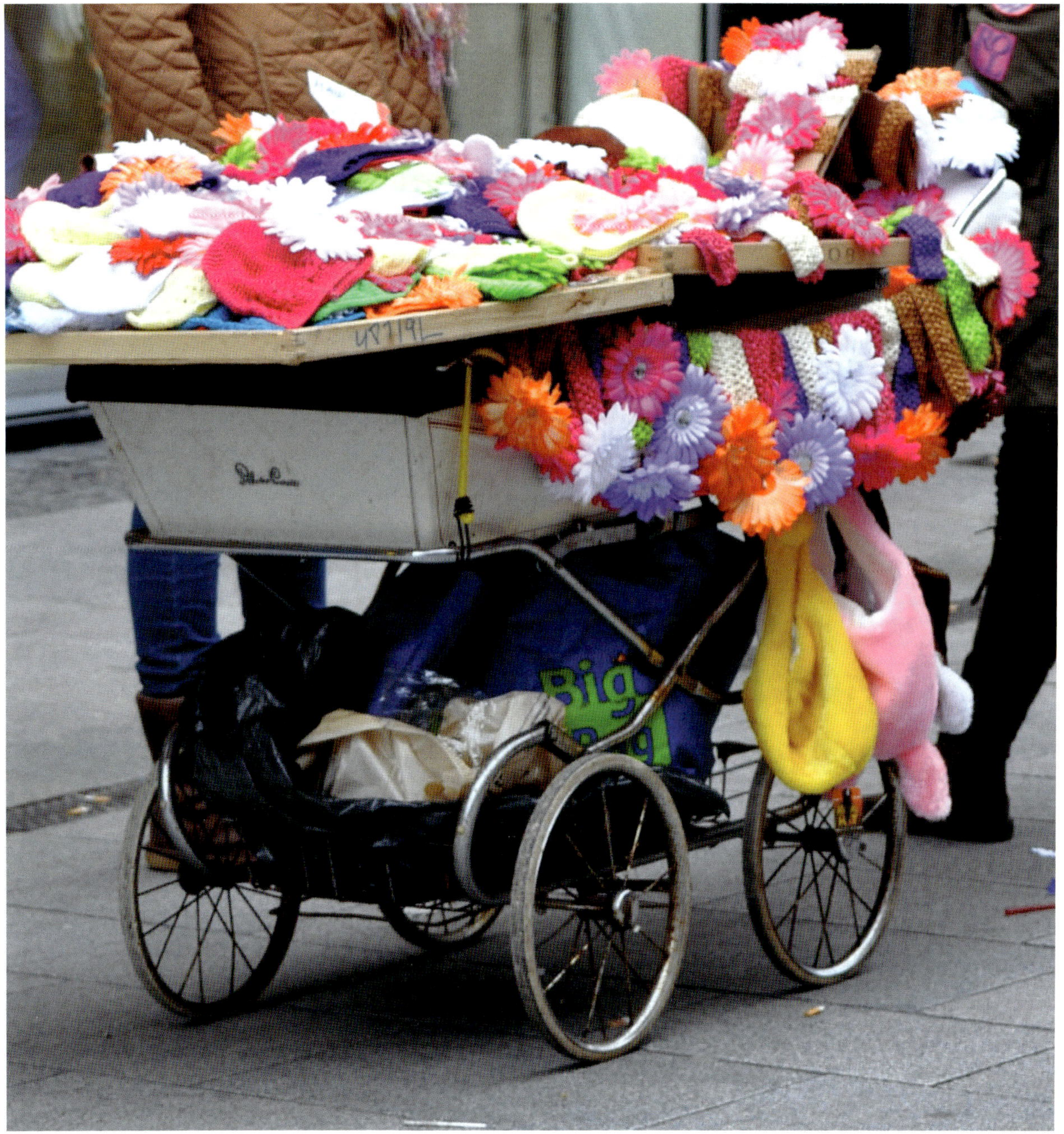

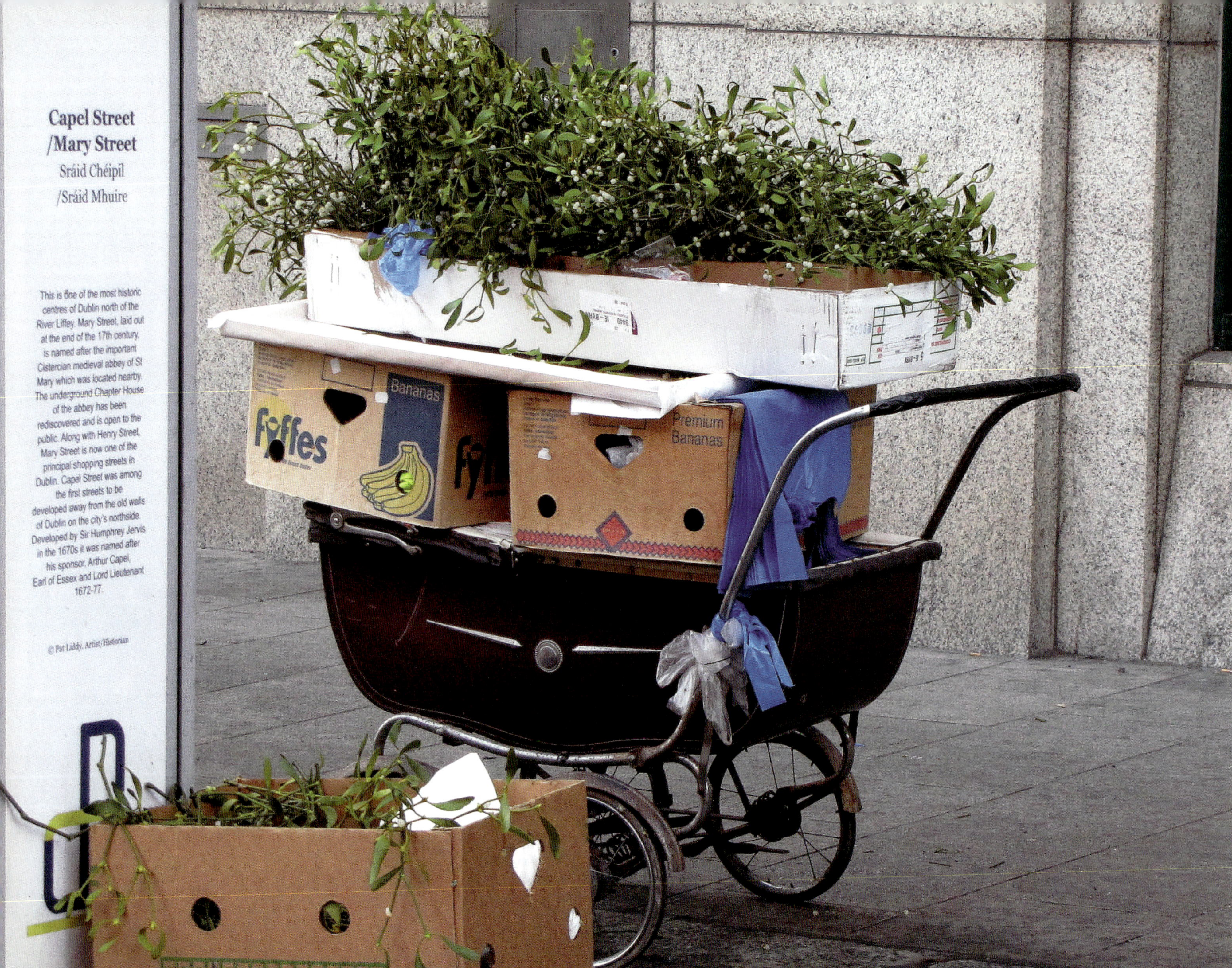
Capel Street
/Mary Street
Sráid Chéipil
/Sráid Mhuire
This is one of the most historic centres of Dublin north of the River Liffey. Mary Street, laid out at the end of the 17th century, is named after the important Cistercian medieval abbey of St Mary which was located nearby. The underground Chapter House of the abbey has been rediscovered and is open to the public. Along with Henry Street, Mary Street is now one of the principal shopping streets in Dublin. Capel Street was among the first streets to be developed away from the old walls of Dublin on the city's northside. Developed by Sir Humphrey Jervis in the 1670s it was named after his sponsor, Arthur Capel, Earl of Essex and Lord Lieutenant 1672-77.
© Pat Liddy, Artist/Historian
Fyffes
Bananas
Premium
Bananas

Bibliography

Cullen, B. (2001). *It's a long way from penny apples.* Dublin: Mercier Press.

Dáil Éireann Oireactas reports.

Dublin City Libraries.

Gilligan, R. (2011). *Tony Gregory.* Dublin: O'Brien Press.

Historical Irish Times.

Irish Independent Archive.

Irish Times.

Kearns, K. (1994). *Dublin tenement life.* Dublin: Gill and Macmillan.

Magennis, T. (1988). Prams. In *Ireland of the Welcomes, (Vol 37,* 26-29). Dublin: Bord Fáilte.

National Library of Ireland, Photographic Archive.

RTE Stills Library.

Ward, C. (2010). *Silver Cross: The story of a great British brand.* Yorkshire: The History Writer.

Postscript

By the time I was expecting my daughter in 2004, the kinds of pram I had admired as a child thirty years previously were no longer being manufactured. However, I was determined to have a 'proper', traditional, pram for my baby! I began to search for prams in online auctions, and eventually discovered a beautiful 30-year old navy Silver Cross Tenby pram for sale in the UK. It was a case of love at first sight. I won the auction, and persuaded my husband to accompany me on the ferry from Dublin to Holyhead to collect it. At the ferry terminal in Wales, the seller and her husband (who was, no doubt, grudgingly roped into the transaction) were waiting for us with a beautiful, shiny, bouncy, large-wheeled, Silver Cross pram with sparkling spokes. Having exchanged embraces with the sellers, and being wished all the best with the birth of our child, we promptly re-boarded the same ferry that had brought us over. The customs officers – three women – whom we had passed when disembarking ten minutes earlier, were quick to spot the new 'passenger' and were approaching quickly. I was suddenly overcome by a fear that they might think we were using the pram to smuggle illegal substances! I need not have worried. All they wanted to do was admire the pram, give it a little push, and reminisce about prams that they had once known.

This was to be my first realisation of the true affection with which these prams are held. With a certain sense of relief, we wheeled our way towards a quiet spot on board. However, our chosen location proved to be less than peaceful, as, much to our amusement, our fellow passengers kept coming over to have a look at the 'baby' in the beautiful pram. In fact the entire staff running a coffee outlet temporarily pulled down the shutters so that they could all come and have a look! The attention attracted by the pram continued when it was used for its intended purpose. When taking my daughter to the shops, or for walks in the park, I was often stopped by people who wanted to admire the pram (and baby!). Older people, in particular, commented on how lovely it was to see a real pram again and told me about the prams they had used for their children. It was clear to me that the evolution of the pram into its modern form had not pleased everyone and that I was far from alone in regretting the demise of the old-fashioned pram. For now, the pram is safely stored in the attic ready for use by the next generation. Who knows, perhaps one day it will find a new lease on life on the streets of Dublin.

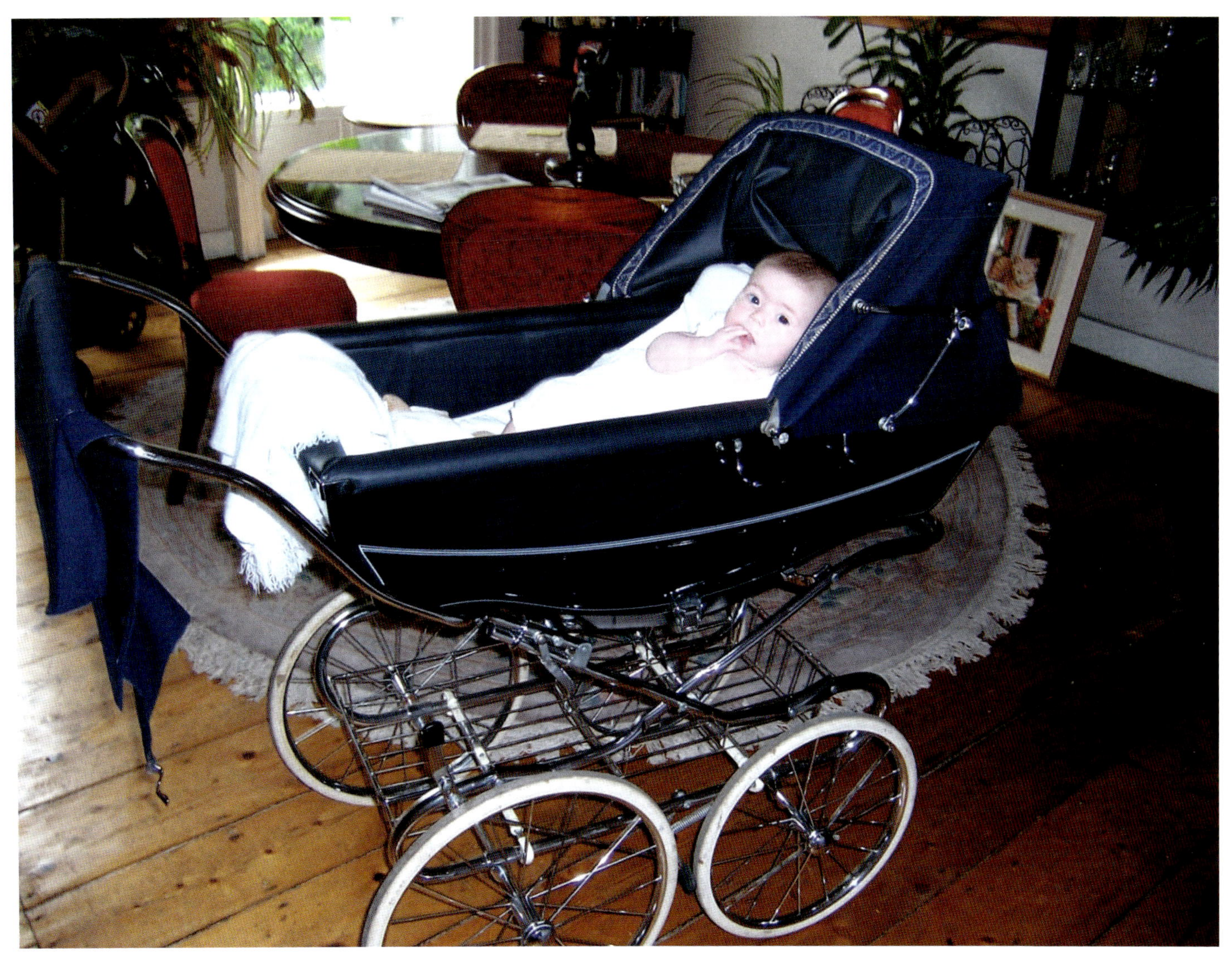

My daughter, Daisy, in her Silver Cross Tenby pram in 2005.